Preventing
Computer Fraud

Preventing Computer Fraud

Dana L. Stern

McGraw-Hill, Inc.

New York San Francisco Washington, D.C. Auckland Bogotá
Caracas Lisbon London Madrid Mexico City Milan
Montreal New Delhi San Juan Singapore
Sydney Tokyo Toronto

Library of Congress Cataloging-in-Publication Data

Stern, Dana L.
    Preventing computer fraud / Dana L. Stern
        p.   cm.
    Includes bibliographical references and index.
    ISBN 0-07-061200-5
    1. Computer crimes.   2. Computer security   I. Title.
HV6773.S74   1993   93-37225
364.1'68—dc20   CIP

1 2 3 4 5 6 7 8 9 0   DOC/DOC   9 9 8 7 6 5 4 3

ISBN 0-07-061200-5
PART OF
0-07-911545-4

The sponsoring editor for this book was Jeanne Glasser, the editing supervisor was Caroline Levine, and the production supervisor was Donald F. Schmidt. It was set in Palatino by McGraw-Hill's Professional Book Group composition unit.

I dedicate this book to my lovely wife Mary Beth, whose help and understanding have made it possible. Additionally, I'd like to thank my father for rendering legal advice and proofing the book.

Special thanks to Mr. Dennis Hathaway of Pinkerton Security and Investigation Services.

In memory of Mr. Joseph Daniel "Danny" Casolaro, who lost his life attempting to report computer fraud— and possibly an even larger conspiracy.

Contents

10. Audits   **217**

11. Communications, Networks, and Telecommunications   **229**

Part 3. Consulting Firms, Checklists, Questionnaires, and Audit Criteria

12. Consulting Firms   **251**

13. Quick Checklist   **257**

Preface

The cost of white-collar crime in the United States alone is estimated at $200 billion annually in lost money, products, and business opportunities. It is my sincere hope that this quick reference book will help raise the awareness of professionals in the business community to computer fraud and thus prevent its proliferation.

The arrival of the computer has created a huge industry. This industry has prospered in part because it has followed business ethics. However, it is not unreasonable to say that some segments of the computer industry have no business ethics at all.

I have seen a sharp increase in computer fraud. Computer fraud can be prevented by a few simple shortcut methods. These methods are presented in Quick Checklist in Chapter 13 and the Quick Network Checklist in Chapter 14. The Quick Network Checklist is a set of guidelines intended to be used by network administrators to maintain a secure network. This book is brief and to the point. I have personally documented many acts of fraud for clients and testified as an expert witness. This book will help you avoid some common pitfalls.

Because there are so many different types of fraud that most ethical businesspeople would not think of, I have presented actual case histories of fraud that I have encountered during my career. These case histories represent millions of dollars worth of fraud. Names of the victimized companies are always withheld. After each case an analysis is presented followed by a summary that lists appropriate preventive measures. In all instances if the appropriate preventive measure had been used, fraud could have been avoided. These situations were not only costly but also embarrassing to the entities involved. Some entities presented are defense contractors, government agencies, charitable institutions, and Fortune 100 corporations.

This book is primarily written for people managing or acquiring computer systems or networks for business or government. However, some issues discussed here may be pertinent to home users of personal computers.

Dana L. Stern

Preventing
Computer Fraud

PART 1

Misrepresentation, Contractual Agreements, Sabotage, Source Code, Copyright, Data Omission, Fraud in Government

1
Misrepresentation

Introduction

Misrepresentation of goods and services is the most common type of fraud I have seen. The reason for this is that it frequently goes undetected. Sometimes it is concealed by victims to avoid recriminations from their own management and possible publicity from the media. The actual amount of misrepresentation of goods and services is considerable. This is because it is easily accomplished by unscrupulous individuals or vendors. The following case studies illustrate this kind of misrepresentation.

In Cases 1, 2, and 3 the victims thought they were dealing with ethical entities that would stand behind goods and services provided by them. Some perpetrators of this type of fraud on sensing a lack of knowledge on the part of their clients will abuse the opportunity to its limits.

Conversely some managers continue to allow themselves to be manipulated by unscrupulous individuals in the hopes that they will perform as originally agreed. Managers of companies which are victims may even fail to report unethical conduct for fear of reprisal from their superiors.

Case 1

I was contacted by a president of a textile manufacturing firm and asked to do an analysis of a failed software development project. The company used a Prime minicomputer. This was one of Prime's office environment computers that did not require special power or air conditioning. Prime hardware is very reliable and continues to be used for business applications today. The existing software used by the manufacturing firm, however, was inefficient and performance of the Prime computer was degraded as a result. The original software was developed internally by the manufacturing firm.

The manufacturing company purchased a new software package to remedy this poor performance. The purchased software package was supposed to improve performance and convert existing software to a fourth-generation language in one day. The consultant responsible for the installation of the new software system was sponsored by the software vendor. Although the consultant was paid by the manufacturer, he represented the software firm and promoted its product. Six months passed and the consultant was still working on site at the textile firm. The system being created by the consultant was still nowhere near completion.

The president of the manufacturing company became suspicious about the progress in the development of the new software when he read an article about a newer version of the product he had purchased. The article said that this newer version had been beta tested on the manufacturer's computer system. A *beta test* is a prerelease evaluation of software conducted at a customer site with their permission. He was shocked to learn that his system had been used without his permission.

I was retained to do an analysis of the failed software development just after the manufacturing company had replaced the consultant with its own programmer. The manufacturing company's programmer and I did an intensive analysis of the software system being developed by the consultant. My first day on site was spent looking at the hardware, software, and available documentation. Additionally, I interviewed the staff that supported the computer system. It was determined very quickly that the system being developed was far from complete. A few menus, data entry screens, and reports had been completed but most of the software system was not finished and would require substantial time and money to complete.

The manufacturing company had spent approximately $100,000 on this system. Internally the manufacturing company did everything it could to make the development of this new system a success.

The vendor of the software package had conducted an audit on the progress of the software development but had never made a formal report to the president of the manufacturing company. The audit revealed that much of the system was yet to be developed. This is an indication that the vendor of the software package knew they were in difficulties and remained silent. The relationship between the software vendor and the consultant they sponsored also represented a conflict of interest.

Financial losses to the manufacturing company were not limited to the cost of software and consulting. Additional losses in production and administrative costs were considerable.

Analysis

This type of situation is quite common and could have easily been avoided. The president of the manufacturing company should have requested a customer list from the vendor. The customers on the list then could have been contacted and surveyed as to their satisfaction with the product. Consulting firms provide this service to a client and can analyze the software.

The real advantage in using a consulting firm is that you can expect an unbiased report from them. They can review part of the source code and do benchmark testing. Established consulting firms stay in business by maintaining high standards and ethics.

I strongly urge anyone who is contemplating buying a software package or system to visit someone who is using the software and see how it is used from day to day. Avoid a quick tour by management at a customer site. Ask questions and watch the members of the staff use the system. Find out what the staff likes and dislikes about the software.

While I like fourth-generation languages and have been a proponent of them, it must be stressed that they can use considerable memory on most computers. In other words, if a company was experiencing degraded performance with an existing system, a fourth-generation language might not help. The software vendor's statement that his product could convert the existing system in one day was an extreme overstatement of its capabilities. (If it sounds too good to be true, it probably is.)

Ultimately, the manufacturer was forced to sue the software vendor to recoup monies lost. Litigation is often lengthy and costly. Even if a judgment is obtained in your favor, it doesn't prevent a vendor from filing bankruptcy. If the party you're litigating against has few assets, you may be wasting your money on legal fees.

Vendor references should be provided to you without reservation. Vendors that have few references after being in business for several years should be avoided. The best references to check are the ones that have been long-standing clients. User groups, associations, and the Better Business Bureau should be contacted as a matter of routine. Vendor financial statements should always be reviewed. It may be necessary to sign a nondisclosure statement from the vendor before receiving this information. Vendors that are financially troubled should be avoided and a Dunn & Bradstreet report on the vendor should be obtained and reviewed.

Customer questionnaires can be especially useful in deciding the worthiness of software, hardware, and vendor. I have used the Vendor Customer Evaluation Questionnaires (software and hardware) in Chapter 15 of this book to decide the worthiness of software and hardware products. Customers can be surveyed in 15 minutes by telephone. Points can be equated to answers from customers of the vendor. When evaluating multiple vendors, this can be especially helpful. The two Vendor Customer Evaluation Questionnaires in Chapter 15 may not fit every situation but can be used for software and hardware evaluation. Either questionnaire can be used as a guide for developing your own.

Case 2

While consulting at a wholesale company, I noticed that some hardware on the system I was working on was old. When I talked with senior management at the company, one official said that acquisition of the equipment was made through the vendor from whom they had purchased accounting and database software. The system consisted of a 486 and 386 personal computer running SCO Xenix. Twenty Wyse terminals were attached to the 486 personal computer. The 386 personal computer was purchased to be a parallel system to the 486 personal computer and to constitute a backup system if necessary. The entire system cost the wholesaler $700,000.

The same official confided to me that the vendor told him he routinely sold old hardware to customers as new because it is fully tested and therefore more reliable. It was further related to me that when an outside consultant was retained to do an analysis of the accounting software he found out that the software was his own and had been illegally used by the vendor. Apparently the vendor had installed a borrowed copy of accounting software and invoiced the wholesaler for the product.

The performance of the entire system, both the hardware and software, was poor. This demonstrates the kind of vendor this company was dealing with.

Analysis

This kind of vendor should be avoided at all costs. Hardware purchases should be received direct from the manufacturer if possible. However, this would not be necessary if you were doing business with a retailer like Computerland, or Comp USA. Warranty information should be filed and registration cards filled out and returned to the manufacturer promptly. Serial numbers of equipment purchased should be kept on file.

When software packages are delivered and installed by a vendor, you should receive documentation, warranty information, product serial number, and sometimes an activation key code. Registration cards are also part of most software packages. Filling out the registration card and returning it to the software company is essential.

Sometimes smaller reputable software vendors load software on to a computer system in house before they ship it to the customer. This enables them to do some testing and debugging in their own facility. This should not be a problem if warranty, serial number, registration cards, and manuals are provided and the manufacturer verifies the product as new.

All equipment has a mean time to failure. Statements declaring used equipment is better than new equipment should be considered ludicrous. The best part of a computer hardware's life span starts when it is removed from the manufacturer's box new! That does not mean that new hardware will not malfunction when it is delivered. If that happens, you're entitled to new equipment from the manufacturer under warranty.

Purchasing equipment from reputable used equipment brokers can have economic advantages. Buying used equipment at reasonable prices for short-term application solutions is a viable strategy. The supplier of used equipment should provide a limited warranty and the equipment should be competitively priced. Before purchasing used equipment, solicit quotes from two used equipment brokers.

Purchasing new personal computers from retailers that specialize in IBM clones can provide quality solutions. Companies like Computerland and Comp USA handle multiple lines of computer hardware and software. These companies stand behind what they sell and have prospered from putting the customer first.

Case 3

This case involved a nonprofit organization that provided social services. The organization had been dealing with a reputable vendor of hardware and software. Because of this vendor's remote location, another vendor was hired by the head of finance to install accounting software on an existing IBC computer. The new vendor told them that they would have to buy another computer if they wanted to run accounting software. An additional computer was purchased at great expense.

This new vendor then deinstalled and removed a tape drive from the original IBC computer without permission. It was then discovered when another consulting firm was contacted that the original IBC computer would have easily run the accounting software.

A high-level executive of the nonprofit organization lost his position over his dealings with this particular vendor. In this particular case, other managers, sensing that the organization was being taken advantage of, took the necessary steps to regain control of their computer systems.

The nonprofit organization tried in vain to get the systems vendor to perform to expected professional business ethics. When the organization realized that this was not going to be possible, the relationship with the systems vendor was severed.

Analysis

This situation is regrettable. Even after the nonprofit organization became aware of the misrepresentation perpetrated on them, they chose to keep the problem quiet. They were hoping they could get the vendor to return the tape drive and support the accounting software. This of course only compounded their problems with the vendor. If a vendor is not performing as required, sever the relationship immediately.

This situation could have been prevented by retaining a reputable consulting firm to do an analysis of the product and vendor. If funds were not available for such service, then conducting an internal survey of the vendor's clients may have helped. Contractual protection for the nonprofit organization would have protected them from this kind of fraud. The removal of equipment from the organization's premises without their permission amounted to theft.

Summary

1. Check customer references of a potential vendor. Use the Vendor Customer Evaluation Questionnaires. See the samples for software and hardware in Chapter 15.

2. Visit other clients of a vendor and observe them using the vendor's product.

3. Retain the services of a reputable consulting firm or consultant to do an analysis of the product to be purchased. Make sure that the consulting firm or consultant retained has no affiliation with the product and is unbiased.

4. Contractually withhold final payment for the product until it is successfully installed and accepted by you.

5. When acquiring software through a vendor, be sure that you have received the documentation, warranty information, serial number, activation key code, and registration card.

6. Receive hardware purchases directly from the manufacturer whenever possible. Be sure all warranty information and registration cards for the equipment are included.

2
Contractual Agreements

Introduction

Contracts in the purest sense list what both parties are going to do to receive goods, services, and monies. I am going to illustrate two particular cases where I was personally hired to remedy after the fact.

In Cases 4 and 5, a contract had been executed between the vendor and the client. In both cases if a competent contract attorney had been hired by the client, the fraud perpetrated by the vendor would have been prevented.

Never suppose that just because a contract is used by a vendor you can expect them to adhere to ethical business practices. On the contrary, some vendors use contracts not only to protect themselves but also to allow them to take advantage of their clients. The lowest level of details regarding what is expected of both parties must be stated in the contract. Never leave out details or agree to them verbally and expect them to be executed by either party to the contract.

Case 4

In this case, I was contacted by a headhunter who asked if I had expertise with a particular computer language. This language was internal to one operating system and was not widely used. The operating system itself was excellent and was used by state of the art hardware at the time.

I ultimately accepted the assignment, which was at the site of a well-known government contractor. The total investment in the combined hardware and software was $2,500,000. This system provided the distribution of telecommunication costs between the contractor's personnel and government personnel on an international network. The system also maintained an inventory of telecommunications equipment, the location of telephones, and their numbers at vendor sites around the country.

The vendor here had been charging unreasonable maintenance costs on the system for about a year. It was my job to end dependence on the vendor and to make the software work. The application had partially failed on my arrival. The bulk of the software was written in an undocumented language that I had experience with from a previous contract. The vendor openly admitted that he picked this language knowing that it was undocumented. However, no specific computer language had been specified in the contract. The vendor, wishing to perpetuate unreasonable maintenance costs, attempted to make the system proprietary by using an undocumented language.

I was able ultimately to unravel this software system and get it working. This ended dependence on this particularly unscrupulous software vendor. The government contractor here couldn't make the entire system work. I was advised early on that the executive responsible for the initial contract nearly lost his job and a pension. This executive trusted what seemed to be an honest and sincere vendor that wished to provide services of the highest quality. Ultimately, this software vendor folded his tent and left town.

Analysis

The contract with the vendor should have stated the computer language to be used. Hourly rates and overtime rates for maintenance should have been defined in the contract with the vendor. The entire contract should have been reviewed by the legal department of the government contractor. Higher levels of management of the government contractor were not fully aware of the circumstances regarding the project. Audits by an independent consulting firm or consultant would have kept management at the proper levels informed on the real progress of this project. The vendor deliberately kept the government contractor in the dark as to the real status of the system and created problems with it to generate revenue for himself. The manager responsible merely went along with the vendor, when this occurred, because he did not want higher levels of management to think there was a problem with the system.

Case 5

This next situation occurred some years ago. I was asked to help a manufacturing company that was having difficulty with its computer system. They had a failed manufacturing software system. The system could only be supported by the vendor because the manufacturer didn't have the source code. *Source code* is the portion of the software that is compiled to create executable code. It's the executable code that runs on most systems.

This was not the most significant aspect of the situation. I frequently consult with attorneys for my clients. Here, I had the contract reviewed by a competent contract attorney. The contract that the manufacturer signed with the software vendor said that the manufacturer was only renting the software. This was a multimillion-dollar manufacturer that did not own its business system. The manufacturer here was unaware of this situation. The financial loss here was not retrievable and affected the financial status of the manufacturer severely. The software was so bad that the material requirements planning (MRP) module failed to work correctly.

Analysis

Both situations could have been avoided by hiring a consulting firm to do the initial analysis of the system being considered for purchase and getting competent legal assistance with contract negotiations. If possible on substantial purchases, develop your own contract for the software or hardware vendor to sign that contains the minutest detail of your functional requirements and the vendors marketing literature. By making the vendors marketing literature part of the contract, all claims regarding the product can be enforced. Payments to vendors should be tied to meeting deliverables successfully and on time.

I would like to add that the software vendor had a full-time staff attorney to negotiate contracts with clients. An attorney that I asked to review the contract between the manufacturer and the software vendor commented that it was the best written contract he'd ever seen. It flawlessly protected the software vendor from litigation and financial responsibility.

Summary

1. Retain a consulting firm when making significant purchases of either hardware or software.

2. Retain legal counsel to review potential contracts if this service is not offered by the consulting firm.

3. Include all marketing literature from the vendor as exhibits in the contract.

4. The contract itself should detail as closely as possible the functional requirements of the system whether it is hardware or software.

5. Withhold 25 to 50 percent of the final payment from the vendor until the system has been accepted as successful.

6. State contractually that for unsuccessful implementations of hardware or software that the vendor is subject to financial penalties.

7. Make provisions in the contract that require payments to vendors dependent upon meeting a schedule of deliverable items.

8. If possible, develop your own contract—don't sign the vendor's contract.

9. Make sure all vendor guarantees and warranties are fully stated with their limitations in the contract.

10. All contracts should be made in triplicate, signed by authorized representatives, and notarized. Always retain the original copy.

3
Sabotage

Introduction

You're probably thinking, "How can sabotage be construed to be fraud?" After reviewing the following case histories, you may recognize a similar situation at your own company or site. Case 6 reveals details of sabotage perpetrated by a vendor on a government contractor. Case 7 reveals details not only of sabotage but also of what amounted to extortion by the vendor.

Sometimes it is a company's own employees that perpetrate sabotage. This may occur in situations where they are forced to use a computer system that they feel they have no ownership in. Ownership is created by allowing employees to define functional specifications of systems they will be working with.

I have also seen situations where employees sabotaged computer systems just to prove they could do it. These misguided individuals believed that they were demonstrating management's inabilities. Employees and management must be on guard continually for this type of behavior from employees.

Case 6

The first situation occurred at the government contractor's site previously described in Chapter 2, Case 4. I had been on site for only 1 week and was still in the midst of my preliminary analysis. The software vendor was allowed to remain on site until they had finished delivering user documentation on the system. Up to this point, I had tested and done backups. Backups were being done correctly and I could restore any file system if necessary. While I was out to lunch Friday of that week, the system went down. I was not there to see the actual event.

When I returned from lunch, I found the software vendors project leader explaining to the manager in charge that he would have to spend most of the weekend fixing the system and that someone had caused the crash. My name wasn't stated but the statement was directed at me. I listened to the projected overtime hours that it was going to take to fix the system. The project leader was estimating six of his personnel at the overtime rate for 60 hours. I would like to point out at this point that the software vendor's project leader and I shared the system administrator password.

I informed the government contractor's manager in charge that I could restore the file system in approximately 1 hour. The manager was skeptical but allowed me to do the restore on the file system. In less than an hour, the system was restored and ready for use.

Analysis

Two things were happening here. The software vendor was first attempting to discredit me and perpetuate his position with the government contractor. Second, the software vendor was attempting to bill for consulting hours that were totally unnecessary. The entire incident was contrived by the software vendor. Someone else might have been victimized right along with the government contractor.

Significantly, the software vendor did not offer any audit trails or logs of any type to substantiate his claims. Additionally, no concise opinion was presented as to what actually happened.

Luckily for the government contractor, the file system had not been updated since the last backup. However, if information had been entered to that particular file system since the last backup, the appropriate documents could have been reentered into the system.

Case 7

This client was a wholesaler, the same one in Chapter 1, Case 2, that was having problems with a vendor. The vendor had installed a 486 and 386 personal computer, about 20 Wyse terminals, and six printers. The installed software consisted of financial and database software, and SCO Xenix. Except for the 486 computer, all of the equipment was used and billed as new. Documentation was provided with the accounting, database, and the SCO Xenix operating system. However, the software was installed so that only the systems vendor could maintain it. Maintenance was billed at $200 per hour. The wholesaler had invested approximately $700,000 in this system, a system that was probably worth $20,000.

The wholesaler had previously attempted to rid themselves of the vendor and hired a consultant. Their 386 personal computer system had not worked for some time although it was supposed to be a parallel system. They tried to use this 386 personal computer to set up a parallel system in an attempt to learn the changes that were in the software that made it proprietary to the vendor. Coincidental to the vendor learning that the wholesaler had hired a consultant, the 486 personal computer mysteriously stopped working. The consultant hired by the wholesaler was unable to find the cause of the system failure on the 486 personal computer. The vendor then demanded thousands of dollars to fix the system on the 486 personal computer and insisted the other consultant be dismissed. The wholesaler floundered without a system for 3 days before the system was restored, only after the demands made by the vendor had been met.

After listening to management at the wholesaler, I decided to help them in gaining their independence from the vendor. Even before starting work, I advised the management at the wholesale company to disconnect the modems connected to the 486 personal computer.

My first day at the site of the wholesale company was spent reviewing their backup procedures. The backup log was all right: files that were to be backed up were listed. However, the light on the tape drive never came on when running the backup procedure. I then discovered that a few backup tapes were given to another vendor to see if there was data on them. The other vendor reported that they were unable to read the backup tapes. All of the backup tapes yielded one label record without any real data. It then became apparent that the SCO Xenix tape utilities had been modified by the systems vendor. Once this was realized, it didn't take long to restore the tape utilities and start performing full backups of the system.

Management at the wholesale company then became aware that all data on their business transactions were being offered to a competitor by the systems vendor. The systems vendor had been backing up the database that belonged to the wholesaler over a modem connection, apparently for some months. Modems at the wholesale company remained unplugged from wall connections the first day that I began helping that company. Modem connections were not reconnected until proper security measures had been put in place, thus protecting the wholesaler's data from further intrusions.

Analysis

In performing analysis of the systems on the 486 personal computer, I discovered some business names on the system that the wholesaler stated were companies owned by the systems vendor. The systems vendor had been using the resources of the wholesaler to conduct business with these other affiliated companies without the permission of the wholesale company.

The actual integrity of the systems on the 486 personal computer was nominal. Because of the proprietary changes made by the vendor, the wholesale company decided to change to a new hardware platform, the International Business Machines (IBM) AS400 and Turning Point software from one of IBM's business partners. For this company, it was the best choice considering the fact that even data from the accounting and database software was unreliable.

The wholesale company started with excellent software systems from established and reputable firms. However, the systems vendor installing them modified them so that the data lacked integrity and the software was corrupted to the point that only the vendor could maintain it. This was a deliberate effort to make the software proprietary to the systems vendor, thus perpetuating their financial hold on the wholesale company.

This is a preventable situation from the very beginning. The systems vendor had perpetrated the entire situation over a 2-year period. The wholesale company should have gained control of the systems vendor early in the implementation process. If the systems vendor was not performing work ethically, the business relationship should have been severed immediately. Since the wholesaler had no previous experience with computer systems, they should have hired a reputable consulting firm to help in the planning and implementation of a system from the very beginning. The money spent on a consulting firm to start with could have saved hundreds of thousands of dollars.

Summary

1. Conduct business with software and hardware vendors pursuant to the provisions of a contract.

2. If conditions under which a vendor is performing work changes, create a written addendum or change order to the contract.

3. If any vendor shows signs of attempting to perpetuate a relationship for financial gain, suspend the relationship. The business relationship may be resumed after an audit that lays to rest any suspicion of this type of activity.

4. If a vendor is not performing up to reasonable expectations, it should be replaced. Never suppose its performance will improve with time.

5. In case of a system failure find the cause by looking at the system messages printed on the system console or the system printer. If the system has a mail module, check to see if mail has been sent to the system administrator.

6. Have regular audits done by an outside consulting firm or consultant.

4
Source Code

Introduction

Source code is that portion of the software that when compiled creates executable objects. When these objects are executed, they then do the tasks they were designed to do. Software source code is usually not sold. The standard practice of vendors is to sell the executable objects. Developers or software vendors retain the source code, ensuring their continued ownership of the software product.

Purchasing Source Code

Occasionally it makes sense to purchase the source code from a software vendor. This is determined by asking yourself the following questions.

1. Is the software being considered for acquisition to be modified internally?
2. Is the developer or software vendor's financial position tenuous?

Purchasing source code can prevent competitors from getting software that was enhanced and engineered at your company's expense. This can occur when software changes are requested of a software vendor and the changes are retained by them in their copy of the source code. If you modify and maintain your own source code for software, you can control the changes or upgrades to the system. This will prevent your competition from being able to use software that has been developed on your system at no expense to them.

Sometimes software is developed that is excellent and needs little maintenance. However, it may be owned by an entity that does not have staying power in the marketplace. In this situation, price and long-term projected use of the software have to be considered when contemplating buying source code.

Escrow

The middle ground in all this is called escrow, which is a contract deposited with a third party, by whom it is to be delivered to the grantee on the fulfillment of some condition. Everyone understands that when you buy a house or piece of commercial property an escrow is opened. The same instrument can be applied to source code. Escrows can provide protection to both buyers and sellers of software systems. Escrows can ensure the buyer's ability to get the source code at a future time at a fixed price.

Case 8

While working as an employee for a telecommunications company, I was asked to create an escrow agreement. The source code represented a $4 million research and development project that created a system for the monitoring of DS1 and DS3 communications in the network. The system was developed by a subcontractor.

After conferring with the principals of both companies, I developed some escrow agreement criteria. Both parties agreed to a bank in the Midwest. After contacting a bank in the Midwest and discussing the escrow functions with a vice president at the bank, I was furnished with a sample escrow agreement. This sample agreement was then modified by an attorney and myself at the telecommunications company. One of the provisions of this document was that source code in the form of magnetic media and hard copy printouts of tables, charts, programs, and data file definitions were to be deposited with the bank.

Analysis

Escrows of this type generally are designed to remain open and are only closed for the following reasons:

1. If the owners or developers of the software become insolvent and file bankruptcy, the source code is released to the buyer of the software.

2. If the owners or developers cease to support or sell the software and voluntarily release the source code to the buyer.

3. The buyer of the software has ceased using the software and is no longer interested in the source code.

4. Litigation against the owners or developers has ended in a judgment releasing the source code to the buyer. Usually this occurs only when owners or developers of software fail to support the product as agreed contractually.

5. The buyers of the software purchase the source code so that they can change the system internally.

6. The buyer must have the option of closing the escrow at his or her discretion.

Case 9

I was retained by an insurance company to see if modifications could be made to the system they were using, which at the time lacked data integrity. The system had just been purchased from a local software vendor on a purchase order. No documentation on the system was available although the software vendor had promised to provide user-level documentation in the immediate future. This particular system ran on a 386 Everex Step personal computer that used the SCO Xenix operating system. Thirty remote users dialed up daily via modems and multiplexers using Wyse 60 terminals or personal computers. The personal computers were set up to use Term software to emulate Wyse 60 terminals. The system had excellent hardware and software for the type of environment in which it was being used. The software provided by the vendor consisted of Subject & Wills database, Xenix Shell, and C programs. Some of the source code resided on the system.

Clients of the insurance company were ending their business relationship with the insurance company because of their dissatisfaction with data integrity of the system. The clients were sometimes unable to generate billing to clients. They were also unable to generate an accurate aging report on outstanding charges to clients.

As it turned out, the software vendor also provided similar services and was a competitor of my client. By not providing quality services, they were eliminating their own competition. My client contemplated buying the source code of this particular system in an effort to provide reliable services to their clients.

The software vendor was willing to sell the source code for $50,000. This was a grossly inflated price for the source code for this particular system. The original system cost under $10,000 for both hardware, software, and communications equipment for remote users.

Analysis

I was not able to help the client in this particular situation because he had already lost a substantial portion of the business. Paying $50,000 for source code was out of the question.

Clearly, this is a situation where a contract should have been signed. The price for source code should have been set at the time the software system was purchased. Thoroughly researching the company with which you are dealing is essential. This kind of research is done as a matter of routine by consulting firms. This is the advantage in using consulting firms to manage software acquisition. It might have saved the insurance company from substantial financial losses.

Summary

1. When acquiring software systems establish the price for source code contractually.

2. If the price for source code is unreasonably high or if you do not anticipate changing the software, then establish an escrow.

3. If changes in software are anticipated that may give competitors an advantage in the market you share, consider getting the source code and performing the changes internally. This type of work also might be done by a third party or consulting firm.

5
Copyright

Introduction

Software developers and the entities they work for are constantly at risk. The risk is in maintaining and proving ownership of the software. While software is protected from the first time the copyright is affixed to source code and documentation, registration of the software cannot be overlooked. *Circular 1, Copyright Basics,* a pamphlet available from the Copyright office states:

> Copyright is a form of protection provided by the laws of the United States (title 17, U.S. Code) to the authors of "original works of authorship" including literary, dramatic, musical, artistic, and certain other intellectual works. This protection is available to both published and unpublished works. Section 106 of the Copyright Act generally gives the owner of copyright the exclusive right to do and to authorize others to do the following:
>
> - *To reproduce* the copyrighted work in copies or phonorecords
> - To prepare *derivative works* based upon the copyrighted work
> - *To distribute copies or phonorecords* of the copyrighted work to the public by sale or other transfer of ownership, or by rental, lease, or lending
> - *To display the copyrighted work publicly,* in the case of literary, musical, dramatic, and choreographic works, pantomimes, and pictorial, graphic, or sculptural works, including the individual images of a motion picture or other audiovisual work

Copyright protects software products that are developed and sold. Once the copyright is obtained for software, the ownership cannot be disputed. Two specific cases on copyrights are presented in this chapter. In Case 10, copyright was applied for to protect a substantial investment in software. The company in this case had spent millions of dollars developing software but had never copyrighted any of the software.

This is followed by Case 11, where software was spirited away from a company to another company. This situation is unique in that the software cost the developer a staggering amount of money. The investment was not protected and ended up in the hands of a competitor.

Case 10

While working at a telecommunications company, I reviewed their primary system for managing one of the largest telecommunications network in this country. The system represented a $3 million investment in software development. No copyright had ever been applied for by them until I volunteered to do the task.

Additionally, the company was attempting to market this system at telecommunications trade shows. While the software was not unique, the system architecture was. Allowing this information to proliferate without protection would have diminished its value in the marketplace.

Analysis

The company had spent millions of dollars on software development. Software developed by them managed not only their telecommunications networks but also other businesses. They were in an extremely competitive business arena. This company competes with all the major telecommunications companies in this country. The company realized that copyrights had to be secured for software they had developed. The company now aggressively pursues copyright, trademark, and patent opportunities and thereby assures itself of return on its investment in creating systems to manage its businesses.

Case 11

While working for an information company as a consultant, I became aware of the theft of source code from this company. This company had a hardware and software system that provided their clients with up-to-the-minute information on business transactions.

This company's original product was based on hardware and software they had developed for the minicomputer environment. Clients of the information company were exerting pressure and requesting a software version of their system that would run on a personal computer.

The information company developed a software package for the personal computer. This company had a competitor that illegally obtained the software that had been developed by the information company. The competitor of the information company managed to get into the market with the personal computer version of the software developed by the information company.

The information company lost its position in the marketplace to the other company. Both the information company and the competitor are currently embroiled in a civil suit at the time of this writing. It has already been established by independent investigation that the software the competitor has was created by the information company.

Analysis

Registering a copyright on software being developed by any company is something that I strongly recommend. A copyright can be applied for even when software is in the testing phase.

Maintaining a secure development environment is also essential. No one programmer should have access to an entire software system. I recommend that no individual programmer working in a development environment should be allowed access to more than one module of software at a time. Once the programmer has completed his or her work with the module, it should be moved to a directory to which that individual does not have access.

This company should have made it policy to affix a copyright notice or statement on all programs as they were created. Usually, the first 10 to 20 lines of a program describe what the program does, who wrote the program, the environment the program is run in, the data files used by the program, and modifications listing date and name of the programmer who made the modifications.

Documentation should also have a copyright notice displayed at the beginning of the document. The initial display presented to the user of the software at the video display terminal should also have a copyright notice or statement.

By prominently displaying the copyright notice or statement the developer may discourage attempts by unscrupulous individuals to use the software illicitly. One of the benefits is that an infringer will not be able to claim that he or she "innocently infringed" a work. Registration receives the benefit of a legal presumption in court, called *prima facie* evidentiary weight. The court will presume that the facts stated in the copyright certificate of registration are true and that the copyright is valid.

What Works Are Protected

Circular 1, Copyright Basics, a pamphlet available from the Copyright office, states:

Copyright protects "original works of authorship" that are fixed in a tangible form of expression. The fixation need not be directly perceptible, so long as it may be communicated with the aid of a machine or device. Copyrightable works include the following categories:

(1) literary works;
(2) musical works, including any accompanying words;
(3) dramatic works, including any accompanying music;
(4) pantomimes and choreographic works;
(5) pictorial, graphic, and sculptural works;
(6) motion pictures and other audiovisual works;
(7) sound recordings; and
(8) architectural works.

These categories should be viewed quite broadly: for example, computer programs and most "compilations" are registrable as "literary works"; maps and architectural plans are registrable as "pictorial, graphic, and sculptural works."

How to Secure a Copyright

Circular 1, Copyright Basics, states:

Copyright Secured Automatically Upon Creation; The way in which copyright protection is secured under the present law is frequently misunderstood. No publication or registration or other action in the Copyright Office is required to secure copyright (see following note). There are however, certain definite advantages to registration. Copyright is secured *automatically* when the work is created, and a work is "created" when it is fixed in a copy or phonorecord for the first time. "Copies" are material objects from which a work can be read or visually perceived either directly or with the aid of a machine or device, such as books, manuscripts, sheet music, film, videotape, or microfilm. "Phonorecords" are material objects embodying fixations of sounds (excluding, by statutory definition, motion picture soundtracks), such as audio tapes and phonograph disks. Thus, for example, a song (the "work") can be fixed in sheet music ("copies") or in phonograph disks ("phono-records"), or both.

If a work is prepared over a period of time, the part of the work that is fixed on a particular date constitutes the created work as of that date.

Note: Before 1978, statutory copyright was generally secured by the act of publication with notice of copyright, assuming compliance with all other relevant statutory conditions. Works in the public domain on January 1, 1978 (for example, works published without satisfying all conditions for securing statutory copyright under the Copyright Act of 1909) remain in the public domain under the current act.

Statutory copyright could also be secured before 1978 by the act of registration in the case of certain unpublished works and works eligible for ad interim copyright. The current Act automatically extends to full term (section 304 sets the term) copyright for all works in which ad interim copyright was subsisting or was capable of being secured on December 31, 1977.

Copyright Registration

Circular 1, Copyright Basics, states:

In general, copyright registration is a legal formality intended to make a public record of the basic facts of a particular copyright. However, except in two specific situations, "registration is not a condition of copyright protection. Even though registration is not generally a requirement for protection, the copyright law provides several inducements or advantages to encourage copyright owners to make registration. Among these advantages are the following:

- Registration establishes a public record of the copyright claim;
- Before an infringement suit may be filed in court, registration is necessary for works of U.S. origin and for foreign works not originating in a Berne Union country. (For more information on when a work is of U.S. origin, request *Circular 93.*);
- If made before or within 5 years of publication, registration will establish *prima facia* evidence in court of the validity of the copyright and of the facts stated in the certificate; and
- If registration is made within 3 months after publication of the work or prior to an infringement of the work, statutory damages and attorney's fees will be available to the copyright owner in court actions. Otherwise, only an award of actual damages and profits is available to the copyright owner.

Registration may be made any time within the life of the copyright. Unlike the law before 1978, when a work has been registered in unpublished form, it is not necessary to make another registration when the work becomes published (although the copyright owner may register the published edition, if desired).

Deposit Requirements

Circular 61, Copyright Registration for Computer Programs, states:

For published or unpublished computer programs, one copy of identifying portions of the program, (first 25 pages and last 25 pages), reproduced in a form visually perceptible without the aid of a machine or device, either on paper or in microform, together with the page equivalent unit containing the copyright notice if any.

For a program less than 50 pages in length, a visually perceptible copy of the entire program. For a revised version of a program which has been previously published, previously registered, or which is in the public domain, if the revisions occur throughout the entire program, the first 25 and the last 25 pages. If the revisions are not contained in the first and last 25 pages, any 50 pages representative of the revised material in the new program, together with the page or equivalent unit containing the copyright notice for the revised version, if any.

The Copyright Office believes that the best representation of the authorship in a computer program is a listing of the program in source code.

Where the applicant is unable or unwilling to deposit a source code listing, registration will proceed under our RULE OF DOUBT policy upon receipt of written assurance from the applicant that the work as deposited in object code contains copyrightable authorship.

If a published user's manual (or other printed documentation) accompanies the computer program, deposit one copy of the users manual along with one copy of the identifying portion of the program.

Special Relief and Trade Secrets

Circular 61, Copyright Registration for Computer Programs, states:

When a computer program contains trade secrets or other confidential material that the applicant is unwilling to disclose by depositing the first and last 25 pages in source code, the Copyright Office is willing to consider special relief requests enabling the applicant to deposit less than or other than the usual 50 pages of source code. Special relief requests for the following three deposit options are presently being granted upon receipt of the applicant's written request to the Chief, Examining Division, for special relief:

- first and last 25 pages of source code with some portions blocked out, provided that the blocked-out portions are proportionately less than the material still remaining;
- at least the first and last ten pages of source code alone, with no blocked-out portions; or
- first and last 25 pages of object code plus any ten or more consecutive pages of object code, with no blocked-out portions.

Location of Copyright Notice

Section 201.20(g),37 C.F.R.

Works Reproduced in Machine-Readable Copies

Circular 61, Copyright Registration for Computer Programs, states:

> For works reproduced in machine-readable copies (such as magnetic tapes or disks, punched cards, or the like), from which the work cannot ordinarily be visually perceived except with the aid of a machine or device, each of the following constitute examples of acceptable methods of affixation and position of notice:
>
> (1) A notice embodied in the copies in machine-readable form in such a manner that on visually perceptible printouts it appears either with or near the title, or at the end of the work;
>
> (2) A notice that is displayed at the user's terminal at sign on;
>
> (3) A notice that is continuously on terminal display; or
>
> (4) A legible notice reproduced durably, so as to withstand normal use, on a gummed or other label securely affixed to the copies or to a box, reel, cartridge, cassette, or other container used as a permanent receptacle for the copies.

Form of Copyright Notice

Form of Notice for Visually Perceptible Copies

According to Circular 61, January 1991, of the U.S. Printing Office, the notice for visually perceptible copies should contain all of the following three elements:

1. The symbol © (the letter C in a circle), or the word "Copyright," or the abbreviation "Copr."

2. The year of first publication of the work. In the case of compilations of derivative works incorporating previously published material, the year date of first publication of the compilation or derivative work is sufficient.

3. The name of the owner of copyright in the work, or abbreviation by which the name can be recognized, or generally known alternative designation of the owner. Example: ©1986 John Doe

Registration Procedures

In General

1. To register a work, send the following three elements in the same envelope or package to the Register of Copyright, Copyright Office, Library of Congress, Washington, DC 20559:
   a. A properly completed application form.
   b. A nonrefundable filing fee of $20 for each application.

c. A nonreturnable deposit if the work is being registered. The deposit requirements vary in particular situations.

If you are registering software or text request Form TX. A copy of this form is included in this text for your convenience. A two-sided copy of the form may be submitted when submitting for a copyright. However, the form should be printed on both sides and be an accurate reproduction of the Form. Free applications forms are provided by the Copyright Office.

A series of pamphlets and forms are available to help firms in understanding, searching, or applying for a copyright. Although the office cannot give legal advice, it can help in providing information on claiming a copyright, what can be copyrighted, notice of copyright, transfer of copyright, and searching records of the Copyright Office.

Contact.   Copyright Office, Library of Congress, Washington, DC 20559. Telephone (202) 479-0700.

How Will I Know If My Application Was Received?

Effective August 1991, Bulletin SL-9 states the following:

> You will not receive an acknowledgment that your application has been received—the Office receives over 600,000 applications annually—but you can expect within 16 weeks of submission (normally much more quickly):
>
> - A certificate of registration to indicate the work has been registered
> - A letter or telephone call from a Copyright Office staff member if further information is needed; or if the application cannot be accepted, a letter explaining why it has been rejected.

If you want to know when the Copyright Office receives your material, send it by registered or certified mail and request a return receipt from the Postal Service. Due to the large volume of mail received by the Office daily, you should allow at least 3 weeks for the return of your receipt.

What Is the Status of My Application?

The Copyright Office states:

> We cannot provide free information about the status of applications that have been in the Copyright Office fewer than 16 weeks. If you

must have this information sooner, contact the Certifications and Document Section, which can provide this information upon payment of applicable fees.

When Is My Registration Effective?

A copyright registration is effective on the date that all the required elements (application, fee, and deposit) in acceptable form are received in the copyright office, regardless of the length of time it takes the Copyright Office to process the application and mail the certificate of registration. You do not have to receive your certificate before you publish or produce your work, nor do you need permission from the Copyright Office to place notice of copyright on your material.

How Many Forms May I Receive?

The Copyright Office states:

Because of budget restrictions we can no longer send unlimited quantities of our application forms and publications. If you need additional application forms or circulars, you may order a limited supply by calling the Copyright Office Hotline anytime day or night at (202) 707-9100 and leaving a message on the recorder. We encourage you to photocopy our circulars and other informational material. You may also photocopy blank application forms; however, photocopied forms submitted to the Copyright Office must be clear, legible, and on a good grade of 8 1/2-inch by 11-inch white paper, suitable for automatic feeding through a photocopier. The forms should be printed, preferably in black ink, head to head (so that when you turn the sheet over, the top of page 2 is directly behind the top of page 1). *Forms not meeting these requirements will be returned.* Please allow 2–3 weeks for delivery of your order.

A sample copyright form follows. The Copyright Office accepts reproductions of the copyright form for submission. Be sure you reproduce the form in a two-sided format.

U.S. Adherence to the Berne Convention

Circular 93 Highlights of U.S. Adherence to the Berne Convention states:

On March 1, 1989, the United States joined the Berne Union by entering into an international treaty called the Berne Convention,

FORM TX

UNITED STATES COPYRIGHT OFFICE

REGISTRATION NUMBER

TX   TXU

EFFECTIVE DATE OF REGISTRATION

Month   Day   Year

DO NOT WRITE ABOVE THIS LINE. IF YOU NEED MORE SPACE, USE A SEPARATE CONTINUATION SHEET.

1

TITLE OF THIS WORK ▼

PREVIOUS OR ALTERNATIVE TITLES ▼

PUBLICATION AS A CONTRIBUTION If this work was published as a contribution to a periodical, serial, or collection, give information about the collective work in which the contribution appeared   **Title of Collective Work ▼**

If published in a periodical or serial give: **Volume ▼**   **Number ▼**   **Issue Date ▼**   **On Pages ▼**

2

a

NAME OF AUTHOR ▼

DATES OF BIRTH AND DEATH
Year Born ▼   Year Died ▼

Was this contribution to the work a "work made for hire"?
☐ Yes
☐ No

AUTHOR'S NATIONALITY OR DOMICILE
Name of Country
OR { Citizen of ▶
Domiciled in ▶

WAS THIS AUTHOR'S CONTRIBUTION TO THE WORK
Anonymous? ☐ Yes ☐ No
Pseudonymous? ☐ Yes ☐ No

If the answer to either of these questions is "Yes." see detailed instructions

NATURE OF AUTHORSHIP Briefly describe nature of the material created by this author in which copyright is claimed. ▼

NOTE

Under the law the "author" of a work made for hire" is generally the employer not the employee (see instructions) For any part of this work that was "made for hire" check "Yes" in the space provided give the employer (or other person for whom the work was prepared) as "Author" of that part and leave the space for dates of birth and death blank.

b

NAME OF AUTHOR ▼

DATES OF BIRTH AND DEATH
Year Born ▼   Year Died ▼

Was this contribution to the work a "work made for hire"?
☐ Yes
☐ No

AUTHOR'S NATIONALITY OR DOMICILE
Name of country
OR { Citizen of ▶
Domiciled in ▶

WAS THIS AUTHOR'S CONTRIBUTION TO THE WORK
Anonymous? ☐ Yes ☐ No
Pseudonymous? ☐ Yes ☐ No

If the answer to either of these questions is "Yes." see detailed instructions

NATURE OF AUTHORSHIP Briefly describe nature of the material created by this author in which copyright is claimed. ▼

c

NAME OF AUTHOR ▼

DATES OF BIRTH AND DEATH
Year Born ▼   Year Died ▼

Was this contribution to the work a "work made for hire"?
☐ Yes
☐ No

AUTHOR'S NATIONALITY OR DOMICILE
Name of Country
OR { Citizen of ▶
Domiciled in ▶

WAS THIS AUTHOR'S CONTRIBUTION TO THE WORK
Anonymous? ☐ Yes ☐ No
Pseudonymous? ☐ Yes ☐ No

If the answer to either of these questions is "Yes." see detailed instructions

NATURE OF AUTHORSHIP Briefly describe nature of the material created by this author in which copyright is claimed. ▼

3

a

YEAR IN WHICH CREATION OF THIS WORK WAS COMPLETED This information must be given in all cases.
◀ Year

b

DATE AND NATION OF FIRST PUBLICATION OF THIS PARTICULAR WORK
Complete this information ONLY if this work has been published.
Month ▶   Day ▶   Year ▶   ◀ Nation

4

See instructions before completing this space

COPYRIGHT CLAIMANT(S) Name and address must be given even if the claimant is the same as the author given in space 2.▼

TRANSFER If the claimant(s) named here in space 4 are different from the author(s) named in space 2, give a brief statement of how the claimant(s) obtained ownership of the copyright.▼

APPLICATION RECEIVED

ONE DEPOSIT RECEIVED

TWO DEPOSITS RECEIVED

REMITTANCE NUMBER AND DATE

DO NOT WRITE HERE OFFICE USE ONLY

MORE ON BACK ▶ • Complete all applicable spaces (numbers 5-11) on the reverse side of this page.
• See detailed instructions.   • Sign the form at line 10.

DO NOT WRITE HERE

Page 1 of _____ pages

EXAMINED BY	**FORM TX**
CHECKED BY	
☐ CORRESPONDENCE Yes	FOR COPYRIGHT OFFICE USE ONLY

DO NOT WRITE ABOVE THIS LINE. IF YOU NEED MORE SPACE, USE A SEPARATE CONTINUATION SHEET.

PREVIOUS REGISTRATION Has registration for this work, or for an earlier version of this work, already been made in the Copyright Office?

☐ Yes ☐ No If your answer is "Yes," why is another registration being sought? (Check appropriate box) ▼

a. ☐ This is the first published edition of a work previously registered in unpublished form.

b. ☐ This is the first application submitted by this author as copyright claimant.

c. ☐ This is a changed version of the work, as shown by space 6 on this application.

If your answer is "Yes," give: **Previous Registration Number** ▼   **Year of Registration** ▼

5

DERIVATIVE WORK OR COMPILATION Complete both space 6a & 6b for a derivative work; complete only 6b for a compilation.

a. Preexisting Material Identify any preexisting work or works that this work is based on or incorporates. ▼

b. Material Added to This Work Give a brief, general statement of the material that has been added to this work and in which copyright is claimed. ▼

See instructions before completing this space.

6

7

REPRODUCTION FOR USE OF BLIND OR PHYSICALLY HANDICAPPED INDIVIDUALS A signature on this form at space 10, and a check in one of the boxes here in space 8, constitutes a non-exclusive grant of permission to the Library of Congress to reproduce and distribute solely for the blind and physically handicapped and under the conditions and limitations prescribed by the regulations of the Copyright Office: (1) copies of the work identified in space 1 of this application in Braille (or similar tactile symbols); or (2) phonorecords embodying a fixation of a reading of that work; or (3) both.

a ☐ Copies and Phonorecords   b ☐ Copies Only   c ☐ Phonorecords Only   See instructions

8

DEPOSIT ACCOUNT If the registration fee is to be charged to a Deposit Account established in the Copyright Office, give name and number of Account.

Name ▼   **Account Number** ▼

9

CORRESPONDENCE Give name and address to which correspondence about this application should be sent. Name/Address/Apt/City/State/Zip ▼

Be sure to give your daytime phone ◀ number

Area Code & Telephone Number ▶

CERTIFICATION* I, the undersigned, hereby certify that I am the

Check one ▶

☐ author
☐ other copyright claimant
☐ owner of exclusive right(s)
☐ authorized agent of _____

Name of author or other copyright claimant, or owner of exclusive right(s) ▲

of the work identified in this application and that the statements made by me in this application are correct to the best of my knowledge.

Typed or printed name and date ▼ If this application gives a date of publication in space 3, do not sign and submit it before that date.

_____ date ▶ _____

☞ Handwritten signature (X) ▼

10

MAIL CERTIFI- CATE TO	Name ▼	• Complete all necessary spaces • Sign your application in space 10
	Number Street Apartment Number ▼	1. Application form 2. Nonrefundable $20 filing fee in check or money order payable to Register of Copyrights 3. Deposit material
Certificate will be mailed in window envelope	City State ZIP ▼	Register of Copyrights Library of Congress Washington, D.C. 20559

11

* 17 U.S.C. § 506(e): Any person who knowingly makes a false representation of a material fact in the application for copyright registration provided for by section 409, or in any written statement filed in connection with the application, shall be fined not more than $2,500.

September 1991—100,000   ☆U.S. GOVERNMENT PRINTING OFFICE: 1991-282-170 40,005

whose full title is the Berne Convention for the Protection of Literary and Artistic Works. Also on March 1, 1989, amendments to the U.S. Copyright law that satisfy U.S. treaty obligations under the Convention took effect. The U.S. law continues to govern the protection and registration of works in the United States. The following discussion outlines the most important amendments in the law.

Effect of U.S. Membership in the Berne Union

Beginning March 1, 1989, copyright in the works of U.S. authors is protected automatically in all member nations of the Berne Union. (As of September 1988, there were a total of 79 member nations in the Berne Union.)

Since members of the Berne Union agree to a certain minimum level of copyright protection, each Berne Union country will provide at least that guaranteed level for U.S. authors.

Members of the Berne Union agree to treat nationals of other member countries like their own nationals for purposes of copyright. Therefore, U.S. authors will often receive higher levels of protection than the guaranteed minimum.

Overall, piracy of U.S. works abroad can be fought more effectively.

Beginning March 1, 1989, works of foreign authors who are nationals of a Berne Union country and whose works were first published in a Berne Union country are automatically protected in the United States.

U.S. Law Amended

In order to fulfill its Berne Convention obligations, the United States made certain changes in its copyright law by passing the Berne Convention Implementation Act of 1988. These changes are not retroactive and are effective only on and after March 1, 1989.

Mandatory Notice of Copyright Is Abolished

Mandatory notice of copyright has been abolished for works published for the first time on or after March 1, 1989. Failure to place a notice of copyright on copies or phonorecords of such works can no longer result in the loss of copyright.

Voluntary Use of Notice Is Encouraged

Placing a notice of copyright on published works is still strongly recommended. One of the benefits is that an infringer will not be able to claim that he or she "innocently infringed" a work. (A successful innocent infringement claim may result in a reduction in damages for infringement that the copyright owner would otherwise receive.)

Notice Unchanged for Works Published Before March 1, 1989

The Berne Convention Implementation Act is not retroactive. Thus, the notice requirements that were in place before March 1, 1989, govern all works first published during that period (regardless of national origin).

- Works first published between January 1, 1978, and February 28, 1989: If a work was first published without notice during this period, it is still necessary to register the work before or within five years after publication and add the notice to copies distributed in the United States after discovery of the omission.

- Works first published before January 1, 1978: If a work was first published without the required notice before 1978, copyright was lost immediately (except for works seeking "ad interim" protection). Once copyright is lost, it can never be restored in the United States, except by special legislation.

Mandatory Deposit

Copyright owners must deposit in the Copyright Office two complete copies or phonorecords of the best edition of all works subject to copyright that are publicly distributed in the United States, whether or not the work contains a notice of copyright. In general, this deposit requirement may be satisfied by registration. For more information about mandatory deposit, request *Circular 7d.*

Registration as a Prerequisite to Suit

Before a copyright infringement suit is brought for a work of U.S. origin, it must be submitted to the Copyright Office for registration.
When is the United States the country of origin for a work?

- Publication first occurred in the United States.

- Publication occurred simultaneously in the United States and a non–Berne Union country. "Simultaneous publication" means within the first 30 days of publication.

- The work is unpublished and all of the authors are nationals of the United States. (U.S. domiciliaries and habitual residents are treated the same as nationals.) In the case of an unpublished audiovisual work, all the authors are legal entities with headquarters in the United States.

- The work is a pictorial, graphic, or sculptural work that is incorporated in a permanent structure located in the United States.

- The work is first published in a non–Berne Union country and all of the authors are U.S. nationals. In the case of a published audiovisual work, all the authors are legal entities with headquarters in the United States.

Although Berne Convention works whose origins are not the United States are exempt from the requirement to register before suit can be brought, a person seeking the exemption bears the burden of proving to the court that the work is not subject to the registration requirement.

Benefits of Registration

Berne Convention works whose country of origins is not the United States need not be registered with the Copyrights Office in order to bring an infringement suit. However, registration receive the benefit of a legal presumption in court, called *prima facie* evidentiary weight. This means that the court will presume:

- That the facts stated in the copyright certificate of registration are true

- That the copyright is valid

Statutory Damages and Attorney's Fees

Another benefit of timely registration is that the copyright owner of works registered for copyright protection within 3 months of publication, or before infringement, is eligible for an award of attorney fees and statutory damages. These damages are now double the amounts previously provided. A copyright owner may elect to receive either actual damages or statutory damages. Where statutory damages are elected, the court determines the amount of the award, within a certain range. The Berne Convention Implementation Act doubles the statutory damages to

- A range between $500 and $20,000 for ordinary infringement
- A maximum of $100,000 for willful infringement
- A minimum of $200 for innocent infringement

Renewal Is Still Required

Works first federally copyrighted before 1978 must still be renewed in the 28th year in order to receive the second term of 47 years. If such a work is not timely renewed, it will fall into the public domain in the United States at the end of the 28th year.

Recordation

Recordation is a prerequisite to an infringement suit. The copyright owner no longer has to record a transfer before bringing a copyright lawsuit in that owner's name.

Benefits of Recordation

The benefits of recordation in the Copyright Office are unchanged.

- Under certain conditions, recordation establishes priorities between conflicting transfers and nonexclusive licenses.
- Under certain conditions, recordation establishes priority between conflicting transfers.
- Recordation establishes a public record of the contents of the transfer or document.

Summary

1. Apply for the copyright as soon as possible.
2. Details of the copyright submission should be kept confidential.
3. During the development of software, avoid allowing a single individual access to the entire system being developed.
4. Apply for a new copyright when significant changes are made to the system or a new version is to be released.
5. Affixation of the copyright notice to documentation and source code should occur as they are being created.

6

Data Omission

Introduction

While implementing systems, it is essential that databases be monitored to ensure that all required data is entered and not withheld. Failure to enter data into a database can be used as a method of concealing questionable transactions.

Mr. Thomas Peltier is the information security advisor for General Motors Corporation. He directs the implementation of corporate information security policies, procedures, and the ongoing security awareness program.

In an article titled "Policy Statement: The Cornerstone To All Procedures" published in the *Computer Security Journal,* Mr. Peltier writes:

> Every data processing installation has the responsibility to publish a set of standards. Many corporations are required by law to set standards; the *Foreign Corrupt Practices Act* (FCPA) of 1977 requires that senior management "establish policies and procedures to safeguard asset loss and produce reliable financial records."[1]

While the FCPA applies to all publicly held companies, the federal government sector has been mandated by the *Computer Security Act* (CSA) of 1987 to

1. Develop guidelines for protecting unclassified but "sensitive" information stored in government computers

2. Formulate a computer security plan

3. Train employees on the threats and vulnerabilities of its computer systems

CSA applies to federal agencies, many government contractors, and some state agencies. All are required to comply with the act's provisions and apply them as required.

From my own practical experience I can state that the FCPA and the CSA are not widely known or enforced. Certainly both of these laws represent the acknowledgment by our lawmakers that entities governed by them are now compelled to "establish policies and procedures to safeguard against asset loss and produce reliable records."

Case 12

I was retained by a government contractor a number of years ago as the Director of management information systems (MIS). I had been informed at the time that this particular government contractor had been the subject of investigative reporting on network television.

My first day on site I spent just talking to the MIS staff. Because of the ongoing investigation, the entire MIS Staff was ready to quit. After reassurances from me they calmed down and agreed to stay. The software was the MADIC manufacturing system running on a Prime computer. MADIC software when properly implemented can be an excellent tool for managing a manufacturing environment. This system was not fully implemented.

The government contractor was unable to account for $25 million worth of government funds for defense contracts they were working on. A government auditing team was on site auditing contracts in progress. I was informed by the head of the on-site auditing team that they would shut the company down and run it themselves if I could not provide certain data to them. I was also given the name of a Federal Bureau of Investigation (FBI) agent to contact, should I uncover anything that was remiss in MIS operations.

In performing analysis of the database used by MADIC, I realized that data had not been entered by various departments that should have been updating the system from the very beginning. The MADIC software had been installed for about a year before I arrived on site. At the end of the first day, an executive asked me if I would create some data on the database. I never create data for a database to get past data entry. After receiving this particular request, I telephoned the FBI agent whose card I had been given and left a message. When the FBI agent returned my telephone call I discussed the request from the executive.

Ultimately, this company was sold to a competitor. I was able to get the MADIC software working and prevented the auditing team from closing it down until the sale of the company was completed, by providing reports they requested. I probably would not have been able to have succeeded with the software had it not been for two extremely competent programmers that I hired. The programmers fixed internally customized portions of the software that were malfunctioning, enabling data entry and reporting.

Analysis

In this particular situation, the highest levels of management at the company were culpable for this situation. It was management's responsibility to ensure that a system of internal controls had been established and maintained. Failure to provide internal controls can be viewed as a breach of management's fiduciary responsibility. Management at the parent corporation realized it and removed that management before I arrived at the company site. The implementation of MADIC manufacturing software needed to be regularly audited as to the progress being made toward full implementation. Integrity of the data that the system maintained in its database should have been verified during an audit. This kind of review and verification of the MADIC manufacturing system should have been performed by an outside consulting firm.

Summary

1. During the implementation of both hardware and software, audits conducted by an outside consulting firm, timed to coincide with the completion of activities and milestones, are essential.

2. Databases should be regularly checked to ensure that data is being entered correctly.

3. Management and supervisors responsible for data on any computer system should be aware of the FPCA and the CSA. The ramifications of the FPCA and the CSA are presented at the beginning of this chapter.

Reference

1. Thomas Peltier, "Policy Statement: The Cornerstone to All Procedures," *Computer Security Journal*, vol. 7, no. 2, 1991. (*Reprinted by permission from Computer Security Institute, 600 Harrison Street, San Francisco, CA 94107.*)

7
Fraud in Government

Introduction

On two separate occasions in my life, I have worked for city government. Working for city government is a privilege. The job not only calls for your best effort in the performance of duties, but also calls for protecting the public trust. On both of these occasions, I was a director of management information systems (MIS).

I think it is important for me to add that many of my professional peers would not accept a position with government and openly state that position. The primary reason for this is that the environment is politically driven and not driven from a technical perspective. Sometimes it is tough enough to get the job done under normal circumstances. The political sniping that goes on in the government sector can border on the ridiculous.

Ms. Lisa Monzolillo and Dr. Richard Cardinalli presented an article titled "Ethics and Computer Crime—A Guide for Managers" in the *Computer Security Journal* in which they state[1]:

> The changing world of technology presents an increased challenge for managers to promote ethical behavior within their companies. Compared to the early years of management information systems when few people truly understood the complex nature of computers, today knowledgeable users have access to a wide variety of systems. The potential for misuse is widespread; no company is safe and increasing security alone will not solve the problem.
>
> Unethical behavior exists at all levels of society, from government corruption to street crime. Managers cannot assume systems professionals will behave differently. One device the manager has is to understand what motivates people to behave in an unethical

manner and manage the situation without expecting it to disap-
pear. The successful manager can create an environment that will
promote ethical behavior.

Case 13

After having finished a 6-month contract, I answered an ad in the classified section of the local newspaper for the position of director of MIS
with a small municipality located in the Midwest. I was interviewed
by the hiring executive for the city and ultimately offered the position.

This city had three basic software systems that supported the police,
utilities, and library. These systems were run on a minicomputer located at the police department. I had a staff of four that reported to me
directly. Two of the staff were computer operators and the other two
were programmers.

The management at the police department and a high-ranking city
administrator wanted to decentralize the computer systems of the city.
The minicomputer was not able to handle the current work load and
degraded performance was being encountered. Additionally, the management at the police department was concerned about having their
data mixed with other city functions.

A consulting firm had been hired by the city to perform a study of
decentralizing the systems. A meeting was held and the recommendations of the consulting firm were presented. The recommendations
made by the consulting firm were to replace functions supported by
the minicomputer with small personal computers running Xenix.

This particular consulting firm primarily used personal computers
that were a trade name of a national retail electronics company. The
personal computers they were recommending were not as powerful as
the 286 or 386 variety.

I wasn't particularly pleased with the recommendations of the consulting company. I realized these personal computers would not perform adequately. The computers being proposed would just not be
powerful enough to support the required systems. The systems that
were to be supported was the municipal court, library, and utilities
department. The police department would retain full control of the
existing minicomputer.

I thought the city's interests were not being served by the recommendations of the consulting firm. I met with the executive I reported
to and voiced these concerns. I felt it was my ethical responsibility to
divulge my concerns. Subsequent to this, another meeting was held
with the high-ranking officials of the city and myself. The ranking city
executive then informed me that he had done a lot of research into
these systems and that he and his assistant felt the recommendations
of the consulting firm were more than valid.

My superior asked me to support the recommendations of the consulting firm in the strongest possible way. I was then directed to support the high-ranking city executive and informed that failure to do so would mean forfeiture of my position. I did not voice my concerns again fearing that I might be endangering my position. I decided that it would not serve my interests to openly oppose high-ranking city officials, thus jeopardizing my family's security. However, personal ethics would not allow me to condone unethical activity.

At a meeting subsequent to this, I was informed by the same high-ranking city official that the consulting firm that had made recommendations to use personal computers running Xenix would actually create the software for these systems. The consulting firm was a small company and I was concerned about their past performance with clients. I voiced this concern to members present at the meeting, but did not gain anyone's attention. Again I was cautioned by the executive to whom I reported to support the goals of high-ranking city officials.

One of the computer operators, who reported to me as it turned out, had actually worked for the consulting firm that had made the recommendations to the city. This individual related to me that the consulting firm had been in financial difficulties. Legal actions had been taken against the firm. I later substantiated the assertions of my computer operator to be true.

The executive I reported to called me and informed me that I and one of my programmers would be taking a seminar on Xenix. The seminar was to be held at a regional education center operated by the national retail electronics company. The programmer and I attended the seminar and became certified on Xenix. I still have the certificate. It was a good experience and I enjoyed the seminar. I developed a friendship with the instructor and a sales representative at the seminar. I was interested in learning all I could about Xenix and the instructor was very helpful.

Later I was scheduled to take a seminar given by a local systems vendor. The seminar was on Info/Basic. It was a 1-day course which I enjoyed. By the end of the day, I was certified on Info/Basic. While at the branch office, I was introduced to one of my predecessors in the director of MIS job with the city. He chatted with me and invited me to a dinner to be held for clients.

The dinner, which was held at a local country club, was the price you paid to hear about new products being offered in the future by the systems vendor. After the marketing people had finished making their pitch I found myself chatting with the prior director of MIS previously mentioned. He informed me that there had been another director of MIS after he had vacated the position. The other director of MIS was now working for the local rapid transit district. This meant there had been three new directors of MIS for this city in the last 6 months. As I left to go home that evening, this prior director of MIS asked me what I thought of the city's new decentralized computer system plan. I informed him that I had some concerns. He said, "I had concerns too, that's why I left."

The next day I contacted the director of MIS for the local rapid transit district. He related that he too had been presented with a decentralized plan by the consulting firm and that he also had reservations about a successful outcome. His reasons for vacating the position with the city were the same as the previous director of MIS.

While no laws had been broken, ethically I did not feel that I could be a part of the high-ranking city official's plans. I began looking for a job, the best course of action in this case. I really felt that my superior had not been honest with me, and the high-ranking city executive's motives in all this were suspect.

The consulting firm was now firmly in the driver's seat to deliver new systems at this time. However, their lead programmer had left their employ over a compensation dispute. This individual had contacted my superior. He was now proposing to provide the utilities, library, and municipal court system on his own. While I felt this act on the part of the programmer was unethical, my supervisor did not and decided to use the programmer's services.

The two programmers that reported to me had already voiced negative opinions about the recommendations of the consulting firm. They also voiced concerns about the former programmer of the consulting firm developing required systems. One of the programmers found another job and resigned after giving a 2-week notice.

My job hunting efforts yielded an opportunity for myself with a reputable consulting firm. I was offered a position at the close of business on the day of my interview. The next day I tendered my resignation to the executive that had hired me.

I offered 2 weeks notice to the city and it was accepted. My friendship with the instructor who had given the Xenix seminar had been close. We met for lunch within a couple of days of my resignation. I dropped the instructor off at the regional education center and met the salesman I had become acquainted with when I had taken the Xenix seminar. He said, "You know the regional manager for our company and a certain high-ranking city executive are good friends and have been working together for some time on getting our systems."

This is exactly what I had suspected all along. The high-ranking city official was not interested in a well-engineered solution to creating systems for the city. He was interested in serving his own interests all along.

Analysis

The national electronics firm that I make reference to was not the problem in this situation. This company certainly offers more powerful systems now. The Xenix operating system is currently used widely and successfully. Decentralization of computer systems for entities like cities and corporations is viable if engineered correctly.

Clearly selection of systems for any municipality must be an unbiased decision. Expenditures of capitol on systems for government should go through a fair and impartial process that allows multiple vendors a chance to respond. Responses from vendors should be reviewed by an impartial entity, preferably a consulting firm committed to unbiased recommendations.

I spoke to my replacement at the city after I got settled at my new job. He was the fourth Director of MIS in a year. He also voiced concerns about the high-ranking city official's plans. This time the city officials listened. The new director of MIS was able to implement a well-engineered solution. I couldn't help but think that it took three directors before him to really make it happen.

The high-ranking city official in this particular instance was attempting to deliberately engineer the situation to serve his own interests and not the interests of the city. Certainly, there was a conflict of interest that he concealed. The unwillingness of two prior directors of MIS to cooperate in the implementation of the same plan should have been heeded by someone.

The attempted coercion on me was entirely unethical on the part of my superior and the high-ranking city official. Holding my position with the city over my head along with the welfare of my family was despicable. No disclosure was made to me regarding the two previous directors of MIS or the high-ranking city official's plans for decentralization of the computer system at the time I was hired.

I did receive letters of recommendation from the police department and the municipal court. Most of the city employees respected me for my actions in this situation.

The case I am going to present now represents conflict of interest, possible theft, and misuse of government funds. This case involves the acquisition of a computer system for a local government agency. The agency involved provided services for a large metropolitan city. Local, state, and federal funds were involved.

Case 14

A consulting firm asked me to take a temporary assignment as director of MIS for a city services department. I interviewed for the position with what seemed like a capable and businesslike administrator that would be my supervisor. I also was interviewed by the departing director of MIS. Both of these individuals assured me there were no problems with the hardware or software system. The departing director of MIS made a point of saying that there had been no unethical activity in regards to implementing the new computer system. I was also assured that the implementation had been handled efficiently and with the cooperation of the administrators involved thus far.

The remaining software requiring implementation dealt with payments collected in the various locations throughout the city. A substantial amount of money was collected every month in the form of payments to city services. The software that remained to be implemented would provide accountability of all monies collected.

I was introduced to the executive in charge of the city services who seemed both efficient and politically astute. The executive encouraged me to finish the implementation of the computer system. I immediately set about reviewing the progress made by the outgoing director of MIS.

The staff I had to work with was not well trained and I immediately went about implementing a training program for them and started them reading the available documentation of the hardware and software. One key member of my staff was rumored to be related to the executive in charge of city services.

Within the first week of the assignment, I was introduced to an executive at the Finance Department for City Services. I was concerned that this individual had the responsibility for backing up the computer system. I informed the executive that this duty would be taken over by someone on my staff and that he was to cease performing the task. The password level required to perform backups would allow system level access to all the data on the computer system.

It didn't take me long to determine that the existing computer was not powerful enough to support the software purchased. I decided to review the contract executed to acquire the hardware and software. It was probably the best written contract I'd ever seen up to that point in my career. The contract protected the City Services Department extremely well. One particular portion of the contract stated that if the response times of the computer system went over 10 seconds that the computer would be upgraded at no charge to the City Services Department. With this in mind, I conducted tests which showed the response times to be greater than 10 seconds.

I informed the administrator I reported to that City Services was entitled to a hardware upgrade at no charge. The administrator asked me to pursue this with the vendor that sold the system to City Services. The vendor of the hardware and software was not responsive at all and pretended ignorance of the contract stipulation regarding upgrades at no charge.

In reviewing the hardware specifications for the computer, I realized that the City Services had overpaid for the system by possibly hundreds of thousands of dollars. This fact was also reported to the administrator I reported to.

I then became aware that the City Services Department was paying rent on a personal computer that was not in their possession. I was informed that this personal computer was in the possession of the previous director of MIS by the vendor that provided the unit. Payments for the personal computer were in arrears by 2 months.

My next discovery was that the previous director of MIS was now working for the vendor that had supplied the new software and hardware for the City Services Department. This was clearly a conflict of interest on the part of the vendor and the previous director of MIS. Later I learned that the previous director of MIS actually had lived with the executive in charge of city services.

The payment module of the software provided accountability for monies collected. The amount of money collected by the city services for a large metropolitan city could be considerable. The unwillingness of the administrators responsible for various projects to implement the payment module was suspect. One administrator actually stated to me that other administrators responsible for the various locations would pay lip service to the computerization of payments, but were not in a hurry for it to happen. The payment module of the system was ready to be used and was just sitting there waiting.

I was then instructed by the administrator I reported to to let the executive at the finance department continue backing up the computer system. The administrator that I reported to informed me that this executive had been hired specifically because of his knowledge of the software being used by the city services.

I began to document everything that had transpired since I started the assignment for the consulting firm. I informed the consulting firm that I worked for that the actions of certain managers within the City Services Department were suspect. I also wrote a memo to a member of the city attorney's staff to advise him of irregularities.

All documents regarding the software and hardware implementation for the city were kept in my office. I kept the office locked and the documents were also locked in my desk. The next day I discovered that documents I had been putting into some chronological order in the course of preparing them for delivery to the district attorney were missing. I immediately made the theft of the documents known to a staff member whom I asked to contact the police. A sergeant with the police department took a report. Shortly thereafter my temporary assignment with the city was terminated.

Analysis

I welcomed the termination of my assignment with City Services. I make it a point professionally to work in environments that observe ethical business practices. This has sometimes meant the difference between working and not working. Certainly the termination was an indication that I knew more than some individuals at City Services wished. The theft of documents from a locked desk in a locked office certainly indicates someone feared discovery of unethical and possibly criminal activities.

This particular incident was discovered after the fact. The conflict of interest involving the previous director of MIS was clearly against the local city ordinances. The vendor that supplied both hardware and software acted irresponsibly in the hiring of the previous director of MIS.

The purchase of a computer system and subsequent overpayment for the city services system was extremely suspect. The disparity between what was contracted for and what was delivered could have amounted to a considerable amount of money.

The removal of property by the previous director of MIS also was an instance of possible theft or the misappropriation of government funds and equipment. The personal computer had been on rental to the City Services Department and now was in the possession of the previous director of MIS. The City Services Department paid for the 2 months rental that was in arrears for the personal computer even though it was not in possession of the equipment.

Allowing an executive in the finance department to perform back-ups of the computer system was very unusual. The particular individual involved had a great deal of knowledge about the computer system, including both hardware and software. The possibility of modifying financial information without anyone knowing certainly existed.

Departmentalization or compartmentalization of security privileges is crucial to the success of any security implemented for a government entity. Allowing the executive in the finance department to have security privileges that clearly went beyond the finance department was extremely suspect. Compartmentalization of security privileges provides the checks and balances necessary for maintaining good security.

Literally there was no data on the system that the executive in the finance department did not have access too. His user privileges should have been limited to his department. Additionally, his ability to modify financial data after the fact should have required journal entries that also updated an audit trail.

Clearly, the administrator that I reported to did not recognize the importance I placed on limiting the data access privileges of the executive in the finance department. The executive in charge of City

Services also did not seem to think that it was inappropriate for the finance department executive to perform backups of the computer system either. The executive in the finance department, a trained and certified accountant, also did not see the implications of his actions.

Security for the computer system and users was not implemented properly. I made a point of making recommendations to ensure data integrity of the system. However, I was not allowed to change the security levels of users. The administrator I reported to and the executive in charge of City Services failed in their fiduciary responsibilities by not letting me implement effective computer security policies.

The City Services Department was being audited by a federal agency when I began my assignment. The fact that no one seemed to object to the executive in the finance department being able to back up the new computer system with the exception of myself is a concern. The fact that the executive in the finance department had virtually unlimited access to the data on the system went unquestioned or undiscovered.

Clearly, the complacency of the auditors conducting the audit was blatant. The auditors did not interview me and did not speak with me. I was assured that I would be able to speak to the auditors; however, this never occurred and I doubted the real effectiveness of an audit that bypassed the director of MIS. The problem that can occur with professional auditors is that they may become complacent and not discharge their duties aggressively. Auditors internal to any entity don't want to rock the boat. Keeping the status quo means less work for them and possibly keeping their jobs as well. This is why I recommend retaining consulting firms to perform audits, particularly consulting firms that are aggressive in researching and verifying the lowest level of details.

While local, state, and federal government entities are audited, that doesn't mean that improprieties are always discovered or even reported. Even when unethical or criminal activities are reported to the proper authorities, that doesn't mean that the suspected culprits will be caught or prosecuted.

My supervisor with City Services should have initiated an immediate audit of all transactions regarding the acquisition of the new computer system. This audit could have been conducted internally by city auditors. Optionally, an audit could have been conducted by auditors provided by a consulting firm. A covert audit should also have been performed to ensure all appropriate information was obtained. Depending on the information obtained and discovered, an investigation by the local police department might have been indicated.

The executive in charge of the City Services Department was remiss in allowing the executive in the finance department to perform backups of the computer system. The vendor who provided the new computer system should have been advised of city ordinances prohibiting the hiring of the previous director of MIS by the executive in charge of the City Services Department. The payments authorized by the executive director in charge of City Services on a personal computer no longer in possession of City Services was suspicious. Certainly, the director was remiss in not requiring administrators responsible for collection of rent monies to use the rent payment module of the software.

The lack of accountability of monies collected and the unwillingness of the various administrators in control of those locations were very suspect. While the foot dragging of some administrators in City Services to implement the payment module of the software was questionable, it did not constitute a criminal act. However, administrators could have been pressured by the executive in charge of the City Services Department to implement the payment module of the system.

These are potentially embarrassing situations for government that are usually handled by termination of the employee who is responsible. On some occasions employees are prosecuted for criminal conduct. Sometimes it is the employee discovering the improprieties who gets terminated. The public trust that government is charged with must be observed and protected by everyone. I believe that each of us must observe high standards of ethical behavior whether we work in private business or government.

This situation certainly involved funds from local, state, and federal sources. It was unfortunate that an entity charged with providing social services serving low-income families and the homeless seemed intent on serving themselves.

In retrospect, many of the employees at City Services were as knowledgeable regarding the discoveries I made as myself. These individuals' priorities were protecting their jobs first, City Services, and then the public trust. Some of the employees admitted to me that they were clearly aware of improprieties and unethical conduct. These same employees were afraid of losing their jobs, should they make disclosures to proper authorities.

The executive in charge of the City Services was ultimately dismissed. The administrator I reported to went on to become the contract administrator of a huge federally funded project. This individual would be responsible for millions of tax dollars.

I never heard anything subsequent to my filing of a police report regarding theft of documents from the desk in my office. The perpetrators in that case clearly had the keys to my office and desk. Since then I never let documents supporting possible mismanagement and criminal activity out of my possession.

Case 15 The INSLAW Affair

Introduction

This case may clearly be an example of the ability of the power to corrupt. While I was not one of the hundreds of journalists that first broke this story, I feel that it has been suppressed and deserves the scrutiny of this country's taxpayers. In this particular case, I present findings and facts already presented in testimony before Congress and information obtained from periodicals. Additionally, I have obtained some background information directly from the victims of the INSLAW Affair.

Mr. William A. Hamilton is the founder and chief executive officer of INSLAW and its predecessor The Institute for Law and Social Research. Mr. Hamilton is a graduate of the University of Notre Dame. In the 1960s, Mr. Hamilton worked as an intelligence analyst and manager for the National Security Agency (NSA).

Mr. Hamilton was the project manager on the development of the first generation of PROMIS software—short for Prosecutor's Management Information System. Mr. Hamilton was awarded the John D. Rockefeller Award for Distinguished Public Service. The selection for the award was made by Princeton University's Woodrow Wilson School.

In the 1980s, Mr. Hamilton positioned INSLAW to become the leading software company serving the legal profession. INSLAW was awarded a contract to install PROMIS software in 20 of the largest U.S. attorney's offices. PROMIS software was installed in courts, jails, and prosecution agencies throughout the country. Additional agreements were made with European countries for strategic partnering, development, and co-marketing.

INSLAW filed suit against the Justice Department in June 1986. On September 28, 1987, the Bankruptcy Court ruled that the Department of Justice (DOJ) had stolen INSLAW's software through "trickery, fraud and deceit" and had unlawfully attempted to cause INSLAW's liquidation. In November 1989, Senior U.S. District Judge William Bryant upheld the Bankruptcy Court's $8 million judgment against the DOJ, ruling that even the uncontested evidence virtually compelled the findings of the Bankruptcy Court "under any standard review." The U.S. District Court decision was reversed by the U.S. Court of Appeals for the District of Columbia in May 1991, on narrow jurisdictional grounds. The U.S. Court of Appeals did not, however, disturb the 399 findings of fact about the DOJ's malfeasance against INSLAW. In January 1992, the U.S. Supreme Court declined to afford INSLAW a hearing on the decision by the U.S. Court of Appeals. In 1989, IBM Corporation made a multimillion dollar loan to INSLAW enabling the corporation to emerge from bankruptcy.

Mr. Colin Brown, the editor in chief of *TC Technical Consultant*, recently interviewed Mr. Hamilton. Mr. Brown then wrote the article, "Spies, Lies and Inslawgate" and a subsequent article entitled "CIA Computer Consultant Alleges Massive Conspiracy." The following paragraphs are reprinted with the permission of TC Publications.

Mr. Brown writes, "The INSLAW case has bizarre ramifications, involving as it does, the death of computer magazine publisher and journalist Mr. Danny Casolaro and the jailing of alleged narcotics trafficker, computer consultant and scientifically fluent Michael Riconosciuto.[2]

TC Technical Consultant questioned Bill Hamilton about the claims Michael Riconosciuto made about modifying the PROMIS software to place an intelligence backdoor in it. This seemed unlikely to us, since the software source code was made available to the purchasers. If any code was modified and recompiled, any backdoor would be overwritten at the compiled level. If the backdoor was visible in the source code itself, it certainly wouldn't be an effective Trojan horse. Hamilton, himself a former NSA employee, made some interesting new statements.

> TECHNICAL CONSULTANT: What sort of machine does the software run on?
>
> BILL HAMILTON: Any UNIX machine, Hewlett-Packard UNIX, RISC 6000, AT&T, AS400 under its own operating system and on mainframes under MVS.
>
> TECHNICAL CONSULTANT: How many modules in the software?
>
> BILL HAMILTON: About 88 programs.
>
> TECHNICAL CONSULTANT: So how did Riconosciuto modify the software if he did?
>
> BILL HAMILTON: I'm inclined to believe he did, although he never came up with any evidence. He talked in our first conversation, about the VAX/VMS version of the PROMIS software.
>
> TECHNICAL CONSULTANT: Did he know where to go in the software to change it?
>
> BILL HAMILTON: We didn't get into that in our first conversation, but in our subsequent conversation he described the software in a plausible way. He described it as top-down structured software, which it is. Someone could have briefed him on it—but he knew what he was talking about.
>
> TECHNICAL CONSULTANT: Would the code have been at the COBOL level or the machine level?
>
> BILL HAMILTON: Source code.

TECHNICAL CONSULTANT: Well, wouldn't it have been recognizable by any government that had it or did you keep the source code?

BILL HAMILTON: No, they kept the source code. Unless they've changed it, INSLAW's name is all through the source code commentary. My guess is it's still there and they all know what it is.

TECHNICAL CONSULTANT: Is it table driven?

BILL HAMILTON: Yes, it's table driven and it's easy to change a lot of things. The tables are actually for changing the database structure. We give the source code under the license. The reason for that is that we have an application generator sub-system which requires the use of source code in order to make the changes.

Colin Brown's subsequent article "CIA Computer Consultant Alleges Massive Conspiracy" sheds even more light on the INSLAW case. Mr. Brown states, "The death of a journalist in West Virginia, plus the jailing of an alleged CIA computer consultant in Washington state may be elements of a much wider scandal that could have serious implications for the Bush White House in 1992."

What started out as an investigation of an apparent case of pirated software has grown to be a project involving hundreds of journalists all over the world. The journalist Joseph Daniel "Danny" Casolaro was found dead August 10, 1992, in a West Virginia motel room. Each of his wrists was slashed seven times and a suicide note was found nearby. The only manuscript of his book, with accompanying notes, was missing.

The book, provisionally titled *The Octopus*, was meant to be an explosive expose of misdeeds by the DOJ and the Reagan administration. *Time* magazine also reported that Casolaro's research centered on gambling and attempted arms deals at the Cabazon Indian reservation near Indio, California. Indeed, the scope of Casolaro's investigation was so large that any one of the areas researched could have been the trigger for a possible hit.[3]

While authorities declared his death a suicide, his relatives definitely stated that Casolaro's mental state was sound, indeed upbeat, after the completion of his book. Casolaro started his work nearly 2 years before, investigating the bankrupting of a small computer software company called INSLAW, allegedly by the U.S. Justice Department. INSLAW, a company headed by Bill and Nancy Hamilton of Washington, D.C., had developed a package known as PROMIS to act as a case management tool for the Justice Department's unwieldy work load.

INSLAW President Bill Hamilton has claimed that Attorney General Ed Meese associate Earl Brian was given control of pirated versions of the PROMIS software by Meese to sell back to different U.S. government agencies for great profit. Two courts have so far agreed with Hamilton, awarding an $8 million judgment, but a higher court of appeal has quashed the award and the verdict, declaring that it was not in the jurisdiction of the lower courts.

Earl Brian owns United Press International (UPI) and Financial News Network (FNN). According to Michael Riconosciuto, a Washington state resident who claims to have modified the COBOL-based software for the Central Intelligence Agency (CIA) and other intelligence agencies, the software was a reward for Earl Brian's role in arranging the so-called "October surprise" gambit—the alleged conspiracy to withhold the American hostages in Iran until after the 1980 election which saw Jimmy Carter removed from power.

The "October surprise" scandal has taken some time to emerge. In a Paris meeting, President Bush is alleged to have met with Ali Akbar Hashemi Rafsanjani, the speaker of the Iranian Parliament, Mohammed Al Rajai, the future President of Iran, and Manucher Ghorbanifar, an Iranian arms dealer with connections to Mossad, the Israeli intelligence agency, according to Navy Captain Gunther Russbacher, who claims to have flown Bush, CIA chief William Casey, and Donald Gregg, a CIA operative, to that location. Russbacher, who made the allegation in May 1991, is now in jail on Terminal Island, convicted on the charge of impersonating a U.S. Attorney.

Michael Riconosciuto is now awaiting trial in a Washington, D.C. jail on charges of conspiracy to sell drugs, charges which Riconosciuto claims are manufactured. Indeed, the charges made against Riconosciuto were made 1 week after he authored and signed an affidavit describing his role in modifying the pirated software.

The affidavit also claimed that he had been contacted by phone and threatened by Peter Videnieks—a Justice Department employee and customs official, who Riconosciuto alleges had intelligence ties—as to the possible consequences of his going public with certain information. According to Riconosciuto, Videnieks was a frequent visitor to the Cabazon Indian reservation near Palm Springs, California and had visited tribal manager John P. Nichols. Nichols was in essence Riconosciuto's boss in a number of enterprises conducted on reservation land, and the PROMIS modification was just one of these projects. According to Riconosciuto, in an interview with *TC Technical Consultant* conducted from jail, the PROMIS software was modified to install a backdoor access for use by American intelligence services. The software was then sold to 88 different countries as a Trojan horse package enabling the United States to access their intelligence systems. According to Riconosciuto, these countries included Iraq and Libya.

Correspondence between Nichols and other companies, if authentic, would indicate that Riconosciuto's claims of his expertise in the area of electronics and armaments appear to be true. Marshall Riconosciuto, Michael's father, is a reputed former business partner of Richard M. Nixon.

Concluding a 3-year investigation of the Justice Department's conduct vis-à-vis INSLAW, on September 10, 1992, the Committee on the Judiciary of the House of Representatives published an investigative report entitled *The INSLAW Affair* (which is reprinted below). The committee corroborated the findings of the two lower federal courts on the theft of the PROMIS software, found that the effort to harm INSLAW began no later than the end of the first month of INSLAW's 3-year contract under the direction of the highest-ranking officials of the Justice Department, and found corroborating evidence substantiating some aspects of the sworn testimony of former covert intelligence operatives that private sector associates of the leadership of the Justice Department illegally sold PROMIS software domestically and internationally to intelligence agencies for their personal gain and in order to further the intelligence and foreign policy objectives of the United States. The Committee stated that the Department's conduct "clearly raises the specter that the Department actions taken against INSLAW in this matter represent an abuse of power of shameful proportions."

This case history is not presented as an indictment of our government. Our government was founded on democratic principles and promotes those principles throughout the world. That does not mean that actions of government officials in any capacity should go unchallenged with respect for the law.

We as Americans must not allow those who would not serve the government ethically and responsibly to remain in office. There are those who roam the halls of power in Washington, D.C. with impunity and may believe they are above the law.

Our judicial systems in this country are the finest in the world. The rights of individuals, companies, corporations, and the government are protected by the judicial system. However, it is not a perfect system.

Sometimes the facts in any case may be hard to uncover, especially in the case of testimony by individuals regarding names, places, dates, and actual events. Having testified myself and observed others, I know that accuracy of testimony can vary, vary from omission of slight details to outright perjury.

Perjury does occur, and the reasons may not always be self-evident at the time of occurrence. Perjury is usually self-serving and occurs when one is attempting to substantiate "facts" that are untrue. Perjury is punishable by law. Prosecution of those committing perjury should be pursued more aggressively.

The Investigative Report by the Committee on the Judiciary touches some prominent individuals in this country. Mr. Edwin Meese and Dr. Earl Brian are prominently mentioned in the report but are not currently under indictment. The reader is urged to carefully reflect on the dissenting and separate dissenting views by members of the

Committee on the Judiciary that is presented in the report.

On the following pages, the actual report published by the Committee on the Judiciary for the House of Representatives is presented. While some changes have been made for the purpose of including the document in this book, it remains an informative account of computer fraud at the highest levels of our government.

Summary:

Individuals in local, state, or federal government suspecting wrongdoing by superiors or fellow workers have a responsibility to do the following things:

1. Suspicions or concerns of possible wrongdoing should be documented and presented verbally and in writing to your superiors first.

2. Do not discuss the circumstances regarding the incident with fellow employees.

3. If you suspect that the wrongdoing may be perpetrated by immediate supervisors or managers, go to the next level, and the next, if necessary. If you are a member of union, notify the shop steward.

4. If you are an employee of local, state, or federal government and suspect criminal activity, report it to the proper law enforcement agency.

5. Maintain a copy of documentation in your possession along with any names, dates, and other pertinent information to the incident.

6. You have a legal and moral responsibility to report illegal or unlawful acts by government employees.

7. If you are not sure of the circumstances but feel something is wrong, consult with an attorney.

References

1. Lisa Monzolillo and Richard Cardinalli, "Ethics and Computer Crime—a Guide for Managers," *Computer Security Journal*, vol. 7, no. 2, 1991. (*Reprinted with permission from Computer Security Institute, 600 Harrison Street, San Francisco, CA 94107.*)

2. Colin Brown, "Spies, Lies and Inslawgate," and "CIA Computer Consultant Alleges Massive Conspiracy," *TC Technical Consultant*, August–September 1992, pp. 6, 10, 11, and 13. (*Reprinted by permission from* TC Publications, *1916 Rockefeller Lane, Suite #2, Redondo Beach, CA 90278.*)

3. Ibid.

Union Calendar No. 491

102d Congress, 2d Session - - - - - - - - - - - House Report 102-857

THE INSLAW AFFAIR

INVESTIGATIVE REPORT
BY THE
COMMITTEE ON THE JUDICIARY

together with

DISSENTING AND SEPARATE DISSENTING VIEWS

SEPTEMBER 10, 1992.—Committed to the Committee of the Whole House on the State of the Union and ordered to be printed

---

U.S. GOVERNMENT PRINTING OFFICE

WASHINGTON : 1992

COMMITTEE ON THE JUDICIARY

JACK BROOKS, Texas, *Chairman*

DON EDWARDS, California
JOHN CONYERS, JR., Michigan
ROMANO L. MAZZOLI, Kentucky
WILLIAM J. HUGHES, New Jersey
MIKE SYNAR, Oklahoma
PATRICIA SCHROEDER, Colorado
DAN GLICKMAN, Kansas
BARNEY FRANK, Massachusetts
CHARLES E. SCHUMER, New York
EDWARD F. FEIGHAN, Ohio
HOWARD L. BERMAN, California
RICK BOUCHER, Virginia
HARLEY O. STAGGERS, JR., West Virginia
JOHN BRYANT, Texas
MEL LEVINE, California
GEORGE E. SANGMEISTER, Illinois
CRAIG A. WASHINGTON, Texas
PETER HOAGLAND, Nebraska
MICHAEL J. KOPETSKI, Oregon
JACK F. REED, Rhode Island

HAMILTON FISH, JR., New York
CARLOS J. MOORHEAD, California
HENRY J. HYDE, Illinois
F. JAMES SENSENBRENNER, JR.,
  Wisconsin
BILL McCOLLUM, Florida
GEORGE W. GEKAS, Pennsylvania
HOWARD COBLE, North Carolina
LAMAR S. SMITH, Texas
CRAIG T. JAMES, Florida
TOM CAMPBELL, California
STEVEN SCHIFF, New Mexico
JIM RAMSTAD, Minnesota
GEORGE ALLEN, Virginia

JONATHAN R. YAROWSKY, *General Counsel*
ROBERT H. BRINK, *Deputy General Counsel*
JAMES E. LEWIN, *Chief Investigator*
JOHN D. COHEN, *Investigator*
ALAN F. COFFEY, JR., *Minority Chief Counsel*

LETTER OF TRANSMITTAL

———

HOUSE OF REPRESENTATIVES,
Washington, DC, September 10, 1992.

Hon. THOMAS S. FOLEY,
Speaker of the House of Representatives,
Washington, DC.

DEAR MR. SPEAKER: By direction of the Committee on the Judiciary, I submit herewith an investigative report entitled "The INSLAW Affair."

JACK BROOKS, *Chairman.*

(III)

CONTENTS

VI

VIEWS

Union Calendar No. 491

102D CONGRESS *2d Session*	HOUSE OF REPRESENTATIVES	REPORT 102-857

THE INSLAW AFFAIR

SEPTEMBER 10, 1992.—Committed to the Committee of the Whole House on the
State of the Union and ordered to be printed

Mr. BROOKS, from the Committee on the Judiciary, submitted the
following

INVESTIGATIVE REPORT

together with

DISSENTING AND SEPARATE DISSENTING VIEWS

BASED ON A STUDY BY THE FULL COMMITTEE

On August 11, 1992, the Committee on the Judiciary approved
and adopted a report entitled, "The INSLAW Affair." The chairman
was directed to transmit a copy to the Speaker of the House.

I. SUMMARY

The Department of Justice has long recognized the need for a
standardized management information system to assist law enforcement offices across the country in the recordkeeping and
tracking of criminal cases. During the 1970's, the Law Enforcement
Assistance Administration (LEAA) funded the development by
INSLAW[1] of a computer software system called the Prosecutor's
Management Information System or PROMIS. This system was designed to meet the criminal prosecutor workloads of large urban jurisdictions; and by 1980, several large U.S. attorneys offices were
using the PROMIS software. At this time, INSLAW (formerly

---

[1] INSLAW, Inc., is a Washington, DC, based company engaged in computer software and systems analysis, particularly case management and decision support applications for legal and
criminal justice oriented organizations.

(1)

called the Institute for Law and Social Research) was a nonprofit corporation funded almost entirely through Government grants and contracts. When President Carter terminated the LEAA, INSLAW converted the company to a for-profit corporation in 1981 to commercially market PROMIS. The new corporation made several significant improvements to the original PROMIS software and the resulting product came to be known as INSLAW's proprietary Enhanced PROMIS. The original PROMIS was funded entirely with Government funds and was in the public domain.

In March 1982, the Justice Department awarded INSLAW, Inc., a $10 million, 3-year contract to implement the public domain version of PROMIS at 94 U.S. attorneys' offices across the country and U.S. Territories. While the PROMIS software could have gone a long way toward correcting the Department's longstanding need for a standardized case management system, the contract between INSLAW and Justice quickly became embroiled in bitterness and controversy which has lasted for almost a decade. The conflict centers on the question of whether INSLAW has ownership of its privately funded "Enhanced PROMIS." This software was eventually installed at numerous U.S. attorneys' offices after a 1983 modification to the contract. While Justice officials at the time recognized INSLAW's proprietary rights to any privately funded enhancements to the original public domain version of PROMIS, the Department later claimed that it had unlimited rights to all software supplied under the contract. (See section of report entitled, "The Department Misappropriated INSLAW Software.")

INSLAW attempted to resolve the matter several times but was largely met with indifference or hostility by Department officials. Eventually, the Department canceled part of the contract and, by February 1985, had withheld at least $1.6 million in payments. As a result, the company was driven to the brink of insolvency and was threatened with dissolution under chapter 7 of the bankruptcy laws. Department officials have steadfastly claimed the INSLAW controversy is merely a contract dispute which has been blown out of proportion by the media. INSLAW's owners, William and Nancy Hamilton, however, have persisted in their belief that the Department's actions were part of a high level conspiracy within Justice to steal the Enhanced PROMIS software.

A. INSLAW ALLEGATIONS

Based on their knowledge and belief, the Hamiltons have alleged that high level officials in the Department of Justice conspired to steal the Enhanced PROMIS software system. As an element of this theft, these officials, who included former Attorney General Edwin Meese and Deputy Attorney General Lowell Jensen, forced INSLAW into bankruptcy by intentionally creating a sham contract dispute over the terms and conditions of the contract which led to the withholding of payments due INSLAW by the Department. The Hamiltons maintain that, after driving the company into bankruptcy, Justice officials attempted to force the conversion of INSLAW's bankruptcy status from Chapter 11: Reorganization to Chapter 7: Liquidation. They assert that such a change in bankruptcy status would have resulted in the forced sale of INSLAW'S assets, including Enhanced PROMIS to a rival computer company

3

called Hadron, Inc., which, at the time, was attempting to conduct a hostile buyout of INSLAW. Hadron, Inc., was controlled by the Biotech Capital Corporation, under the control of Dr. Earl Brian, who was president and chairman of the corporation. The Hamiltons assert that even though the attempt to change the status of INSLAW'S bankruptcy was unsuccessful, the Enhanced PROMIS software system was eventually provided to Dr. Brian by individuals from the Department with the knowledge and concurrence of then Attorney General Meese who had previously worked with Dr. Brian in the cabinet of California Governor Ronald Reagan and later at the Reagan White House. According to the Hamiltons, the ultimate goal of the conspiracy was to position Hadron and the other companies owned or controlled by Dr. Brian to take advantage of the nearly 3 billion dollars' worth of automated data processing upgrade contracts planned to be awarded by the Department of Justice during the 1980's.

Information obtained by the Hamiltons through sworn affidavits of several individuals, including Ari Ben-Menashe, a former Israeli Mossad officer, and Michael Riconosciuto, an individual who claims to have ties to the intelligence community, indicated that an element of this ongoing criminal enterprise by Mr. Meese, Dr. Brian and others included the modification of the Enhanced PROMIS software by individuals associated with the world of covert intelligence operations. The Hamiltons claim the modification of Enhanced PROMIS was an essential element of the enterprise, because the software was subsequently distributed by Dr. Brian to intelligence agencies internationally with a "back door" software routine, so that U.S. intelligence agencies could covertly break into the system when needed. The Hamiltons also presented information indicating that PROMIS had been distributed to several Federal agencies, including the FBI, CIA, and DEA.

B. Committee Investigation

Due to the complexity and breadth of the INSLAW allegations against the Department of Justice, the committee's investigation focused on two principal questions: (1) Did high level Department officials convert, steal or otherwise misappropriate INSLAW's PROMIS software and attempt to put the company out of business; and, (2) did high level Department of Justice officials, including Attorney General Edwin Meese and then Deputy Attorney General Lowell Jensen, and others conspire to sell, transfer, or in any way distribute INSLAW's Enhanced PROMIS to other Federal agencies and foreign governments?

1. DID THE DEPARTMENT CONVERT, STEAL OR MISAPPROPRIATE THE PROMIS SOFTWARE?

With regard to the first question, there appears to be strong evidence, as indicated by the findings in two Federal court proceedings as well as by the committee investigation, that the Department of Justice "acted willfully and fraudulently," [2] and "took, con-

---

[2] *INSLAW, Inc.*, v. *United States*, opinion of U.S. District Court Judge William Bryant, at p. 52a.

4

verted and stole,"[3] INSLAW's Enhanced PROMIS by "trickery, fraud and deceit."[4] It appears that these actions against INSLAW were implemented through the project manager from the beginning of the contract and under the direction of high level Justice Department officials.

Just 1 month after the contract was signed, Mr. C. Madison "Brick" Brewer, the PROMIS project manager, raised the possibility of canceling the INSLAW contract. During an April 14, 1982, meeting of the PROMIS Project Team, Mr. Brewer, and others discussed terminating the contract with INSLAW for convenience of the Government. Mr. Brewer did not recall the details of the meeting but said that if this recommendation was made, it was made "in jest."[5] Based on notes taken at this meeting by Justice officials, Bankruptcy Court Judge George Bason found that Mr. Brewer's recommendation to terminate the INSLAW contract, "...constituted a smoking gun that clearly evidences Brewer's intense bias against INSLAW, his single-minded intent to drive INSLAW out of business...."[6] By his own admission, Mr. Brewer became upset when INSLAW claimed that it had made enhancements to the public domain version of PROMIS using private funds. In his view, under the contract all versions of PROMIS were the Government's property. It is clear from the record that Mr. Brewer and Mr. Videnieks (the PROMIS contracting officer), supported by high level Justice officials continued to confront INSLAW at every turn. As Senior District Court Judge Bryant stated in his ruling on the case: "There was unending contention about payments under this contract and the rights of the respective parties."

Over the life of the contract, INSLAW made several attempts to reach an agreement with the Department over its proprietary rights to the Enhanced PROMIS software. The Department, however, steadfastly refused to conduct any meaningful negotiations and exhibited little inclination to resolve the controversy. In the meantime, INSLAW was pushed to the brink of financial ruin because the Department withheld at least $1.6 million in critical contract payments on questionable grounds, and in February 1985 was forced to file for protection under chapter 11 of the Bankruptcy Code in order to stay economically viable. INSLAW at this time had installed PROMIS at the 20 largest U.S. attorneys' offices across the country as required by the contract.[7] The Department had earlier canceled installation of PROMIS at the 74 smaller offices.

While refusing to engage in good faith negotiations with INSLAW, Mr. Brewer and Mr. Videnieks, with the approval of high level Justice Department officials, proceeded to take actions to misappropriate the Enhanced PROMIS software. These officials knew that INSLAW had installed Enhanced PROMIS at the 20 sites. Yet, without notice, and certainly without permission, the Depart-

---

[3] *INSLAW, Inc.,* v. *United States,* Ch 11. Case No. 85-00070, Adv. No. 86-00069, transcript of oral decision at 9 (Bankr.D.D.C. September 28, 1987).
[4] *INSLAW, Inc.,* v. *United States,* 83 B.R. 89 (Bktcy. D. Dist. Col. 1988) at 158 (Finding 399).
[5] Sworn statement of C. Madison Brewer, In the matter of: Office of Professional Responsibility Investigation No. 88-0137, June 29, 1988, p. 35.
[6] *INSLAW, Inc.,* v. *United States,* 83 B.R. 89 (Bktcy. D. Dist. Col. 1988) at 123 (Finding 165).
[7] There were two additional sites (Southern District of California and District of New Jersey) which were used as pilot sites prior to the award of the March 1987 contract to INSLAW.

5

ment of Justice illegally copied INSLAW's Enhanced PROMIS software and installed it eventually at 25 additional U.S. attorneys' offices. The Department reportedly also brought another 31 U.S. attorneys' offices "on-line" to Enhanced PROMIS systems via telecommunications. INSLAW first learned of these unauthorized actions in September 1985, and notified the Department that it must remove the Enhanced PROMIS software or arrange for license agreements. When the Department refused, INSLAW subsequently filed a claim against Justice in the Federal Bankruptcy Court which eventually led to the Bankruptcy's Court's finding that the Department's actions "...were done in bad faith, vexatiously, in wanton disregard of the law and the facts, and for oppressive reasons...to drive INSLAW out of business and to convert, by trickery, fraud and deceit, INSLAW's PROMIS software." When the case was appealed by the Department, Senior District Court Judge William Bryant concurred with the Bankruptcy Court and was very critical of the Department's handling of the case. In his ruling, at 49a, Judge Bryant stated:

> The Government accuses the bankruptcy court of looking beyond the bankruptcy proceeding to find culpability by the Government. What is strikingly apparent from the testimony and depositions of key witnesses and many documents is that *INSLAW performed its contract in a hostile environment that extended from the higher echelons of the Justice Department to the officials who had the day-to-day responsibility for supervising its work.* [Emphasis added.]

Recently, the posture of some Department officials has been to attempt to exonerate the Department's handling of the INSLAW matter by citing the fact that the Court of Appeals has vacated the Bankruptcy and District Courts' judgment involving illegal misconduct of the Department including violations of the automatic stay provisions of the Bankruptcy Code. However, the D.C. Circuit's opinion was grounded primarily on jurisdictional questions and did not address the substantive merits of the findings of fact and conclusions of law of either the Bankruptcy Court or the ruling of the U.S. District Court.

Based on the facts presented in court and the committee's review of Department records, it does indeed appear that Justice officials, including Mr. Brewer and Mr. Videnieks, never intended to fully honor the proprietary rights of INSLAW or bargain in good faith with the company. The Bankruptcy Court found that:

> ...[The Department] engaged in an outrageous, deceitful, fraudulent game of cat and mouse, demonstrating contempt for both the law and any principle of fair dealing. [Finding No. 266 at 138.]

As the Bankruptcy and District Courts found on the merits, it is very unlikely that Mr. Brewer and Mr. Videnieks acted alone to violate the proprietary rights of INSLAW in this matter. In explaining his own actions, Mr. Brewer, the project manager, has repeatedly stated that he was not acting out any personal vendetta against INSLAW and that high level Department officials including Lowell Jensen were aware of every decision he made with regard to the contract. Mr. Brewer stated, under oath that "...there was

6

somebody in the Department at a higher level, looking over the shoulder of not just me but the people who worked for me ...."[8] The PROMIS Oversight Committee, headed by Deputy Attorney General Lowell Jensen, kept a close watch over the administration of the contract and was involved in every major decision. Mr. Jensen, who worked with former Attorney General Edwin Meese in the Alameda County district attorneys' offices, stated under oath that he kept the Attorney General regularly informed of all aspects of the INSLAW contract. The PROMIS Oversight Committee readily agreed with Mr. Brewer's recommendation to cancel part of INSLAW's contract for default because of the controversy regarding the installation of PROMIS in word processing systems at the 74 smaller U.S. attorneys' offices. Mr. Brewer's proposal was ultimately rejected only because a Justice contracts attorney advised the oversight committee that the Department did not have the legal authority to do so. Curiously, the recommendation to find INSLAW in default occurred shortly after INSLAW and the Department signed a modification to the contract (Mod. 12), which was supposed to end the conflict over proprietary rights.

Mr. Jensen, who is currently a Federal District Court judge in San Francisco, served at the Justice Department successively as Assistant Attorney General in charge of the Criminal Division, Associate Attorney General and Deputy Attorney General between 1981 and 1986. The Bankruptcy Court found that he "had a previously developed negative attitude about PROMIS and INSLAW" from the beginning (Findings No. 307–309) because he had been associated with the development of a rival case management system while he was a district attorney in California, and that this experience, at the very least, affected his judgment throughout his oversight of the contract. During a sworn statement, Judge Jensen denied being biased against INSLAW, but averred that he did not have complete recollection of the events surrounding his involvement in the contract. However, based on the committee's own investigation it is clear that Judge Jensen was not particularly interested or active in pursuing INSLAW's claims that Department officials were biased against the company and had taken action to harm the company. Perhaps most disturbing, he remembered very few details of the PROMIS Oversight Committee meetings even though he had served as its chairman and was certainly one of its most influential members. He stated that after a meeting with former Attorney General Elliot Richardson (representing INSLAW) regarding the alleged Brewer bias, he commissioned his deputy, Mr. Jay Stephens, to conduct an investigation of the bias charges. Based on this investigation, Judge Jensen said he concluded that there were no bias problems associated with the Department's handling of the INSLAW contract.

This assertion, however, contradicted Mr. Stephens, who testified during a sworn statement that he was never asked by Judge Jensen to conduct an investigation of the Brewer bias allegations raised by Mr. Richardson and others. Mr. Stephens' recollection of the events was sharp and complete in stark contrast to Judge Jensen's. As a result, many questions remain about the accuracy and

---

[8]*INSLAW, Inc., v. United States*, 83 B.R., op cit., p. 17.

7

completeness of Judge Jensen's recollections and statements. As for the PROMIS Oversight Committee, committee investigators were told that detailed minutes were not kept at any of the meetings, nor was there any record of specific discussions by its members affecting the INSLAW contract. The records that were available were inordinately sparse and often did not include any background of how and why decisions were made.

To date, former Attorney General Meese denies having knowledge of any bias against INSLAW by the Department or any of its officials. He stated, under oath, that he had little, if any, involvement with the INSLAW controversy and that he recalls no specific discussion with anyone, including Department officials about INSLAW's contract with Justice regarding the use or misuse of the PROMIS software. This statement is in direct conflict with Judge Jensen's testimony, that he briefed Mr. Meese regularly on this issue and that Mr. Meese was very interested in the details of the contract and negotiations.

One of the most damaging statements received by the committee is a sworn statement made by Deputy Attorney General Arnold Burns to Office of Professional Responsibility (OPR) investigators in 1988. In this statement, Mr. Burns stated that Department attorneys had already advised him (sometime in 1986) that INSLAW's claim of proprietary rights in the Enhanced PROMIS software was legitimate and that the Department had waived any rights in these enhancements. Mr. Burns was also told by Justice attorneys that the Department would probably lose the case in court on this issue. Accepting this statement, it is incredible that the Department, having made this determination, would continue to pursue its litigation of these matters. More than $1 million has been spent in litigation on this case by the Justice Department even though it knew in 1986 that it did not have a chance to win the case on merits. This clearly raises the specter that the Department actions taken against INSLAW in this matter represent an abuse of power of shameful proportions.

2. WAS THERE A HIGH LEVEL CONSPIRACY?

The second phase of the committee's investigation concentrated on the allegations that high level officials at the Department of Justice conspired to drive INSLAW into insolvency and steal the PROMIS software so it could be used by Dr. Earl Brian, a former associate and friend of then Attorney General Edwin Meese. Dr. Brian is a businessman and entrepreneur who owns or controls several businesses including Hadron, Inc., which has contracts with the Justice Department, CIA, and other agencies. The Hamiltons and others have asserted that Dr. Brian conspired with high level Justice officials to sell PROMIS to law enforcement and intelligence agencies worldwide.

Former Attorney General Elliot Richardson, counsel to INSLAW, has alleged that the circumstances involving the theft of the PROMIS software system constitute a possible criminal conspiracy involving Mr. Meese, Judge Jensen, Dr. Brian, and several current and former officials at the Department of Justice. Mr. Richardson maintains that the individuals involved in the theft of the Enhanced PROMIS system have violated a plethora of Federal crimi-

8

nal statutes, including but not limited to: (1) 18 U.S.C 654 (officer or employee of the United States converting the property of another); (2) 18 U.S.C 1001 (false statements); (3) 18 U.S.C 1621 (perjury); (4) 18 U.S.C 1503 (obstruction of justice); (5) 18 U.S.C 1341 (mail fraud) and (6) 18 U.S.C. 371 (conspiracy to commit criminal offenses). Mr. Richardson further contends that the violations of Federal law associated in the theft of Enhanced PROMIS, the subsequent coverup and the illegal distribution of PROMIS fulfill the requirements for prosecution under 18 U.S.C. 1961 et seq. (the Racketeer Influenced and Corrupt Organizations—(RICO)—statute).

As discussed earlier, the committee's investigation largely supports the findings of two Federal courts that the Department "took, converted, stole" INSLAW'S Enhanced PROMIS by "trickery, fraud and deceit," and that this misappropriation involved officials at the highest levels of the Department of Justice. The recent ruling by the D.C. Circuit Court of Appeals does nothing to vitiate those conclusions, the product of an extensive record compiled under oath by two Federal jurists. While the Department continues to attempt to explain away the INSLAW matter as a simple contract dispute, the committee's investigation has uncovered other information which plausibly could suggest a different conclusion if full access to documents and other witnesses were permitted. Several individuals have stated under oath that the Enhanced PROMIS software was stolen and distributed internationally in order to provide financial gain to Dr. Brian and to further intelligence and foreign policy objectives for the United States. While it should be acknowledged at the . outset that some of the testimony comes from individuals whose past associations and enterprises are not commendable, corroborating evidence for a number of their claims made under oath has been found. It should be observed that these individuals provided testimony with the full knowledge that the Justice Department could—and would probably be strongly inclined to—prosecute them for perjury if they lied under oath. Moreover, we note that the Department is hardly in a position to negate summarily testimony offered by witnesses who have led less than an exemplary life in their choice of associations and activities. As indicated by the recent prosecution of Manuel Noriega, which involved the use of over 40 witnesses, the majority of whom were previously convicted drug traffickers, a witness' perceived credibility is not always indicative of the accuracy or usability in court of the information provided. Although the committee's investigation could not reach a definitive conclusion regarding a possible motive behind the misappropriation of the Enhanced PROMIS software, the disturbing questions raised, unexplained coincidences and peculiar events that have surfaced throughout the INSLAW case raises the need for further investigation.

One area which requires further investigation is the allegations made by Mr. Michael Riconosciuto. Mr. Riconosciuto, a shady character allegedly tied to U.S. intelligence agencies and recently convicted on drug charges, alleges that Dr. Brian and Mr. Peter Videnieks secretly delivered INSLAW's Enhanced PROMIS software to the Cabazon Indian Reservation, located in California, for "refitting" for use by intelligence agencies in the United States and

9

abroad.[9] When Dr. Brian was questioned about his alleged involvement in the INSLAW case, he denied under oath that he had ever met Mr. Riconosciuto and stated that he had never heard of the Cabazon Indian Reservation.

C. ADDITIONAL QUESTIONS

Suspicions of a Department of Justice conspiracy to steal INSLAW's PROMIS were fueled when Danny Casolaro—an investigative writer inquiring into those issues—was found dead in a hotel room in Martinsburg, WV, where he was to meet a source that he claimed was critical to his investigation. Mr. Casolaro's body was found on August 10, 1991, with his wrists slashed numerous times. Following a brief preliminary investigation by local authorities, Mr. Casolaro's death was ruled a suicide. The investigation was reopened later as a result of numerous inquiries from Mr. Casolaro's brother and others regarding the suspicious circumstances surrounding his death.

The Martinsburg Police investigation subsequently concluded in January 1992, that Mr. Casolaro's death was a suicide. Subsequently, Chairman Brooks directed committee investigators to obtain sworn statements from the FBI agent and two former Federal Organized Crime Strike Force prosecutors in Los Angeles who had information bearing on the Casolaro case. Sworn statements were obtained from former Federal prosecutors Richard Stavin and Marvin Rudnick on March 13 and 14, 1992. After initial resistance from the Bureau, a sworn statement was taken from FBI Special Agent Thomas Gates on March 25 and 26, 1992.

Special Agent Gates stated that Mr. Casolaro claimed he had found a link between the INSLAW matter, the activities taking place at the Cabazon Indian Reservation, and a Federal investigation in which Special Agent Gates had been involved regarding organized crime influence in the entertainment industry.

Special Agent Gates stated that Mr. Casolaro had several conversations with Mr. Robert Booth Nichols in the weeks preceding his death. Mr. Nichols, according to documents submitted to a Federal court by the FBI, has ties with organized crime and the world of covert intelligence operations. When he learned of Mr. Casolaro's death, Special Agent Gates contacted the Martinsburg, WV, Police Department to inform them of the information he had concerning Mr. Nichols and Mr. Casolaro. The Martinsburg Police have not commented on whether or not they eventually pursued the leads provided by Special Agent Gates.

Based on the evidence collected by the committee, it appears that the path followed by Danny Casolaro in pursuing his investigation into the INSLAW matter brought him in contact with a number of dangerous individuals associated with organized crime and the world of covert intelligence operations. The suspicious circumstances surrounding his death have led some law enforcement professionals and others to believe that his death may not have been a suicide. As long as the possibility exists that Danny

---

[9] Mr. Riconosciuto provided an affidavit to the Hamilton's stating that Mr. Videnieks had worked for the CIA and had threatened him with retribution if he talked to committee investigators.

10

Casolaro died as a result of his investigation into the INSLAW matter, it is imperative that further investigation be conducted.

D. Evidence of Possible Coverup and Obstruction

One of the principal reasons the committee could not reach any definitive conclusion about INSLAW's allegations of a high criminal conspiracy at Justice was the lack of cooperation from the Department. Throughout the two INSLAW investigations, the Congress met with restrictions, delays and outright denials to requests for information and to unobstructed access to records and witnesses since 1988. The Department initially attempted to prevent the Senate Permanent Subcommittee on Investigations from conducting an investigation of the INSLAW affair. During this committee's investigation, Attorney General Thornburgh repeatedly reneged on agreements made with this committee to provide full and open access to information and witnesses. Although the day before a planned committee meeting to consider the issuance of a subpoena the Department promised full access to documents and witnesses, the committee was compelled to subpoena Attorney General Thornburgh to obtain documents needed to complete its investigation. Even then, the Department failed to provide all the documents subpoenaed, claiming that some of the documents held by the Department's chief attorney in charge of the INSLAW litigation had been misplaced or accidentally destroyed. The Department has not provided a complete accounting of the number of documents missing nor has it conducted an investigation to determine if the documents were stolen or illegally destroyed.

Questions regarding the Department's willingness and objectivity to investigate the charges of possible misconduct of Justice employees remain. That Justice officials may have too readily concluded that witnesses supporting the Department's position were credible while those who did not were ignored or retaliated against was, perhaps, most painfully demonstrated with the firing of Anthony Pasciuto, the former Deputy Director, Executive Office of the U.S. Trustees.

Mr. Pasciuto had informed the Hamiltons that soon after INSLAW filed for chapter 11 bankruptcy in 1985, the Justice Department had planned to petition the court to force INSLAW into chapter 7 bankruptcy and liquidate its assets including the PROMIS software. His source for this information was Judge Cornelius Blackshear who, at the time, was the U.S. Trustee for the Southern District of New York. Judge Blackshear subsequently provided INSLAW's attorneys with a sworn statement confirming what Mr. Pasciuto had told the Hamiltons. However, following a conversation with a Justice Department attorney who was representing the Department in the INSLAW case,[10] Judge Blackshear recanted his earlier sworn statement. Moreover, Judge Blackshear, under oath, could not or would not provide committee investigators with a plausible explanation of why he had recanted

---

[10] In an October 26, 1988, FBI Interview of James Garrity, Garrity (who was Judge Blackshear's attorney) stated that DOJ lawyer Dean Cooper had called him (Garrity) and said that Judge Blackshear's testimony was wrong and that DOJ was concerned that something should be done to correct it. Mr. Garrity informed Judge Blackshear of this information who later recanted his testimony. Mr. Garrity was an attorney with the Department at that time.

11

his earlier statements to INSLAW, Mr. Pasciuto and others regarding the Justice Department's efforts to force INSLAW out of business. He did confirm an earlier statement attributed to him that his recantation was a result of "his desire to hurt the least number of people." However, he would not elaborate on this enigmatic statement.

Similarly, Mr. Pasciuto, under strong pressure from senior Department officials, recanted his statement made to the Hamiltons regarding Judge Blackshear. It appears that Mr. Pasciuto may have been fired from his position with the Executive Office of U.S. Trustees because he had provided information to the Hamiltons and their attorneys which undercut the Department's litigating position before the Bankruptcy Court.[11] This action was based on a recommendation made by the Office of Professional Responsibility (OPR). In a memorandum to Deputy Attorney General Burns, dated December 18, 1987, the OPR concluded that:

> In our view, but for Mr. Pasciuto's highly irresponsible actions, the department would be in a much better litigation posture than it presently finds itself. Mr. Pasciuto has wholly failed to comport himself in accordance with the standard of conduct expected of an official of his position.

Mr. Pasciuto now states he regrets having allowed himself to be coerced by the Department into recanting and has stated under oath to committee investigators that he stands by his earlier statements made to the Hamiltons that Judge Blackshear had informed him that the Department wanted to force INSLAW out of business. Certainly, Mr. Pasciuto's treatment by the Department during his participation in the INSLAW litigation raises serious questions of how far the Department will go to protect its interests while defending itself in litigation. Not unexpectedly, Mr. Pasciuto's firing had a chilling effect on other potential Department witnesses who might have otherwise cooperated with the committee in this matter. Judge Blackshear, on the other hand, was not accused of wrongdoing by the Department even though he originally provided essentially the same information as had Mr. Pasciuto.

Despite this series of obvious reversals, the Department, after limited investigation, has apparently satisfied itself that the sworn statements of its witnesses, including Judge Blackshear, have somehow been reconciled on key issues such that no false statements have been made by any of these individuals. This position is flatly in opposition to the Bankruptcy Court's finding that several Department officials may have perjured themselves which was never seriously investigated by the Department. In addition, there are serious conflicts and inconsistencies in sworn statements provided to the committee that have not been resolved. Equally important, the possibility that witnesses' testimony were manipulated by the Department in order to present a "united front" to the Congress and the public on the INSLAW case needs to be fully and honestly explored. The potential for a conflict of interest in the Department's

---

[11] In a January 20, 1988, letter to Mr. Pasciuto from B. Boykin Rose, Associate Deputy Attorney General, Mr. Pasciuto was informed he was being terminated. Mr. Rose describes Mr. Pasciuto's providing information to the Hamiltons as "atrocious judgment."

12

carrying out such an inquiry is high, if not prudently manifest, and independent scrutiny is required.

E. JUDGE BASON'S ALLEGATIONS AGAINST THE DEPARTMENT

Judge Bason testified, under oath, before the Economic and Commercial Law Subcommittee that the Department's actions against its critics may have extended into blocking his reappointment as a bankruptcy judge in 1988 because of his ruling in INSLAW's case. Judge Bason was replaced by Martin Teel, Jr., who, prior to his appointment, was a Justice Department attorney heavily involved in the Department's litigation of the INSLAW case. [12] The committee was unable to substantiate Judge Bason's charges. If such undue influence did occur, it was subtle and lost in the highly private manner in which judge selection procedures are conducted. While sworn statements were not taken, the committee investigators interviewed several of the judges involved in the selection process. The judges who agreed to provide interviews all stated that they had little firsthand knowledge in which to evaluate the candidates, including the incumbent judge. As a result, the members of the Judicial Council had to rely on the findings of the Merit Selection Panel headed by Judge Norma Johnson.

The Merit Selection Panel's findings were provided to the Judicial Council by Judge Johnson whose oral presentation was instrumental in the final selection. Judge Johnson had previously worked at the Department of Justice with Stuart Schiffer, who led the Department's attempt to have the District Court remove Judge Bason from the INSLAW case. Mr. Schiffer is also the official who argued vociferously against the appointment of an independent counsel on the INSLAW case in a memorandum to Deputy Attorney General Arthur Burns. Judge Johnson also served in the D.C. Superior Court with Judge Tim Murphy from 1970 through 1980. Judge Murphy subsequently worked directly for Mr. Brewer on the PROMIS contract. The committee, however, has not at this date found any evidence that Judge Johnson had specific discussions with Mr. Schiffer or anyone else at the Department of Justice about Judge Bason, the INSLAW case or the bankruptcy judicial selection process.

The committee's investigation revealed that the selection process was largely informal, undocumented and highly subjective. For example, several members of the Judicial Council indicated that one of the primary factors influencing the nonreappointment of Judge Bason, was the poor administrative condition of his court. These same members admitted that they had no firsthand knowledge of the administrative condition and based this opinion on the reports of the Merit Selection Panel and Judge Johnson. This was corroborated by the discovery of a confidential memorandum written by a member of the Merit Selection Panel which was highly critical of

---

[12] The procedures for the selection of a bankruptcy judge include: (1) Public notice of the vacancy, (2) applicants submit an application illustrating they meet the minimum qualifications to the circuit executive, (3) the applications are reviewed by a Merit Selection Panel, led by a district judge and appointed by the Judicial counsel or counsel delegates, (4) the panel evaluates the applicants and selects the four most qualified candidates based on a review of applications and interviews of the applicants and interested parties, and (5) the selections are forwarded to the Judicial Council, which reviews the report of the panel and recommends at least three nominees to the Court of Appeals which makes the final selection.

13

Judge Bason and the administrative condition of the Bankruptcy Court. While this memorandum had been seen by several judges during the selection process, committee investigators were unable to determine who authored it. The committee's investigation did not reveal any evidence to support the criticisms raised in the memorandum. Martin Bloom, Clerk of the Bankruptcy Court, indicated in his sworn statement to committee investigators that under Judge Bason, the administrative condition of the court vastly improved. These sentiments were echoed by Chief Judge Aubrey Robinson who consistently complimented Judge Bason on his efforts to improve the administrative condition of the Bankruptcy Court in his remarks to the Annual Judicial Conference.

F. CONCLUSION

The history of the Department's behavior in the INSLAW case dramatically illustrates its (1) reflexive hostility and "circle the wagons" approach toward outside investigations; (2) inability or unwillingness to look objectively at charges of wrongdoing by high level Justice officials, particularly when the agency itself is a defendant in litigation; and, (3) belligerence toward Justice employees with views that run counter to those of the agency's upper management. The fact that the Department failed to recognize a need for an independent investigation of the INSLAW matter for more than 7 years is remarkable. Failure to do so has effectively shielded officials who may have committed wrongdoing from investigation and prosecution.

As already documented and confirmed by two Federal judges, the Department's actions in the INSLAW case have greatly harmed the company and its owners. These actions, as they pertain to the dispute with INSLAW over the misappropriation of the PROMIS software, were taken with the full knowledge and support of high level Justice officials. The harm to the company was further perpetuated by succeeding high level officials, such as former Attorney General Richard Thornburgh, who not only failed to objectively investigate the serious charges raised by the Hamiltons and their attorney, former Attorney General Elliot Richardson, but also delayed and rebuffed effective and expeditious outside investigation of the matter by Congress.

The Department of Justice is this nation's most visible guarantor of the notion that wrongdoing will be sought out and punished irrespective of the identity of the actors involved. Moreover, its mandate is to protect all private citizens from illegal activities that undermine the public trust. The Department's handling of the INSLAW case has seriously undermined its credibility and reputation in playing such a role. Congress and the executive must take immediate and forceful steps to restore public confidence and faith in our system of justice, which cannot be undermined by the very agent entrusted with enforcement of our laws and protections afforded every citizen. In view of the history surrounding the INSLAW affair and the serious implications of evidence presented by the Hamiltons, two court proceedings in the judicial branch and the committee's own investigation, there is a clear need for further investigation. The committee believes that the only way in which INSLAW's allegations can be adequately and fully investigated is

14

by the appointment of an independent counsel. The committee is aware that on November 13, 1991, Attorney General Barr appointed Nicholas Bua, a retired Federal judge from Chicago, as his special counsel to investigate and advise him on the INSLAW controversy. The committee eagerly awaits Judge Bua's findings; however, as long as the investigation of wrongdoing by former and current high level Justice officials remains under the ultimate control of the Department itself, there will always be serious doubt about the objectivity and thoroughness of the inquiry.

II. COMMITTEE INVESTIGATION, PRIOR STUDIES, HEARINGS AND SUBCOMMITTEE PROCEEDINGS

On December 5, 1990, Chairman Brooks convened a hearing of the Subcommittee on Economic and Commercial Law to review Attorney General Thornburgh's repeated refusal to provide the committee full and open access to all INSLAW documents and records. Representatives from the GAO, Mr. Steven R. Ross, the General Counsel to the Clerk of the U.S. House of Representatives (accompanied by Mr. Charles Tiefer, Deputy General Counsel, and Mr. Michael Long, Assistant Counsel), former Attorney General Elliot L. Richardson (of Milbank, Tweed, Hadley & McCloy), Mr. William and Mrs. Nancy Hamilton (INSLAW's corporate officers), and Judge George F. Bason testified at the hearing. [13]

Messrs. Richardson and Hamilton outlined their allegations of a criminal conspiracy in the Department's handling of the INSLAW contract and the theft of the Enhanced PROMIS software. Judge Bason testified that he believed that his failure to be reappointed as bankruptcy judge was the result of improper influence on the court selection process by the Justice Department because of his findings in favor of INSLAW in its bankruptcy proceedings. Mr. Ross refuted the Justice Department's rationale for withholding documents related to possible wrong doing by Justice officials involved with the INSLAW contract. GAO representatives described a wide range of deficiencies in the Department's Information Resources Management Office and its administration of the ADP contracts.

After the December 1990 hearing, the Attorney General once again vowed to cooperate with the committee. By June 1991 however, it was clear that the Department was not going to provide the committee with a substantial number of the documents that had been requested. As a result, Committee Chairman Brooks announced plans to address this and other issues related to INSLAW at the full committee hearings on the Department of Justice Authorization for Appropriations hearings scheduled for July 11 and 18, 1991.

On July 11, 1991, Congressman John Conyers, Jr., chairman of the Government Operations Committee; Congressman Frank Horton, the ranking minority member of that committee; and Congressman Robert Wise, Jr., chairman of the Subcommittee on Government Information, Justice, and Agriculture, testified before the committee. Also appearing before the committee were Mr. Steven

---

[13] Hearing, House Judiciary Committee's Subcommittee on Economic and Commercial Law, December 5, 1990, Serial No. 114.

15

Ross, General Counsel to the Clerk of the U.S. House of Representatives; Charles Tiefer, Deputy General Counsel to the Clerk; and GAO officials: Milton Socolar, Richard Steiner, and Richard Fogel.

The Attorney General, who was scheduled to appear before the committee on July 18, 1991, was asked to be prepared to provide an executive branch perspective on the interbranch conflicts over GAO and Judiciary Committee access to Department documents, and to discuss the INSLAW case.[14]

On July 18, 1991, the committee reconvened to review the Department's fiscal year 1992 authorization for appropriations request and to hear the testimony of Attorney General Thornburgh. However, according to the chairman, the Attorney General notified the committee the night before the hearing that he refused to attend on the grounds that the committee press release announcing the hearing had been unduly aggressive and contentious and not in keeping with the tenor of an oversight hearing. The chairman added that "the Attorney General seems to be objecting to a robust interchange of views that is an essential part of the give-and-take at the heart of the political process."

On July 25, 1991, the Subcommittee on Economic and Commercial Law met to authorize the issuance of two subpoenas to the Department of Justice; one for INSLAW documents and the other for a copy of an Office of Legal Counsel Opinion regarding FBI's authority to arrest individuals overseas. The subcommittee authorized issuance of a subpoena by a vote of 10 to 6.[15] On July 31, 1991, the Subcommittee on Economic and Commercial Law received most of the subpoenaed INSLAW documents from the Attorney General. The Department however, claimed that 51 documents or files were missing and could not be found.[16] To date, the subcommittee has not received an adequate explanation from the Department on how the documents came to be missing.[17]

III. CONFLICTS BETWEEN THE DEPARTMENT AND INSLAW RESULT IN THE MISAPPROPRIATION OF INSLAW'S ENHANCED PROMIS

On November 2, 1981, the Department issued a request for proposals (RFP) for installing public domain PROMIS on minicomputers and word processors. Prior to the issuance of the RFP, several vendors, including INSLAW, advised the Department not to try to perform PROMIS functions on word processing equipment because the case management activities were computation-intensive and needed to be performed on full function microcomputers.[18]

One reason why such an approach was inherently flawed was because PROMIS involved over 500,000 lines of Common Business

[14] House Judiciary Committee hearing, July 11, 1991, Serial No. 12, p. 3.
[15] Statements of Chairman Jack Brooks before the Subcommittee on Economic and Commercial Law, "Meeting to Authorize Issuance of a Subpoena for Documents From the Department of Justice," July 25, 1991.
[16] July 30, 1991, letter from Assistant Attorney General W. Lee Rawls to the Honorable Jack Brooks, Chairman, Committee on the Judiciary.
[17] Statement of Chairman Jack Brooks before the Subcommittee on Economic and Commercial Law, "Meeting on the Return of Subpoenas," July 31, 1991.
[18] *INSLAW, Inc.,* v. *United States of America and the U.S. Department of Justice,* Findings of Fact and Conclusions of Law (Case No. 85–00070) Adversary Proceeding No. 86–0069, p. 59.

16

Oriented Language (COBOL) program code and required a very large-capacity computer at that time. INSLAW further advised the Department to move toward the use of full function micro-computers that could perform both case management and word processing. However, word processors remained in the Department's plan. Only 2 of the 104 firms that requested the RFP submitted proposals in the 30 days allowed—INSLAW and Systems Architects, Inc. INSLAW was selected for the contract since Systems Architects, Inc., was considered to be non-responsive to the RFP.[19]

Even before the contract was awarded, there was discussion between the Department and INSLAW over a period of 2 months on the subject of public domain software as opposed to privately funded enhancements. INSLAW was explicit in stating to the Department that its version of PROMIS had been enhanced with private funds and future enhancements funded outside the Department's contract were expected.[20]

In March 1982, INSLAW was awarded a $10 million, 3-year contract to install the public domain version of PROMIS on minicomputers in 20 large U.S. attorneys' offices and on word processors in 74 smaller offices. According to Judge Bryant, of the U.S. District Court for the District of Columbia, in commenting on the Department's appeal of the Bankruptcy Court's ruling:

> ...the contract sought proposal for (1) implementing the computerized "pilot version" of PROMIS as supplemented by the BJS [Bureau of Justice Statistics] enhancements in 20 "large" U.S. attorneys' offices; (2) creating and implementing a noncomputerized version of that software for word processors in the remaining U.S. attorneys' offices; and (3) providing necessary training, maintenance and support for 3 years.[21]

Shortly after receiving the contract to implement PROMIS at the 94 U.S. attorneys' offices, INSLAW's counsel sent a detailed letter to Mr. Stanley Morris, then an Associate Deputy Attorney General at the Department. This letter, with an attached memorandum written by Mr. Hamilton, notified the Department of INSLAW's intent to market an enhanced version of PROMIS as a fee-generating product to public and private sector customers.[22] This claim to exclusive proprietary rights by INSLAW would naturally require the Department to pay INSLAW license fees if it chose to use Enhanced PROMIS. INSLAW based this claim on the fact that several non-Federal sources paid for continued funding of PROMIS' development and implementation.[23]

---

[19] Memorandum to the File from Mr. Peter Videnieks, Contracting Officer, Department of Justice, illegible date, pp. 1–2.

[20] Memorandum of the U.S. District Court for the District of Columbia concerning the consolidated appeal of the final judgment entered by the U.S. Bankruptcy Court in favor of INSLAW, November 22, 1989, p. 22a. Also see January 14, 1982, letter from Dr. Dean C. Merrill, INSLAW vice president, to Mr. Peter Videnieks, Department contracting officer, p. 9.

[21] Ibid., p. 21a.

[22] Letter with attached memorandum to Mr. Stanley E. Morris, Associate Deputy Attorney General and a member of the PROMIS Oversight Committee, from Mr. Roderick M. Hills, Latham & Watkins, April 2, 1982.

[23] In a memorandum to INSLAW's counsel, an INSLAW employee stated that, during the period from May 1981 to May 1982 INSLAW developed a number of enhancements using over $1 million of private funds and that no Federal funds were expended on these enhancements.

17

As detailed by the Bankruptcy Court in its chronology of events surrounding the INSLAW matter, Mr. C. Madison (Brick) Brewer had just assumed the departmental position of PROMIS project manager at the time of contract award. Mr. Brewer reacted negatively to INSLAW's efforts to protect its proprietary interest and in retaliation considered canceling the Department's contract with INSLAW just 1 month after it was initiated. A Department team meeting, including Messrs. Brewer, Videnieks (Justice Contracting Officer), and Rugh (Acting Assistant Director for Office of Management Information Systems Support—OMISS), was held on April 14, 1982, in Mr. Brewer's office to discuss Mr. Hamilton's "scurrilous"[24] memo. According to Mr. Videnieks' notes of the meeting:

> Discussed INSLAW's "PROMIS II" memo... Termination for Convenience discussed.[25]

Mr. Brewer apparently also discussed other reprisals against INSLAW on its other contracts with the Department.[26] However, when subsequently questioned in the course of litigation, there developed a severe memory loss with respect to the Department witnesses' recollection of this meeting, as noted by Judge Bason:

> All of the DOJ witnesses who attended the April 14, 1982, meeting professed a total lack of memory about it. They testified they had no recollection of any such meeting. This court disbelieves that testimony. None of them could offer any credible explanation, or indeed any explanation, of the meaning of Videnieks' handwritten notes other than what this court finds to be their meaning in this Finding of Fact No. 165. These notes constitute a "smoking gun" that clearly evidences Brewer's intense bias against INSLAW, his single-minded intent to drive INSLAW out of business, and Rugh's and Videnieks' complicity.[27]

In an apparent effort to respond to the concern raised by Department officials over whether the Department or INSLAW would own any enhancements to the PROMIS software, INSLAW's attorney, Mr. James Rogers, wrote on May 26, 1982, to Associate Deputy Attorney General, Stanley E. Morris. In this letter, Mr. Rogers provided a detailed description of what the company planned to do to market the software commercially, and asked that the Department respond to INSLAW to "ensure that these representations are correct." Mr. Rogers went on to explain:

> [Y]ou expressed concern about the software itself, PROMIS 82, which INSLAW proposes to license to users for a fee commencing in June of 1982. We are prepared to make the following representations, which should alleviate the Department's concerns:
> PROMIS 82 is the sum of only three parts:

Memorandum to Jim Rogers, Latham, Watkins & Hills, from Joyce Deroy, June 17, 1982, Exhibit 1.
[24] *INSLAW, Inc.,* v. *United States*, 83 B.R. 89 (Bktcy. D. Dist. Col. 1988) at 123 (Finding 165).
[25] Ibid., at 123 (Finding 165).
[26] Findings of Fact and Conclusions of Law, No. 165, at 84.
[27] Ibid., at 84–85.

18

(1) the "Original PROMIS," that is, the public domain software as of May 15, 1981 as memorialized in tapes delivered to the Bureau of Justice Statistics;

(2) enhancements undertaken by INSLAW at private expense after the cessation of LEAA funding; and

(3) the so-called printed inquiry enhancement, which was created under contract to the Bureau of Justice Statistics and delivered to the Department of Justice on May 17, 1982.

It is apparent that both Mr. Brewer and Mr. Videnieks, the PROMIS contracting officer, reacted very strongly to INSLAW's notice that it had developed Enhanced PROMIS with private funding. There followed a very antagonistic meeting between Mr. Brewer and INSLAW representatives soon after INSLAW's assertions of proprietary claims to PROMIS.[28] Messrs. Brewer and Videnieks continued to believe that, because the Department was currently funding the implementation of PROMIS, they could ignore INSLAW's proprietary interest in the privately funded enhancements made to the PROMIS software.

However, in an August 1982 response to INSLAW, Mr. Stanley Morris, the Department's Associate Deputy Attorney General, stated that the original PROMIS, as well as an enhancement known as printed inquiry,[29] was in the public domain. He added that, to the extent that any other enhancements to PROMIS were privately funded by INSLAW and not specified to be delivered to the Department, INSLAW could assert whatever proprietary rights it might have.[30]

A. PROJECT MANAGER BREWER: AN INHERENT BIAS AND POTENTIAL CONFLICT OF INTEREST

For those who have formally reviewed the INSLAW matter, both in the judicial and legislative branches, the selection of Mr. Brewer by Mr. William P. Tyson of the Executive Office of U.S. Attorneys (EOUSA) to serve as the PROMIS project manager looms as a curious choice when matters of the conflict of interest, appearance and actual, are considered.[31] Indeed, Mr. Brewer worked for Mr. Hamilton between 1974 and 1976 as general counsel for the Institute for Law and Social Research, a not-for-profit corporation owned by Mr. Hamilton which later became INSLAW. Mr. Hamilton has testified that in this capacity, Mr. Brewer was unable to perform the duties required of him; and, as a result, he was asked to leave.[32] Mr. Hamilton testified that he provided Mr. Brewer with a suffi-

---

[28] Findings of Fact and Conclusions of Law, No. 168, 170, pp. 85–86 and sworn statement of C. Madison Brewer, September 13, 1990, p. 74.

[29] "Printed inquiry" enhancement refers to special enhancements made to PROMIS pursuant to a Bureau of Justice Statistics contract with INSLAW.

[30] On August 11, 1982, Morris responded:

"We agree that the original PROMIS, as defined in your letter of May 26, 1982, is in the public domain. We also agree that the printed inquiry enhancement is in the public domain. To the extent that any other enhancements to the system were privately funded by INSLAW and not specified to be delivered to the Department of Justice under any contract or other arrangement, INSLAW may assert whatever proprietary rights it may have." [Letter from Mr. Stanley E. Morris, Associate Deputy Attorney General to James Rogers, Esq., August 11, 1982, p. 1.]

[31] Mr. Brewer started with the EOUSA in January 1982 and officially became the PROMIS project manager in April 1982.

[32] Findings of Fact and Conclusions of Law, No. 101, 103, pp. 110–11.

19

cient time period to find a job rather than summarily forcing him out of the company. After the initial conflict with Mr. Brewer flared up over the PROMIS software enhancement issue in April 1982, INSLAW formally complained to Mr. Morris that Mr. Brewer was biased against INSLAW because he had been asked to resign his position with the company; and that in any event, the Department should have placed another official in charge of managing the project who was not tainted with past direct (and very possibly negative) associations with the company. Mr. Hamilton strongly believed that Mr. Brewer harbored antagonistic feelings about his past working relationship with Mr. Hamilton. Department officials were apparently impervious to these concerns and stated that Mr. Brewer's skills and prior employment with INSLAW were important factors in his hiring by the Department. Mr. McWhorter, Deputy Director of the EOUSA, who was involved in Mr. Brewer's hiring, believed that Mr. Brewer's employment by INSLAW qualified him to:

> ...run the implementation of a case tracking system for U.S. attorneys to...basically direct the implementation of a case tracking system in U.S. attorneys offices. [33]

It is difficult to understand, however, how Mr. McWhorter could make this statement. By Mr. Brewer's own admission, he had very little, if any, experience in managing computer projects and Government ADP procurement law at the time he was hired. Perhaps even more damaging, while under oath to committee investigators, he admitted to a lack of experience or detailed understanding of computers or software:

> ...I was not a computer person. We talked about my role, viewed as being liaison, the person who would make things happen, a coordinator. It was not contemplated that I would, by osmosis or otherwise, learn computer science. [34]

Even after interviewing Mr. Brewer's supervisor (Mr. Tyson) and other Department personnel involved with his hiring, committee investigators were unable to determine how Mr. Brewer came to be considered for the position. Still unexplained—given the appearance of a conflict of interest created by his past employment with Mr. Hamilton and his total lack of experience and training in ADP contracting—is why the Department would have considered him prepared, much less best qualified, for the job.

As project manager throughout the implementation of the contract, Mr. Brewer was involved in all major contract and technical decisions—including the development of the Department's position on INSLAW's claim of proprietary software enhancements made to the public domain version of PROMIS. Significantly, Mr. Brewer, also reported on the progress on the contract to the Department's PROMIS Oversight Committee, a senior level decisionmaking committee organized in 1981 as part of the Department's overall control point for the PROMIS project. [35]

---

[33] Deposition of Laurence S. McWhorter, June 12, 1987, pp 11-12.
[34] Sworn statement of C. Madison Brewer, September 13, 1990, p. 39.
[35] The PROMIS Oversight Committee reviewed and approved plans developed by Mr. Brewer and the EOUSA for implementing the PROMIS software into the EOUSA district offices. The
Continued

20

Investigations by both the Senate and GAO into the INSLAW matter flagged serious concerns about Mr. Brewer's appointment and the possible conflict of interest his appointment represented. The Permanent Subcommittee on Investigations (PSI) drew the same conclusion as the GAO's audit manager that Mr. Brewer's appointment as project manager created an undeniable appearance of a conflict of interest that should have been avoided at all costs by the Department. The PSI report stated:

> The staff finds that the Department exercised poor judgment in ignoring the potential for a conflict of interest in its hiring of the PROMIS project director [Brewer], and then, after receiving allegations of bias on his part, in failing to follow standard procedures to investigate them in a timely manner. [36]

The potential conflict of interest was an unsatisfactory situation irrespective of his admittedly negative feelings about his forced resignation from the company. Had Mr. Brewer taken actions which could have been construed to unduly favor INSLAW throughout the life of the contract, similar questions of potential conflict could just as easily have arisen either from within the Department or from outside competitors of the company. In either situation, the Department had placed itself in an undeniable ethical situation that could have been easily avoided had it followed basic procedures to prevent any possible appearance of a conflict. On this point, Judge Jensen stated that:

> I would think that the better path of wisdom is not to do that [hire an alleged fired employee to direct the contract of his former employer] if that's possible to do...I think that it's better to have these kinds of issues undertaken by people who don't have questions raised about them one way or the other whether they are biased in favor of or against the people they deal with. [37]

While phrased in the abstract, Judge Jensen and other Department officials apparently ignored the circumstances surrounding Mr. Brewer's departure from INSLAW and did not consider the po-

---

committee membership originally consisted of the Associate Attorney General (Rudolph W. Giuliani), the Associate Deputy Attorney General (Stanley E. Morris), the Director of EOUSA (William P. Tyson), and Justice Management Division's (JMD) Assistant Attorney General for Administration (Kevin D. Rooney). The Associate Attorney General was the Chairman of the Committee. See memorandum from Mr. Kevin D. Rooney, Assistant Attorney General for Administration and Mr. William P. Tyson, Acting Director, EOUSA to Deputy Attorney General Edward C. Schmults, August 13, 1981, p. 3 (hereinafter Rooney and Tyson memorandum).

It is important to note that Mr. Jensen was heavily involved in the Department's PROMIS project. Mr. Brewer has testified that Judge Jensen, who was the Assistant Attorney General for the Criminal Division between 1981 and early 1983, attended most, if not all, of the PROMIS Oversight Committee meetings as a participant and, later, as the chairman of the committee. Mr. Brewer indicated that Judge Jensen attended these meetings before he became Associate Attorney General (and Chairman of the Oversight Committee) because PROMIS implementation was a very high priority program, and representation from all departmental offices was required. During early 1983, as Associate Attorney General and later as Deputy Attorney General, Judge Jensen was ranking Chairman of that Committee and one of its most influential members throughout the life of the PROMIS contract. Sworn statement of C. Madison Brewer, September 13, 1990, pp. 114–15.

[36] Staff Study of Allegations Pertaining to the Department of Justice's Handling of a Contract with INSLAW, Inc., by the Permanent Subcommittee on Investigations, Senate Committee on Governmental Affairs, September 1989, p. VII.

[37] Office of Professional Responsibility Deposition of Judge Lowell Jensen, June 19, 1987, p. 34.

21

tential bias or conflict of interest issues either before or after his hiring. In fact, Mr. Brewer stated that no formal inquiry into these charges was made by the Department until after the contract expired in 1985. On the issue of his departure from INSLAW, Mr. Brewer stated under oath to OPR investigators that:

> At no time did he [Mr. Hamilton] ever say you are fired and at no time did he [Mr. Hamilton] ever indicate great dissatisfaction with my performance.
> I don't believe anything Mr. Hamilton did regarding my employment or relationship with the Institute...was wrong. I never felt that I was discharged, let alone wrongfully discharged.

Mr. Brewer again asserted this position under oath to committee investigators:

> I never thought that he asked me to leave. It has always been my understanding that I was not asked to leave....I have never viewed my departure from the Institute as either being a discharge, or forced.

However, in other parts of his testimony to OPR and the committee investigators he appears to acknowledge that Mr. Hamilton asked him to leave. For example, he stated to OPR:

> ...it has been my view that Mr. Hamilton obviously wanted me gone. I had been sending these signals, if not directly indicating a job dissatisfaction, since April, and it was now February, almost 1 year later and I was still extricating myself.

Mr. Brewer's statements that he was not asked to leave are also contradicted by other witnesses' statements on this point. As indicated above, according to Mr. Hamilton, Mr. Brewer was unable to perform the duties required of him and; as a result, he was asked to leave.[38] Mr. Hamilton's account was corroborated by Mr. John Gizzarelli, Jr., who stated under oath that Mr. Hamilton mentioned that Mr. Brewer had been asked to resign and Mr. Hamilton asked for advice on how Mr. Brewer could be removed while preserving his professional dignity and feelings.[39]

Mr. Brewer appears to contradict his own assertions that he was never asked to leave by Mr. Hamilton. At trial, Mr. Brewer stated under oath that:

> ...on one occasion Mr. Hamilton came and said to me, "can you go to lunch?" I explained that I couldn't....And he said, "Well, what I have to say over lunch I can say right now. I think you ought to find [an] alternative—that you ought to leave the Institute."

The circumstances surrounding Mr. Brewer's departure from the institute appears to have had a major influence over his views about INSLAW and its president, Mr. Hamilton. Several witnesses asserted that Mr. Brewer exhibited considerable bias against INSLAW and Mr. Hamilton during critical points of the contract.

---

[38] Findings of Fact and Conclusions of Law, pp. 49–52.
[39] Testimony of John Gizzarelli at trial, July 22, 1987, p. 473.

22

When asked about his relationship to Mr. Hamilton, Mr. Brewer stated:

> He was very supportive, and I thought that he was a very dynamic and creative person, a very skilled communicator and a very talented individual, but as to some aspects of life, one who did not have a realistic viewpoint on some things...he had said some things to me on occasion that made me think that he was somewhat of a zealot about his pursuits and the things he did....Mr. Hamilton is a difficult person to deal with, or that he is not realistic.... [40]

However, several witnesses provided a considerably different description of Mr. Brewer's feelings toward INSLAW and Mr. Hamilton. Mr. Gizzarelli stated under oath that:

> I also had occasional contact with Mr. Brewer during the period of his employment with INSLAW...specifically, he thought that Mr. Hamilton was insane. And I think he meant that literally. He did make comments about his rationality, his sanity, thought he wasn't capable of leading an organization. The tenor of his remarks were to me very startling.
>
> * * * * * * *
>
> ...mental observation...was used to describe a person for whom that process might be advisable, mental observation being a psychiatric evaluation to determine whether or not a person is or is not afflicted with a psychosis. And Mr. Brewer used that term to describe Mr. Hamilton. He said he was M.O., [mental observation] which is a colloquialism—means he should be examined by a psychiatrist.
>
> * * * * * * *
>
> After he became the project manager...a flood of memories about his prior involvement with INSLAW and his characterization of Bill Hamilton came back, and I was afraid that his bias would be overwhelming—would overwhelm him. [41]

Mr. Gizzarelli later stated by memorandum to Mr. Dean Merrill that Mr. Brewer:

> ...has made no secret of his dislike of Bill Hamilton. In his present job, he is in a position to demonstrate his dislike. Bill, however, has kept his distance from the project and probably will continue to do so, until and unless there are large problems which Bill—in his role as president—must deal with personally. It is entirely possible—and I believe likely—that Brick will escalate the level of controversy until he draws Bill into the project, at which time he will be able to "lord it over him" and show who's boss.

[40] Sworn statement of C. Madison Brewer, September 13, 1990, pps. 11 and 75.
[41] Gizzarelli sworn testimony, pp. 474–476.

23

I don't think Brick will ever be at peace with his feelings about Bill and therefore, with us.[42]

Mr. Harvey Sherzer, INSLAW's attorney, made similar assertions about Mr. Brewer's bias against INSLAW during the trial:

...I think the most descriptive answer is to say that Mr. Brewer exhibited an animus toward INSLAW and toward Mr. Hamilton.

He viewed with...skepticism and negativism and some hostility INSLAW's allegations with regard to its financial condition. And I recall specifically that I reached the conclusion at that time that, and I recall expressing it to him, that he had a problem, that he seemed to think there was something wrong with a contractor benefiting from a government contract. Let me be more specific on that point. The gist of what he seemed to be saying was that by performing this contract INSLAW and Mr. Hamilton, specifically, was making an effort to expand the company...And there seemed to be a negative inference toward INSLAW's ability to use the base created by this contract to expand.

And I recall explaining to him that that was perfectly legitimate, and, indeed, that the Government often in its efforts to support congressionally the appropriations for the space program and other programs often points out that a byproduct of a space program is a better toaster oven because various alloys [are] created or what have you. It's a common phenomenon whereby the...by-product of Government work is the ability to benefit both the company the Government and the community generally in a broader way. And Mr. Brewer seemed to resent the fact that INSLAW might use the benefits of this large contract to expand its company, which at that time it was doing.[43]

On this same issue the Bankruptcy Court concluded that:

On the basis of the...evidence taken as a whole, this court is convinced beyond any doubt that...Brewer was consumed by hatred for and an intense desire for revenge against Mr. Hamilton and INSLAW, and acted throughout this matter in a thoroughly biased and unfairly prejudicial manner toward INSLAW.

In reviewing Judge Bason's substantive findings of fact and conclusions of law, the District Court also concluded that:

The nature and circumstances of his separation from that employment are somewhat in dispute, but it is clear that Brewer was not happy in his job when he left it after being urged to do so by Hamilton.

* * * * * * *

INSLAW attributed its troubles to an acute bias on the part of Brewer, who according to it was intent on running the company out of business. INSLAW lodged many com-

---

[42] Memorandum from Mr. John Gizzarelli to Mr. Dean Merrill, July 1, 1982, pp. 1–3.
[43] Testimony of Harvey G. Sherzer, INSLAW's attorney, June 30, 1987, pp. 63–64.

24

plaints of bias and made several request of DOJ to investigate these complaints and give some relief from what it perceived to be grossly unfair treatment. DOJ made no meaningful response to these complaints, and INSLAW's fortunes did not change.

INSLAW's problems began soon after the contract was awarded and immediately after its assertion of proprietary enhancements to public domain PROMIS. Mr. Brewer's animosity toward INSLAW was strongly manifested in a meeting (April 19, 1982) to discuss INSLAW's proposal to market its Enhanced PROMIS software, as noted in an INSLAW memorandum on the meeting:

Brewer...seized upon this issue and launched into a tirade which was very emotional, unorganized and quite illogical. He said that:

"1. the memo was typical of INSLAW and Bill Hamilton and that it was self-serving and unnecessary.

"2. that how did they know that we might say work was not finished under our Government contracts and the next week copyright the work and begin selling it back to the Justice Department.

"3. that the press release about the contract award was not accurate in that it described West Virginia as a successful implementation when in fact, they had spent an additional 20K on the project and Lanier was doing all the work....

"7. that the memo had caused all kinds of problems in Justice and had many people upset.

"8. that if you ask Namely, Illinois Criminal Justice Coordinating Council, Michigan Prosecuting Attorney's Association, Andy Voight and others, they would tell you that INSLAW did not do good or successful work.

"9. that Bill Hamilton started the PROMIS system as an employee of the D.C., U.S.A.O. and that all of the software was developed with Federal funds and what right did Hamilton have to try to claim ownership of the software."

All of these comments were based with an obvious dislike of Bill Hamilton and a resentment for the success of INSLAW personified in him.[44]

After this meeting, INSLAW complained to Associate Deputy Attorney General Morris that Mr. Brewer was obviously biased against INSLAW because he had been asked to leave his employment at the company. On this basis, INSLAW requested that Mr. Brewer be recused from further Department consideration of the proprietary software enhancement issue. Subsequently, Mr. Morris decided to remove Mr. Brewer from face-to-face negotiations with INSLAW officials on the enhancement issue. By note dated May 27, 1982, Mr. Laurence McWhorter, Deputy Director of the Executive Office of U.S. Attorney, stated that he was directed by Mr. Morris to "take the point outside the Department" on the proprietary enhancement issue. It is clear from this action that Mr. Morris was concerned about the possibility of an appearance of a con-

---

[44] April 21, 1982, INSLAW Memorandum to File from J. F. Kelly and J. Doroy.

25

flict of interest with having an ex-employee of INSLAW operating as the Department's project manager on a contract involving the same company. However, this solution was only superficial because Mr. Brewer continued to have substantive influence over the management and administration of the INSLAW contract. Mr. Brewer acknowledged under oath that he remained involved in the Department negotiations with INSLAW on all important issues including the enhancement issue throughout the life of the contract. He also stated that Mr. Hamilton had "shot himself in the foot" and created considerable "ill will" within the Department by asserting that INSLAW had proprietary interest in the PROMIS software.[45] INSLAW's expanding problems with the Department are detailed in the following sections of the report.

B. BREWER AND VIDENIEKS THREATEN INSLAW

During the contract negotiations the Department acknowledged INSLAW's cash-poor situation by inserting a contract clause that enabled INSLAW to receive payment in advance of the Department receiving and approving finished products.[46] During November 1982, the Department learned that INSLAW had assigned Government invoices to a financial institution to secure a line of credit, and Mr. Videnieks, by letter dated November 10, 1982, asserted to INSLAW that it was in default of the advance payments clause of the contract.[47]

Cancellation of the advance payments would have had a devastating impact on INSLAW. Mr. Videnieks told committee investigators under oath that:

> I think I was advised at the same time....that INSLAW may indeed have difficulty in meeting the December payroll, and I think in general I was advised that they were in bad financial condition.[48]

INSLAW, at that point, was supporting the Department's utilization of PROMIS with its proprietary enhanced software through time-sharing on a mainframe. The Department, lacking the hardware to implement public domain PROMIS, moved to obtain a copy of INSLAW's proprietary Enhanced PROMIS software, as described in an internal memorandum dated March 7, 1983:

> Of course, an INSLAW failure at any time prior to contract completion would have a detrimental effect on the implementation project. Currently, programmatic risk is very high. So long as INSLAW continues to support U.S. attorneys' offices in a timesharing mode, withholds time-sharing [the enhanced] PROMIS software, and fails to

---

[45] Sworn statement of C. Madison Brewer, September 13, 1990, pp. 155–156.
[46] The advance payments clause (N)(1) from contract states that: "The amount of advance payments at any time outstanding hereunder shall not exceed:
$280,000.00 during the first 12 months of contract performance;
$380,000.00 during months 13 through 20 of contract performance;
$280,000.00 during months 21 through 30 of contract performance; and
$100,000.00 for the balance of the performance of the contract."
[47] Mr. Brewer stated that the reason for considering terminating INSLAW's advance payment account was that a loan INSLAW had with the Bank of Bethesda, pursuant to which a lien was placed on payments received by INSLAW from the account (not the account itself), was contrary to the contract and placed the Government in financial risk.
[48] Sworn statement of Peter Videnieks, November 5, 1990, p. 62.

26

complete delivery of at least one system operating on a Government furnished Prime computer and at least one system operating on a Government-furnished Lanier word processor, programmatic risk will remain high.[49]

Mr. Videnieks told committee investigators under oath that:

> We were afraid if they indeed were for financial reasons required to close their doors...then we would have to revert to a manual PROMIS in these U.S. attorneys offices. So the reason for requesting copies of this data and documentation were to be able to continue, if indeed INSLAW were to close its doors, automated PROMIS on Government computers.[50]

An internal Department analysis notes, however, that:

> Because DOJ's computers were not in place, DOJ purchased time on INSLAW's computer. INSLAW retained the software to use for time-sharing purposes in its offices and had not yet delivered it to the various U.S. attorneys' offices.[51]

Judge Bryant pointed out that:

> On November 19, 1982, DOJ's technical representative formally requested a copy of the PROMIS software that was then in use by the U.S. attorneys' offices. According to the Justice Department the request was motivated by concern over the financial viability of INSLAW. It is without dispute that because the Government had not obtained the minicomputer hardware for each office, INSLAW arranged for the largest U.S. attorneys' offices to use PROMIS on a time-sharing basis.

Mr. Brewer stated in a December 9, 1982, memorandum that he was concerned with the possibility of INSLAW's bankruptcy, the possible need for in-house EOUSA personnel to take over the PROMIS project, and the possibility of terminating the PROMIS contract. In December 1982, Mr. Videnieks demanded that INSLAW turn over all computer programs and supporting documentation relating to the contract.[52] INSLAW responded that it would not do this without the Department modifying the contract to acknowledge that proprietary enhancements had been inserted into the Department's public domain version of PROMIS. INSLAW required this acknowledgment because INSLAW's other timesharing customers also used this proprietary version of PROMIS.

The Department responded that the contract called for software in which the Government had unlimited rights, and asked that INSLAW identify those portions of the software that it claimed

---

[49] March 7, 1983, Department of Justice internal memorandum, entitled "PROMIS Implementation Contract, Programmatic Risk related to possible failure of INSLAW as a business entity."

[50] Sworn statement of Videnieks, op cit.

[51] Report of the Investigation by the Office of Professional Responsibility in the INSLAW Matter, from Mr. Robert B. Lyon, Jr., Acting Counsel, Office of Professional Responsibility, to Mr. Harold G. Christensen, Deputy Attorney General, March 31, 1989. OPR Footnote 13, pp. 24–25.

[52] Letter from Mr. Peter Videnieks, contracting officer, to Mr. John Gizzarelli, INSLAW, Inc., December 6, 1982, p. 1.

27

were proprietary. INSLAW offered to provide the enhanced software if the Department agreed to INSLAW's rights and controlled its dissemination. Mr. Videnieks stated to committee investigators that the Department believed that it had unlimited rights to any versions of PROMIS, and data rights restrictions would not satisfy INSLAW's obligation under the contract.[53]

INSLAW proposed that the Department use its enhanced software at the 94 U.S. attorneys offices at no additional cost, but that the Government not disseminate the Enhanced PROMIS beyond those offices. The Department objected to this proposal and made a counter-proposal that a contract modification be made which, in exchange for the software and documentation requested previously, the Department would agree not to disseminate Enhanced PROMIS beyond the 94 offices and the EOUSA pending resolution of the enhancement dispute.[54]

Mr. Videnieks further proposed that, if INSLAW could demonstrate that the software contained enhancements to which the Department was not entitled, the Department would either direct that INSLAW remove the enhancements or negotiate with INSLAW regarding inclusion of the enhancements.[55]

C. INSLAW ATTEMPTS TO DEMONSTRATE ENHANCEMENT OWNERSHIP

INSLAW and the Department ostensibly resolved their dispute by "good-faith" action on a contract modification (Mod. 12) dated April 11, 1983. As a result, DOJ agreed to continue to provide advance payments to INSLAW.[56] According to Judge Bryant, under this agreement:

> The parties reaffirmed their understanding that their initial contract governs the rights to the disputed software.

By letters dated April 5, and April 12, 1983, INSLAW attempted to demonstrate that its enhancements were privately funded, but the Department did little to assist INSLAW in determining what documentation would be acceptable.[57] By letter dated April 21, 1983, Mr. Videnieks reiterated that the contract entitled the Government to a version of PROMIS with no restrictions, and demanded that INSLAW:

> ....provide all information necessary to demonstrate that the change was developed both at private expense and outside the scope of INSLAW's performance of any Government contract.

---

[53] Report of the Investigation by the Office of Professional Responsibility in the INSLAW Matter, March 31, 1989, p. 27.

[54] March 18, 1983, letter to Harvey Sherzer, Esq., INSLAW's attorney, from Peter Videnieks, p. 2.

[55] Ibid., p. 2.

[56] Funds were placed by the Department into an account at the Bank of Bethesda. INSLAW could withdraw funds from the account (based on expenses incurred) only after a voucher was signed by Mr. Videnieks.

[57] Letters from Mr. Harvey G. Sherzer, INSLAW counsel, Pettit & Martin, to the Department, April 5, 1983 and April 12, 1983.

28

INSLAW sent another proposed methodology to demonstrate private funding by letter dated May 4, 1983.[58] Mr. Videnieks responded that INSLAW's methodology was unacceptable because it did not identify enhancements developed without Federal funds.[59] Mr. Videnieks never provided INSLAW with a methodology on standards by which INSLAW could demonstrate his evidence requirements.

Mr. Jack Rugh, the Department's Acting Assistant Director for Office of Management Information Systems Support (OMISS), analyzed the INSLAW submissions supporting its contentions that Enhanced PROMIS had been privately funded. Mr. Rugh stated under oath during the Bankruptcy Court hearing that it was his opinion that the methodology used by INSLAW to support its assertion was flawed and that the company's presentation *"probably"* [emphasis added] lacked accounting records to support its claims. Mr. Rugh further stated that he could not recall if he had informed INSLAW of his concerns regarding their lack of accounting records to substantiate their claims. Mr. Rugh said that although he could see no reason why he would withhold this information from INSLAW, he could see no reason for including it.[60] Mr. Rugh stated, however, that INSLAW had an excellent method of documenting the changed (enhanced) source code, so that those changes could be considered proprietary if they were attributed to a particular private source.[61] This admission caused the bankruptcy judge to conclude:

> This process of comparing the enhancements proofs with the previously-provided PROMIS software could have been performed easily by INSLAW with DOJ's assistance in the summer of 1983, when INSLAW attempted to negotiate this issue with DOJ and submitted to DOJ its memoranda proving specific enhancements. All of the documents used by INSLAW in this proceeding to identify the funding of its enhancements existed at the time the negotiations should have occurred. As Mr. Rugh conceded at trial, the proofs offered by INSLAW would have satisfied him that the enhancements were indeed privately funded. (Rugh, T. 1517–1520). DOJ was required to negotiate then, in 1983, as Videnieks specifically had proposed under Modification 12, (see PPFF 228–236) but instead it wrongfully and cynically failed either to negotiate in good faith or even to reveal to INSLAW any purported concerns of Messrs. Rugh and Videnieks at that time with INSLAW's proposed method of proof (see PPFF 246–250).[62]

Mr. Videnieks never accepted any INSLAW attempts at defining proprietary enhancements, and Department officials concluded that the Department had the same unlimited rights to Enhanced PROMIS as it had with public domain PROMIS. This posture was

---

[58] Letter from Mr. Harvey G. Sherzer, INSLAW counsel, Pettit & Martin, to Mr. Peter Videnieks, contracting officer, May 4, 1983.

[59] Letter from Mr. Peter Videnieks, contracting officer, to Mr. Harvey G. Sherzer, Esq. Pettit & Martin, June 10, 1983, p. 2.

[60] Testimony given during *INSLAW, Inc.* v. *United States*, by Mr. Jack Stanley Rugh, July 28, 1987, p. 1513.

[61] Ibid., pp. 1517–1518.

[62] *INSLAW, Inc.* v. *United States*, 83 B.R. 89 (Bktcy D. Dist. Col. 1988) at 107 (Finding 83). Also see INFRA for Terms of Modification 12.

29

made clear from a variety of sources, including Messrs. Brewer and Videnieks. In a sworn statement before this committee, Mr. Brewer responded to the following questions:

> Question: At this April 19th meeting, do you recall making the statement that the Department had unlimited rights to the software?
> Mr. ˙Brewer: That was our position throughout this whole thing, yes.
> Question: What is your view today on that?
> Mr. Brewer: I maintain that we negotiated for and received unlimited rights and data.

Mr. Videnieks also believed that the Department had title to Enhanced PROMIS, which he characterized while discussing his position regarding Modification 12 in a sworn deposition before this committee:

> Initially, I'm the one who wanted no modification. I wanted only a letter saying, "Give us the data," because if we—we don't need any signatures, if we can get the goods. My words. The goods were ours under the contract. All we would have to pay for to effect delivery of those goods were reproduction costs.
> Brewer, I believe, wanted a supplemental agreement but not a modification. I didn't want any of them. But the legal advice was that Bill Snider [the Department's legal counsel] felt strongly that there should be a Modification 12, but my opinion was supported by Patricia Rudd, who was the Chief Procurement Officer at that time.
> So we in Procurement, the hands-on people, thought that the contract as it stands had the mechanism in there for satisfying the Program Officer's needs. But the lawyers on all sides felt that we needed to write escrow agreements and make the thing look pretty, I guess. [63]

Mr. Videnieks, by letter dated July 21, 1983, told INSLAW that:

> We agree with you that Modification No. P0012 to the Contract continues to limit dissemination of that version of the PROMIS computer software specified in the modification. Modification No. P0012 will continue to apply in the event that the Government invokes the provisions of Clause 22, "Disputes," in that the Government will limit dissemination pending a Contracting Officer's Final Decision in the matter. [64]

On December 29, 1983, in spite of a report that there was progress with INSLAW counsel on resolution of the contract problems, Judge Jensen and other members of the PROMIS Oversight Committee approved the termination of the word processing portion of the contract for default based on their view that INSLAW had failed to perform this portion of the contract. [65] However, in

---

[63] Sworn statement of Mr. Peter Videnieks, November 5, 1990, p. 94.
[64] Letter to Mr. H. G. Sherzer, INSLAW's Attorney, from Mr. Peter Videnieks, contracting officer, July 21, 1983.
[65] Findings of Fact and Conclusions of Law, No. 316 and 317, p. 144.

30

February 1984, Department procurement counsel William Snider issued a written legal opinion showing that the Department lacked sufficient legal justification for a default termination. Instead, the PROMIS Oversight Committee approved the termination of the word processing portion of the contract for convenience. Shortly thereafter, Mr. Brewer notified Mr. Hamilton by telephone that Judge Jensen had decided to only terminate the word processing portion of the INSLAW contract at the 74 smaller U.S. attorneys offices for convenience of the Government. [66]

D. THE DEPARTMENT MISAPPROPRIATED INSLAW'S SOFTWARE

The Department's position that it owned Enhanced PROMIS was founded on amendments to the RFP [67] that (1) made available to all offerors copies of the pilot project software and (2) stated that the RFP does not anticipate redevelopment of the public domain PROMIS software used in the pilot offices. The RFP also stated that:

> All systems enhancements... performed pursuant to this contract shall be incorporated within the systems which have already been installed in the U.S. attorneys' offices, including systems installed pursuant to other contracts....

According to Department officials, this language was included to ensure that offices already using PROMIS would benefit from the enhancements and modifications to the Government-furnished software during performance of the new contract. Unfortunately, this language may also have blinded Department management to the idea that INSLAW had made privately funded enhancements that were its property, notwithstanding the Department's claims to the contrary.

INSLAW attempted to convince Department officials that it held proprietary rights to Enhanced PROMIS over a period of several years, but to no avail. The Department steadfastly ignored INSLAW's requests, and even fought two judgments that it believed were in error based on technical, legal issues rather than on the merits of the case. Department officials have continued to maintain that they enjoy total control of Enhanced PROMIS since they obtained it from INSLAW in 1983.

After Modification 12 was signed and the Department obtained Enhanced PROMIS and terminated the installation of PROMIS at the 74 smaller U.S. attorneys offices, INSLAW again attempted to define its enhancements to the Department while the Department continued to use INSLAW's software and services. Each attempt was rebuffed by Mr. Videnieks. He issued a series of determinations in response to INSLAW's claims between November 1984 and September 1986. Finally, almost 3 years after signing Modification 12, Mr. Videnieks declared, on February 21, 1986, that INSLAW had no enhancements that were proprietary to it, and denied INSLAW's claim of $2.9 million for licensing fees.

---

[66] Ibid., p. 144.
[67] RFP amendments 1 and 2, November 9, 1981, and November 16, 1981, respectively.

31

The Bankruptcy Court took the position that the Department obtained INSLAW's Enhanced PROMIS through "fraud, trickery, and deceit." As stated by Judge Bason:

> Under Modification 12, it is undisputed that INSLAW delivered Enhanced PROMIS to DOJ on the basis of an explicit commitment by DOJ which had three components: first, to bargain in good faith to identify the proprietary enhancements; second, to decide within a reasonable time which enhancements it wanted to use; and third, to bargain in good faith with INSLAW as to the price to be paid for such enhancements. On the basis of the foregoing and all of the evidence taken as a whole, this court finds and concludes that the Department never intended to meet its commitment and that once the Department had received Enhanced PROMIS pursuant to Modification 12, the Department thereafter refused to bargain in good faith with INSLAW and instead engaged in an outrageous, deceitful, fraudulent game of "cat and mouse," demonstrating contempt for both the law and any principle of fair dealing. [68]

The Department's unilateral claim of ownership rights to Enhanced PROMIS, coupled with Mr. Videnieks' denial of INSLAW's claims to proprietary enhancements, demonstrates at the very least, a mechanistic approach to procurement policy that always favors the Department, which just happens to be in a most favored negotiating position at every turn. At worst, it reflects a biased view that denied due process and full and fair consideration, for whatever reason. Most disturbing, Mr. Brewer and Mr. Videnieks, the persons in charge of the PROMIS project, refused to consider the software ownership concepts involved in INSLAW's assertions. The judge, in the Bankruptcy Court's *findings of fact and conclusions of law,* stated:

> Brewer was not given and had not considered INSLAW's January 13, 1982 letter, or any of the pre-contract correspondence between INSLAW and Videnieks; therefore, Brewer's subsequent positions regarding INSLAW's proprietary rights were taken without consideration of this letter. [69]

This position which seemed to be predicated more in the fear of giving up an advantageous position, than reaching a determination on the merits, is corroborated in an August 15, 1984, memorandum, in which Mr. Brewer stated that:

> ...the proposal would substantially alter our rights in data (*e.g.,* we would become a licensee—and thus give up *the unlimited rights we currently enjoy*). [Emphasis added.] [70]

---

[68] *INSLAW, Inc.,* v. *United States*, 83 B.R. 89 (Bktcy D. Dist. Col. 1988) at 138 (Finding 266).
[69] Ibid., at 118 (Finding 141).
[70] Memorandum from Mr. C. Madison Brewer, Director, OMISS, EOUSA, to Mr. Kamal J. Rahal, Director, Procurement and Contracts Staff, Justice Management Division, August 15, 1984.

32

This belief, was shared by other officials at the Department. In its analysis of an INSLAW proposal, dated April 30, 1985, an EOUSA analysis stated:

> ...it appears [to the Department] that there are no proprietary enhancements.
>
> All...proposals received from INSLAW....attempt to force the Department into acknowledging INSLAW's proprietary interest in the U.S. attorneys' version of PROMIS by offering a license agreement for software maintenance. To accept INSLAW's proposal would, in effect, ratify INSLAW's claim that the software is proprietary; not only the micro-computer version which INSLAW proposes to develop, but also the Prime mini-computer version currently operational in 20 districts.[71]

Also, in a November 15, 1985, counter proposal to an INSLAW settlement offer, Justice Management Division's General Counsel hewed to the inflexible position that:

> 1. The United States will not pay INSLAW any additional money for software obtained pursuant to this contract.
>
> 2. INSLAW will recognize that the United States has the right to unrestricted use of the software obtained or delivered under this contract for any Federal project, including projects that may be financed or conducted by instrumentalities or agents of the Federal Government such as its independent contractors.
>
> 3. The Department of Justice will agree not to make or permit any disclosure or distribution of the software other than as described above [in 2. above] or as required by Federal law.[72]

Between August 29, 1983, and February 18, 1985, INSLAW implemented Enhanced PROMIS in 20 U.S. attorneys offices.

Yet, even as negotiations were underway, the Department, between June 24, 1985, and September 2, 1987, installed Enhanced PROMIS software at 25 additional sites.[73] According to INSLAW's counsel, Elliot Richardson, Enhanced PROMIS was illegally copied to support an additional two sites and subsequently 31 additional sites were brought "on line" via telecommunications. This action was considered an explicit breach of the bankruptcy rules governing the respective actions of creditors and debtors in a reorganization situation. As stated in the findings of facts, the automatic stay provisions of the Bankruptcy Code prohibit "any act to obtain possession of property of the estate or of property from the estate or

---

[71] Analysis of INSLAW's Unsolicited Proposal of April 19, 1985, an analysis by the Executive Office for U.S. Attorneys, dated April 30, 1985, p. 8. This analysis was transmitted to Mr. Jay Stephens, the Deputy Associate Attorney General, by Mr. William P. Tyson, the EOUSA Director, on May 2, 1985.

[72] Letter from Ms. Janice A. Sposato, General Counsel, JMD, Department of Justice, to Mr. Harvey Sherzer, Esq., INSLAW counsel, November 15, 1985.

[73] Report of the Investigation by the Office of Professional Responsibility in the INSLAW Matter; from Mr. Robert B. Lyon, Jr., Acting Counsel, Office of Professional Responsibility, to Mr. Harold G. Christensen, Deputy Attorney General, March 31, 1989, pp. 36. The report refers to 23 additional sites but this did not include the two PROMIS pilot sites which also installed INSLAW's enhanced software.

33

to exercise control over property of the estate."[74] The Department violated the provisions of the stay by installing Enhanced PROMIS at the additional sites, and also accomplished this deed over the known protests of INSLAW. On September 9, 1985, Mr. Hamilton told the Department that:

> I am extremely disturbed and disappointed to learn that the Executive Office for U.S. Attorneys has begun to manufacture copies of the PROMIS software for customization and installation in additional U.S. attorneys offices, specifically those in St. Louis, Missouri, and Sacramento, California. This action occurs at the very time that the Department of Justice and INSLAW are attempting to resolve, by negotiation, INSLAW's claim that the U.S. attorneys version of PROMIS contains millions of dollars of privately-financed enhancements that are proprietary products of INSLAW and for which INSLAW has, to date, received no compensation.[75]

Not only did the Department proceed with the national installation of Enhanced PROMIS, but it also may have used its "unlimited rights" posture as a pretextual basis for its national and international distribution of Enhanced PROMIS outside of the Department. Details of this distribution are discussed in section IV of this report.

According to Judge Bryant:

> Although INSLAW and the Justice Department negotiated over the enhancements that INSLAW indicated that it had included in the proprietary version of PROMIS, the parties could not agree that the enhancements had been paid for with non-government funds. While INSLAW made several efforts to demonstrate the private financing of the enhancements, the Government did not accept its methodology for allocating funding. When asked to provide an alternative methodology that would be acceptable, the Government declined.[76]

The Department proceeded in its unilateral actions despite internal advice that INSLAW's claims were not frivolous and in fact, likely to be sustained in a court challenge. Pursuant to a letter dated July 9, 1986, from Senator Mathias, Mr. Arnold Burns, the Deputy Attorney General, conducted an inquiry into the status of the INSLAW litigation and was told that INSLAW wanted the Department to pay royalties. As a result of this briefing, Mr. Burns suggested that the issue should be turned around and that a claim against INSLAW should be made for INSLAW to pay royalties to the Government since he believed that PROMIS was the Department's property. Department research provided a shocking result to Mr. Burns:

---

[74] Findings of Fact and Conclusions of Law, p. 196. Although this finding was upheld by the District Court, the Circuit Court of Appeals found on May 17, 1991, that the automatic was not violated.

[75] Letter from Mr. William A. Hamilton, INSLAW president, to the Honorable H. Lawrence Wallace, Assistant Attorney General for Administration, Department of Justice, September 9, 1985, p. 1.

[76] *INSLAW, Inc.,* v. *United States,* opinion of U.S. District Court Judge William Bryant, at p. 25a.

34

...the answer that I got, which I wasn't terribly happy with but *which I accepted,* was that there had been a series of old correspondence and back and forthing [sic] and stuff, that in all of that, *our lawyers were satisfied that INSLAW could sustain the claim in court,* that we had waived those rights, not that I was wrong that we didn't have them but that *somebody in the Department of Justice,* in a letter or letters, as I say in this back and forthing [sic], had, in effect, *waived those rights.*[77] [Emphasis added.]

Considering that the Deputy Attorney General was aware of INSLAW's proprietary rights, the Department's pursuit of litigation can only be understood as a war of attrition between the Department's massive, tax-supported resources and INSLAW's desperate financial condition, with shrinking (courtesy of the Department) income. In light of Mr. Burns' revelation, it is important to note that committee investigators found no surviving documentation (from that time frame) which reveal the Department's awareness of the relative legal positions of the Department and INSLAW, on INSLAW's claims to proprietary enhancements referred to by Mr. Burns.

E. INSLAW DECLARES BANKRUPTCY AND PURSUES LITIGATION

By February 1985, at least $1.6 million in contract payments had been withheld by the Department and INSLAW was forced to file for chapter 11 reorganization in the Bankruptcy Court for the District of Columbia.[78] On June 9, 1986, INSLAW filed a Complaint for Declaratory Judgment, and for an order Enforcing Automatic Stay[79] and Damages for Willful Violation of Automatic Stay in the Bankruptcy Court.[80] In its pleadings, INSLAW asserted that Mr. C. Madison Brewer, who was responsible for implementing PROMIS throughout the Department, was instrumental in propelling INSLAW into bankruptcy, and that he thereafter hindered INSLAW in its development of a reorganization plan.[81] INSLAW also alleged that the Department had improperly converted and exercised control over INSLAW's proprietary Enhanced PROMIS and that its concerns were made known to the highest levels of Department management, without any departmental response.[82]

On July 20, 1987, the court began a trial that lasted 2½ weeks and involved sworn statements from over 40 witnesses and thousands of pages of documentary evidence.[83] On September 28, 1987, Bankruptcy Court Judge Bason issued an oral ruling on liability,

---

[77] Sworn statement of Arnold I. Burns, by OPR, March 30, 1988, pp. 7–13. It is presumed that Mr. Burns is discussing a period of time around his confirmation date in July 1986.

[78] Memorandum from Elliot Richardson, Esq. to Special Counsel Judge Nicholas J. Bua, January 14, 1992, p. 8.

[79] The automatic stay is one of the fundamental debtor protections provided by the bankruptcy laws. It stops all collection efforts, all harassments, and all foreclosure actions, giving the debtor temporary relief from creditors. The automatic stay allows the Bankruptcy Court to centralize all disputes concerning property of the debtor's estate so that reorganization can proceed orderly and efficiently, unimpeded by uncoordinated proceedings in other arenas.

[80] Staff Study Of Allegations Pertaining To The Department of Justice's Handling Of A Contract With INSLAW, Inc., by the Permanent Subcommittee on Investigations of the Committee on Governmental Affairs, U.S. Senate, September 1989, p. 5.

[81] Ibid.

[82] Ibid.

[83] Ibid., p. 9.

35

concluding that a key Department official was biased against INSLAW and that the Department "took, converted, and stole" INSLAW's Enhanced PROMIS by "trickery, fraud, and deceit."[84] On January 25, 1988, the bankruptcy judge issued his written order on liability, which documented his September 1987 oral ruling. On February 2, 1988, the court issued an order awarding INSLAW $6.8 million in damages and $1.2 million in attorneys' fees.

Department violated the Bankruptcy Court's automatic stay: During INSLAW's period of chapter 11 bankruptcy, the Department proceeded to copy and use INSLAW's Enhanced PROMIS, and even spread its use—in violation of the automatic stay. By letter dated March 14, 1986, shortly after INSLAW declared bankruptcy, INSLAW's counsel notified the Department's contracting officer that:

> ...any continued use by the Department of the [Enhanced] PROMIS software without the consent of INSLAW and the use of the software without any agreement as to the payment of license fees contravene INSLAW's property rights, its rights as a debtor in possession under the Bankruptcy Code and is a wrongful exercise of control over property of the debtor's estate in violation of the automatic stay now in effect. Furthermore, the Department's disclosure and dissemination of the PROMIS software to third parties will substantially dissipate, if not completely waste, the commercial value of this major INSLAW asset. We will hold the Department of Justice liable for any such loss of the value of INSLAW's property rights and if necessary will take such actions as are required to prevent such a loss.... If the Department of Justice causes a loss in the commercial value of INSLAW's principal asset, PROMIS, it may be responsible for destroying the company.[85]

The Bankruptcy Court found that the Department had violated the automatic stay by not negotiating a license fee for Enhanced PROMIS after INSLAW declared bankruptcy:

> ...INSLAW is entitled to automatic stay protection for its enhancements under the bankruptcy laws, and appropriate relief for violations of the automatic stay by DOJ.

* * * * * * *

> Under 11 U.S.C. 362(h), [a]n individual injured by any willful violation of a stay provided by this section shall recover actual damages, including costs and attorneys' fees and, in appropriate circumstances, may recover punitive damages.

---

[84] Ibid.
[85] Letter from Mr. Leigh S. Ratiner, INSLAW counsel, to Mr. Peter Videnieks, contracting officer, March 14, 1986, pp. 1–2.

36

* * * * * * *

A "willful" violation does not require a specific intent to violate the automatic stay. Rather, the statute provides for damages upon a finding that the defendant knew of the automatic stay and that the defendant's actions which violated the stay were intentional. Whether the party believes in good faith that it had a right to the property is not relevant to whether the act was "willful" or whether compensation must be awarded.

* * * * * * *

The judge concluded that the Department was liable for actual damages, including costs and attorneys' fees, and that INSLAW could recover punitive damages.

F. DISTRICT COURT JUDGE WILLIAM BRYANT'S DECISION ON APPEAL OF THE BANKRUPTCY COURT'S RULING

The Department appealed the Bankruptcy Court rulings in the U.S. District Court for the District of Columbia. On November 22, 1989, the District Court upheld the Bankruptcy Court's orders regarding liability and damages against the Department. District Court Judge William Bryant in his ruling stated:

> The government accuses the bankruptcy court of looking beyond the bankruptcy proceedings to find culpability by the government. What is strikingly apparent from the testimony and depositions of key witnesses and many documents is that INSLAW performed its contract in a hostile environment that extended from the higher echelons of the Justice Department to the officials who had the day-to-day responsibility for supervising its work. [86]

In its decision upholding the ruling of the Bankruptcy Court, the District Court:

> Emphasized that the Department knew Enhanced PROMIS represented INSLAW's central asset and that ownership of the software was critical to the company's reorganization.
> Held that the Department's unilateral claim of ownership and its installation of Enhanced PROMIS in offices around the United States violated the automatic stay.
> Concurred with the bankruptcy court's conclusion that the Department never had any rights to Enhanced PROMIS.

The District Court also agreed with Bankruptcy Judge Bason's finding that:

> ...the government acted willfully and fraudulently to obtain property that it was not entitled to under the contract....

and found

---

[86] *INSLAW, Inc.*, v. *United States*, opinion of U.S. District Judge William Bryant, at pp. 49a–50a.

37

...convincing, perhaps compelling support for the findings set forth by the bankruptcy court..... The cold record supports his [Bason's] findings under any standard of review. [87]

The District Court also found that the Department unlawfully violated the automatic stay provision of the Bankruptcy Code and agreed that the Department attempted to convert INSLAW's bankruptcy standing from a chapter 11 reorganization to a chapter 7 liquidation. The court also upheld the Bankruptcy Court's order regarding assessed damages as a result of the Department's unlawfully exercising control over and proliferating INSLAW's Enhanced PROMIS and upheld the award of attorneys' fees, but reduced compensatory damages by $655,200. [88]

DEPARTMENT'S POSITION AGAINST JUDGE'S DECISION IS REBUTTED ON APPEAL

The Department's legal defense was found to be deficient on appeal by District Court Judge Bryant. [89] The Department contended that the Bankruptcy Court lacked jurisdiction over INSLAW's claim because the Department had not waived its immunity from monetary judgments against the United States. Judge Bryant ruled against the Department's position stating that the Department's actions throughout the litigation suggested a calculated decision to assert a claim against INSLAW until it appeared that the Department had more to lose than gain.

The Department also argued that the Bankruptcy Court should have referred the case to the Department of Transportation Board of Contract Appeals (DOTBCA) for judgment because INSLAW's claims were based on contract law. However, Judge Bryant found that the INSLAW case did not involve a contract claim but was grounded in bankruptcy law, whereby INSLAW sought relief for violations of the automatic stay provisions of bankruptcy laws. Judge Bryant also found that Bankruptcy Judge Bason used his discretion to decide the legal ownership of Enhanced PROMIS that was necessary for determining whether there had been a violation of the automatic stay.

The Department also argued that INSLAW did not prove that the automatic stay had been violated. However, Judge Bryant concluded that the facts established in the Bankruptcy Court support the multiple violations of the automatic stay that the Bankruptcy Court found. Judge Bryant stated that the Department knew that PROMIS represented INSLAW's principal asset and that, without ownership of the software, the company's economic viability was threatened. Judge Bryant found that the Department acted willfully and fraudulently to obtain property that it was not entitled to under the contract and that, once the software was in the possession of the Department, there was no evidence that it ever negotiated in good faith over the proprietary enhancements claimed by INSLAW. Judge Bryant noted that, instead of following the proce-

---

[87] *INSLAW, Inc.,* v. *United States,* opinion of U.S. District Court Judge William Bryant, at 50a.

[88] *INSLAW, Inc.* v. *United States,* opinion of U.S. District Judge William Bryant at pp. 56a.

[89] *INSLAW, Inc.* v. *United States,* opinion of U.S. District Judge William Bryant at pp. 31a–56a.

38

dure established by the Bankruptcy Code for resolving the ownership dispute and seeking relief from the automatic stay, the Department had pursued a course of self-help by claiming Enhanced
PROMIS to be its property and installing it throughout the United
States.

The Department also charged that Judge Bason exhibited the appearance of bias and should have recused himself, and requested
a new trial based on this assertion. The Department also accused
Judge Bason of using the bankruptcy proceeding to find culpability
by the Government. Judge Bryant responded that the Department
had previously been denied its reversal request by the District
Court and, considering the earlier denial, no new trial would be
granted. Judge Bryant further stated that, while the bankruptcy
review must focus on Department actions taken after INSLAW
filed for bankruptcy, the Department's actions cannot be understood without understanding the events leading up to the bankruptcy. *He added that what was strikingly apparent from the evidence was that INSLAW performed its contract in a hostile environment from the higher echelons of the Justice Department to the officials who had responsibility for supervising its work.* Judge Bryant
also noted that Judge Bason's attention to detail, in both his oral
and written rulings, demonstrated a mastery of the evidence and
provided compelling support for his findings. Judge Bryant concluded that the record adequately supported the bankruptcy judge's
findings under any standard of review.

The Department also stated that the award of damages by the
Bankruptcy Court exceeded its authority and urged that no attorney fees be awarded. However, Judge Bryant determined that the
Bankruptcy Court discharged its responsibility to assess damages
based on the evidence provided at trial, and its decision was sup-
portable.

G. APPEALS COURT REVERSES INSLAW'S VICTORY ON PRIMARILY JURISDICTIONAL GROUNDS

On October 12, 1990, the Department appealed the District
Court decision to the U.S. Court of Appeals for the District of Columbia. The Department raised some of the same issues previously
raised in its appeal to the District Court and requested a reversal
on the basis of the facts found in the Bankruptcy Court. In its brief
for the appellants, the Department stated that:

> In the district court, the Government set out the clear
> errors underlying these findings of facts at great length
> and with great specificity. The district court's decision is
> deficient in not discussing any of these specific conten-
> tions. Of necessity, our factual contentions on appeal are
> more limited. [90]

The following issues were raised by the Department on appeal to
the Court of Appeals: (1) that the Department's use of computer
software in its possession did not violate the automatic stay and
was more properly the subject of a contract dispute under the Contract Disputes Act, which should be heard in DOTBCA; (2) that

---

[90] October 12, 1990, brief for the appellants, p. 16.

39

since there was no motion to convert INSLAW from a chapter 11 to a chapter 7, there was no violation of the automatic stay; (3) that the Department did not file a claim and therefore, did not waive its sovereign immunity; and (4) that damage awards for violation of the automatic stay can only be paid to individuals not corporations.[91]

On May 7, 1991, a panel of the U.S. Court of Appeals for the District of Columbia reversed both the Bankruptcy Court's and District Court's judgments on primarily jurisdictional grounds the Circuit Court found that the Bankruptcy Court was an inappropriate forum to litigate the issues it decided and furthermore that the Department had not violated the automatic stay and dismissed INSLAW's complaint against the Department. The Court of Appeals noted that both courts found that the Department had "fraudulently obtained and then converted Enhanced PROMIS to its own use." The court further noted that: "Such conduct, if it occurred, is inexcusable."[92]

On October 9, 1991, INSLAW filed an appeal for a writ of certiorari to the Supreme Court of the United States. On January 13, 1992, the Supreme Court denied the writ.

H. DEPARTMENT ASSERTS ERRONEOUS POSITION BEFORE DOTBCA

In addition to initiating proceedings in the Bankruptcy Court, INSLAW pursued remedies under the Contract Disputes Act. INSLAW filed notices of appeals with the Department of Transportation Board of Contract Appeals (DOTBCA) in February 1985, and in May and November 1986. On June 23, 1986, the first complaint was filed before DOTBCA. Additional claims were filed on September 19, 1986, and August 24, 1987.

INSLAW's claims before DOTBCA fell into six categories: (1) computer time-sharing charges associated with the computer center operated by INSLAW and used by several U.S. attorneys' offices; (2) contract target fees and voucher payments withheld by the Department and additional fees due INSLAW as a consequence of changes in the scope of work ordered by the Department; (3) indirect costs, including overhead; (4) direct costs; (5) costs, including legal fees, allegedly incurred by INSLAW because of the termination for convenience by the Department of the word processing portion of the contract; and (6) costs incurred because the Department withheld payments.

These claims were held in abeyance pending the outcome in the bankruptcy adversary proceeding. INSLAW's claims against the Department totaled $1,589,562 and the Department's claims against INSLAW totaled $1,216,752. On November 13, 1991, DOTBCA established October 13, 1992, as the trial date to hear INSLAW's case.[93]

Unfortunately, the Department took the spurious position that it has successfully defended itself against assertions of illegality, as

[91] Ibid., pp. 16, 24, 28, 30, 45.
[92] *INSLAW, Inc.* v. *United States, et al.,* case No. 90–5053 and *United States of America* v. *INSLAW, Inc., et al.,* case No. 90–05052, U.S. Court of Appeals decision on the appeal, May 7, 1991, p. 15.
[93] Proceedings of a hearing before the DOTBCA *In the matter of INSLAW, Inc.* v. *Department of Justice, et al.,* case No. 1609, November 13, 1991, p. 49.

40

defined in two courts and based on some of its own internal analysis, by having convinced the Appeals Court to vacate the earlier courts' decisions based on jurisdictional grounds—a ruling that had absolutely no bearing on the truth of the matter adjudicated on the basis of the substantial evidence presented. The Department is operating under the belief that it has been exonerated of any misconduct. In a November 13, 1991, hearing before DOTBCA, Department counsel stated that:

> I think those trials speak for themselves, and every order has been vacated....[94]

However, the DOTBCA judge responded:

> There is one problem. The fact that a judge or a court doesn't have jurisdiction doesn't mean that the court is completely ignorant. True, Mr. Bason [the bankruptcy court judge] and Mr. Bryant [the judge that heard the initial appeal] did not have jurisdiction, but *they did make some very serious findings on the basis of sworn testimony.* They had been truly vacated, and it may be that all the statutes to run have run and they can't go anywhere. *Those cases may be dead forever. But it has left a cloud over the respondent* [the Department]. [Emphasis added.][95]

Thus, still another adjudicating judge found that the rulings of the two courts that reviewed the INSLAW litigation ran counter to the Department's intransigent approach to recognizing formerly what its own internal analysis had suggested in confidence. When asked for his reaction to the finding of the District Court, Attorney General Meese responded that the ruling:

> ...seems totally at odds with everything I have learned and been told while I was in the Department of Justice...that there was any wrongdoing on the part of Justice people.[96]

Department counsel at the DOTBCA hearings responded to the judge by stating that:

> Your Honor, with all due respect, those orders were vacated. And the effect of the vacating is to make them void. They have no force in effect whatsoever. *They are as if they never happened.* They—it would be improper for a court or a board or any other judicial tribunal to rely, in any way, shape or form, on those decisions. [Emphasis added.][97]

Certainly, the Department may be correct in asserting that there is presently no legal force to the courts' rulings on terms of enforceability. But that result is because of the jurisdictional defects, and not the merits of the case, which had been adjudicated in two separate forums. However, it is not correct for the Department to conclude that the INSLAW matter has been resolved or that it should

[94] Ibid., p. 37.
[95] Proceedings of a hearing before the DOTBCA *In the matter of INSLAW, Inc. v. Department of Justice, et al.*, case No. 1609, November 13, 1991, p. 37.
[96] Sworn statement of Mr. Edwin Meese, July 12, 1990, p. 48.
[97] Proceedings of a hearing before the DOTBCA *In the matter of INSLAW, Inc. v. Department of Justice, et al.* case No. 1609, November 13, 1991, p. 37.

41

be considered as if it "never happened." The Department has not yet compensated INSLAW for its illegal and improper use of software that was found to be proprietary to INSLAW by two courts. Furthermore, Justice officials cannot escape accountability merely because the Appeals Court has reversed the lower court's rulings based on a procedural ruling.

As the DOTBCA judge concluded, there definitely remains a cloud over the Department's handling of INSLAW's proprietary software. Department officials should not be allowed to avoid accountability through a technicality or a jurisdiction ruling by the Appeals Court and INSLAW deserves to receive equitable consideration of its claims.

An impartial inquiry needs to be undertaken to assess the facts and potential culpability of the actions involved. Strategic gamesmanship has no place when the full weight and resources of the enforcement arm of the Government is pitted against a private interest, whose financial ability to litigate may have been compromised by the very departmental actions in dispute. In addition, should the Department not resolve this matter fairly and expeditiously, the dispute should be referred through a bill to the Chief Judge of the Claims Court whereby the statute of limitations can be suspended. To recover in such a case a claimant must show that (1) the Government committed a negligent or wrongful act, and (2) this act caused damage to the claimant.[98]

The litigation of a congressional reference case is fully adversarial once the pleading is complete. It proceeds like any other court case through discovery, pretrial, trial, the submission of requested findings and briefs, and decision. After the case is heard, a hearing officer's report is submitted to the Congress, together with the findings of facts. The hearing officer must provide sufficient conclusions to inform Congress:

> ...whether the demand is a legal or equitable claim or a gratuity, and the amount, if any, legally or equitable due from the United States to the claimant.[99]

There is a distinct possibility that the extent of damages to INSLAW (particularly the Department's distribution of INSLAW's proprietary PROMIS) will never be fully known. Department documents provide evidence of distribution of PROMIS to at least one foreign government. There are also numerous allegations of widespread distribution to other foreign governments.

I. DEPARTMENT ENCOURAGES CONTRACT MEDIATION WHILE IT HINDERS SETTLEMENT

It is important to document that another equivocal effort to mediate the INSLAW dispute was initiated on June 28, 1990, when the Department requested the Appellate Court to consider INSLAW for the Appellate Mediation Program.[100] This action on

---

[98] See Shane, supra at 304.

[99] 28 U.S.C. § 2509(c).

[100] The Appellate Mediation Program operates under a court order issued on November 28, 1988, and amended on April 19, 1989. The program is intended to benefit the parties by providing a forum which encourages the settlement of cases, or at least the resolution or simplification

Continued

42

the Department's part appeared significant because it was it's first mediation request out of the 13 appeals submitted since January 1989. However, the success of this program requires that confidentiality be ensured throughout the mediation process. Information concerning cases screened by the Chief Staff Counsel's Office is not to be shared with judges or with anyone outside the court. The judges do not know which cases are selected for mediation. [101]

However, for some unexplained reason, the Department failed to comply with this most basic requirement. On October 3, 1990, Ms. Linda Finklestein, Circuit Executive of the District of Columbia Circuit Court, contacted INSLAW's counsel and referred to an October 1, 1990, Washington Post article, which revealed that mediation had been requested by one of the parties. The article, cited to a departmental spokesman stated:

> that the department has requested that the matter [INSLAW] be considered for mediation by the appeals court, in an attempt to settle the long-running dispute. [102]

This disclosure was completely contrary to the standards of the Appellate Program pursuant to the order of the court. The effect was to force INSLAW to withdraw from the program after only 3 months. It is difficult to understand the Department's strategy by this action. It may be that the Department wanted to maintain the facade of working diligently to settle a sticky contract dispute while working behind the scenes to sabotage it and keep pressure on INSLAW by forcing it to expend additional resources on legal support during the mediation process. If this is the case, the Department was successful. But the Department also succeeded in maintaining a near-flawless record of seeking delay over resolution and raising the level of suspicion about its motives to a point where the public trust in the untarnished pursuit of justice is subject to grave doubts.

IV. SIGNIFICANT QUESTIONS REMAIN UNANSWERED ABOUT POSSIBLE HIGH LEVEL CRIMINAL CONSPIRACY

A. ALLEGATIONS OF CONSPIRACY AND INTRIGUE CONTINUE TO SURROUND THE INSLAW CONTROVERSY

The Hamiltons have alleged that high level Department officials conspired to steal the PROMIS software system. According to their allegations, the theft involved a number of stages which included: (1) the failure of the Department to comply with the terms and conditions of the contract with INSLAW; (2) attempts to force into bankruptcy and force the sale of PROMIS through liquidation of the company; (3) the attempted hostile buyout of INSLAW by a computer company owned by Dr. Earl Brian, a friend and former associate of Attorney General Meese; (4) the providing of the Enhanced PROMIS system to Dr. Brian by high level Department officials; (5) the modification of the PROMIS system by individuals as-

---

of some of the issues, through an independent and neutral mediator. Source: Brochure issued by the court entitled, "Appellate Mediation Program."
   [101] Ibid.
   [102] October 1, 1990, Washington Post article, entitled: "Obsessed by a Theory of Conspiracy," p. 24.

43

sociated with the world of covert intelligence operations so that Enhanced PROMIS could be distributed worldwide to intelligence and law enforcement organizations; and finally, (6) the actual distribution of the Enhanced PROMIS software system domestically and internationally with the knowledge and support of the CIA and Justice Department.

The Hamiltons have asserted that the first step in the conspiracy to steal the PROMIS system occurred when the Department intentionally failed to comply with the terms and conditions of the contract that it had entered into with INSLAW. The Hamiltons believe that INSLAW's contract with Justice did not include the enhanced version of the PROMIS software. In November 1982, the Department demanded that INSLAW turn over the enhanced version of PROMIS stating that INSLAW had no title to it. Further, the Hamiltons have asserted the Department's project manager, C. Madison Brewer, and the contracting officer, Peter Videnieks, directed by Deputy Attorney General D. Lowell Jensen, Attorney General Edwin Meese and other high level officials, resisted any type of negotiated arrangement with INSLAW in order to put the company out of business. The Hamiltons claim that by withholding $2 million in contract payments to INSLAW during this dispute, the Department intentionally forced INSLAW into bankruptcy. The Hamiltons have asserted that the Department then attempted to convert INSLAW from chapter 11 to chapter 7 bankruptcy, so that it could force the sale of INSLAW'S assets, including Enhanced PROMIS, to a rival computer company controlled by Dr. Brian.

The Hamiltons have contended that high level officials in the Department of Justice conspired to steal the PROMIS software system. As an element of this alleged theft, these officials, which included former Attorney General Edwin Meese and Deputy Attorney General Lowell Jensen, forced INSLAW into bankruptcy by intentionally creating a sham contract dispute over the terms and conditions of the contract which led to the withholding of payments due INSLAW by the Department. After driving the company into bankruptcy, the Hamiltons have claimed that Justice officials attempted to force the conversion of INSLAW's bankruptcy status from chapter 11 to chapter 7. They have stated that this change in bankruptcy status would have resulted in the forced sale of INSLAW's assets, including PROMIS, to a rival computer company called Hadron, Inc., which at this time was attempting to conduct a hostile buyout of INSLAW. Hadron, Inc., was controlled by the Biotech Capital Corporation which was under the control of Dr. Earl Brian, who was president and chairman of the corporation. This is the same company in which Mrs. Ursula Meese had invested with money loaned to her by Mr. Edwin Thomas, a mutual friend and associate of Mr. and Mrs. Meese and Dr. Brian. [103] The Hamiltons have asserted that even though the attempt to change the status of INSLAW's bankruptcy case was unsuccessful, the Enhanced PROMIS software system was eventually provided to Dr. Brian. This was allegedly done by individuals from the Department with the knowledge and concurrence of then Attorney General Meese

---

[103] Report of the independent counsel concerning Edwin Meese III, September 20, 1984, pp. 34–35.

44

who had earlier worked with Dr. Brian in the cabinet of California Governor Ronald Reagan and later at the Reagan White House. According to the Hamiltons, the ultimate goal of the conspiracy was to position Hadron, Inc., and the other companies owned or controlled by Dr. Brian, to take advantage of the nearly 3 billion dollars' worth of automated data processing upgrade contracts planned to be awarded by the Department of Justice during the 1980's.

Mr. Meese and Dr. Brian served together in the cabinet of then California Governor Ronald Reagan from 1970 through 1974. Dr. Brian was the controlling shareholder in Biotech Capital Corporation which in turn had a substantial stake in a computer firm called Hadron, Inc. At that time, Dr. Brian was chairman and president of Biotech Capital Corporation and was on the board of directors of Hadron, Inc. The Hamiltons have asserted that after the election of 1980, Dr. Brian moved quickly to put Hadron, Inc., in a position to take advantage of ties to Mr. Meese and others in the newly elected administration. The Hamiltons have claimed that Hadron, Inc.'s first post-election moves were to acquire companies supporting Federal law enforcement efforts to control the smuggling of drugs across the Mexican border. Hadron, Inc., entered into several Government contracts with U.S. Customs and various intelligence agencies. The Hamiltons have claimed that in April 1983, Dominic Laiti, president and chairman of Hadron, Inc., contacted them and attempted to purchase Enhanced PROMIS. When they declined to sell PROMIS, he told them that he had ways of making them sell. The Hamiltons have alleged that Mr. Laiti also told them that as a result of contacts at the highest level of the Reagan administration, including Edwin Meese, Hadron, Inc., was able to obtain the Federal Government's case management software business. The Hamiltons have asserted that after declining to sell the PROMIS system, INSLAW became the target of a hostile buyout attempt.

The Hamiltons have alleged that after the Enhanced PROMIS software was stolen, it was illegally disseminated within the Department of Justice, to other Federal Government agencies and to governments abroad. This dissemination included the distribution of PROMIS to U.S. intelligence agencies, the FBI and the DEA. The Hamiltons have also claimed that the PROMIS software was sold to foreign governments for use by their intelligence and law enforcement agencies. The Hamiltons have strongly asserted that prior to PROMIS being distributed, it was modified by individuals connected with covert U.S. intelligence operations. These modifications possibly allowed for the creation of a "back door" into the system which would allow U.S. intelligence agencies to break into the systems of these foreign governments whenever they wished.

The Hamiltons have alleged that the Department furthered the conspiracy, when Department officials and others, including Judge Cornelius Blackshear, William Tyson, Thomas Stanton, Laurence McWhorter and William White, committed perjury and obstruction of justice during the investigation of the theft of PROMIS and during the trial in front of Judge Bason.

Former Attorney General Elliot Richardson, counsel to INSLAW, has described the circumstances surrounding the INSLAW case as

45

a possible criminal conspiracy involving Edwin Meese, Judge Lowell Jensen, Dr. Earl Brian and several current and former officials at the Department of Justice. Mr. Richardson has stated that the individuals involved in the theft of the PROMIS system, the subsequent coverup and its illegal distribution may have violated several Federal criminal statutes including: (1) 18 U.S.C. § 654 (officer or employee of the United States converting the property of another); (2) 18 U.S.C. § 1001 (false statements); (3) 18 U.S.C. § 1621 (perjury); (4) 18 U.S.C. § 1503 (obstruction of justice); (5) 18 U.S.C. § 1341 (mail fraud); and, (6) 18 U.S.C. § 371 (conspiracy to commit offense). Mr. Richardson also believes that the circumstances surrounding the INSLAW case fulfill the requirements necessary for prosecution under 18 U.S.C. 1961 et seq. (the Racketeer Influenced and Corrupt Organization—(RICO)—statute).[104]

As discussed in the first section of this report, the committee investigation largely supports the findings of two Federal courts that the Department "took, converted, stole" INSLAW'S Enhanced PROMIS by "trickery, fraud and deceit," and that this misappropriation had to involve officials at the highest levels of the Department of Justice. The Department deliberately ignored INSLAW's proprietary data rights, took the Enhanced PROMIS software and improperly distributed it to numerous Justice Department offices that were not entitled to use it under the Department's contract with the company. Certainly, this was a high risk venture in which Department officials had to have known would be vigorously challenged by the Hamiltons. Nonetheless, the Department expended enormous time, energy and money pursuing its conflict with INSLAW including almost 7 years of litigation. The Department took this course of action even though high level Justice officials knew, at least as early as 1986, that INSLAW had legitimate proprietary rights to the Enhanced PROMIS software and that the Department would not likely win the case in court on its merits. This raises the troubling question of why the Department would go to such great lengths to contest a relatively small $10 million procurement when there are certainly more pressing criminal justice matters to attend to. The inability of the Department to provide a plausible answer to this key question has fueled concerns that a more sinister explanation exists.

While the Department continues to explain the INSLAW conflict as a simple contract dispute, the committee's investigation has uncovered or identified information which suggests a different and much more involved explanation.

B. Enhanced PROMIS May Have Been Disseminated Nationally and Internationally

After INSLAW became a for-profit organization, its business objective was to enhance revenues from the licensing,[105] sale or leas-

---

[104] Memorandum to Special Counsel, Judge Nicholas J. Bua from Elliot L. Richardson, Esq., January 14, 1992, pp. 1–16.
[105] Courts have defined a "license" in the following ways:
"...a right granted which gives the grantee permission to do something which he could not legally do absent such permission; leave to do a thing which the licensor [the party granting the license] could prevent....[G]enerally speaking, [it] means a grant of permission to do a par-
Continued

46

ing of PROMIS and maintenance fees earned by its PROMIS software on a worldwide scale. INSLAW's international sales of PROMIS were conducted under the corporate name INSLAW International, [106] which licensed PROMIS in Ireland, Scotland, Australia, Holland and Italy. [107] Nationally, INSLAW's objective was to market PROMIS to state and local jurisdictions, the Federal Government, and private businesses such as law firms. [108]

As previously discussed, INSLAW had long asserted—and was supported in the courts—that it owned proprietary rights to its enhanced version of PROMIS that were turned over to the Department in April 1983. It was the court's position that the Department stole and improperly distributed INSLAW's Enhanced PROMIS. Although later overturned by the Circuit Court, the Bankruptcy and District Courts held that the Department had violated an automatic stay and was liable for license fees for unlawfully using Enhanced PROMIS (as described in other sections of this report). [109] It also appears, however, that the Department's distribution of PROMIS may have gone far beyond its own boundaries because there are documentation and corroborating statements which indicate that PROMIS may have been distributed by Department officials to locations worldwide.

On April 15, 1983, Mr. Brick Brewer asked Mr. Jack Rugh, the Acting Assistant Director, OMISS, EOUSA, about any discussions that he may have had regarding the availability of the various Federal versions of PROMIS to organizations other than U.S. attorneys' offices. In a Department memorandum dated April 22, 1983, Mr. Rugh wrote that:

> Since INSLAW made their claim of proprietary interest in our enhanced version of PROMIS, I have qualified the possibility of the availability of that version. Prior to that claim, *I told several of the organizations discussed below, that EOUSA enhancements could be provided to them at some future date.* [Emphasis added.]
>
> As part of our solicitation for computer equipment, Government owned versions of PROMIS were made available to potential bidders for use in benchmarking their equipment. All four LEAA versions (DEC, IBM, Wang, and Burroughs) as well as the EOUSA Prime pilot version were supplied. . . . *No restrictions were placed on the usage of that software.* [Emphasis added.]
>
> Also as part of our computer buy, a copy of the EOUSA Prime pilot version of PROMIS was supplied to Mr. Dave Hudak who contracted with us to develop certain bench-

---

ticular thing, to exercise a certain privilege, or to carry on a particular business or to pursue a certain occupation." 160 P.2d 37, 39.

"In the law of property, a license is a personal privilege or permission with respect to some use. . . ." 230 S.W. 2d 770, 775.

"Because a license represents only a personal right, it is generally not assignable." 34 N.Y.S. 693.

(Source: Law Dictionary, Mr. Steven H. Gifis, Barron's Educational Series, Inc., Woodbury, New York.)

[106] Memorandum to INSLAW from Peabody, Rivin, Lambert & Meyers, April 16, 1979, p. 1.

[107] Memorandum of interview with Mr. Hamilton, January 30, 1992, p. 1.

[108] Letter from William Hamilton to the Honorable Harold R. Tyler, February 23, 1979, p. 1.

[109] INSLAW and the courts were unaware that Deputy Attorney General Burns had determined in 1986 that INSLAW owned its enhanced version of PROMIS and the Department would lose in court on this issue.

47

mark programs. *Again no restrictions were placed on soft-ware usage.* [Emphasis added.]

In early 1982, I supplied a copy of the EOUSA Prime pilot version of PROMIS to Bob Bussey of the Colorado District Attorneys' Council, at Brick's [Brewer's] request....*Subsequently, I discussed the availability of our PROMIS enhancements, funded through the LEAA contract, once they were installed on our Prime equipment with Mr. Bussey.* I also provided him with a copy of the LEAA DEC version of PROMIS in early 1983. [Emphasis added.]

I provided Jean Gollatz from the Pennsylvania State Government with a copy of our computer RFP in early 1982...I have told Ms. Gollatz on several occasions that our Prime pilot version of PROMIS is available for their use, and that *our enhanced Prime version should be available by mid-summer, 1983.* [Emphasis added.]

I have discussed the availability of EOUSA Prime pilot version of PROMIS *as well as the enhanced version* with Don Manson of the Bureau of Justice Statistics on a number of occasions. *Mr. Manson is particularly interested in providing a copy of our enhanced software to the U.S. Virgin Islands.* [Emphasis added.]

During the week of April 11, 1983, INSLAW demonstrated PROMIS in the Boston U.S. attorneys' office to a group of people from the State of Massachusetts. Joe Creamer, our system manager in Boston, called me late in the week. *He said someone from State [the State Government] had called him to ask about the availability of PROMIS software from sources other than INSLAW.* I told Joe that the LEAA versions and our Prime pilot version were certainly available, but that there was a current dispute with INSLAW regarding our enhanced version. I do not know if Joe provided this information to the State. [Emphasis added.]

I have held a number of informal discussions with personnel in the Criminal Division *regarding their possible use of our enhanced version of PROMIS and the possibility of their using one of our optional Prime machines.* We have also discussed the possibility of cooperating on PROMIS software maintenance and enhancements in the future. [Emphasis added.][110]

A Department memorandum also shows that the Department made at least the LEAA version of PROMIS available to an interested party from a foreign government. In a memorandum dated May 6, 1983, Mr. Rugh stated:

Reference my memorandum to file dated April 22, 1983, on the same subject. *Brick Brewer recently instructed me to make a copy of an LEAA version of PROMIS available to Dr. Ben Orr, a representative of the Government of Israel.* Dr. Orr called me to discuss that request after my earlier memorandum was written. *I have made a copy of*

---

[110] Jack S. Rugh, Acting Assistant Director, OMISS, EOUSA, memorandum to file, April 22, 1983.

48

*the LEAA DEC version of PROMIS and will provide it
along with the corresponding documentation, to Dr. Orr before he leaves the United States for Israel on May 16.* [Em-
phasis added.] [111]

Given the international dimensions to the decisions, it is difficult
to accept the notion that a group of low-level Department personnel
decided independently to get in touch with the Government of Israel to arrange for transfer of the PROMIS software. At the very
least, it is unlikely that such a transaction occurred without the
approval of high level Department officials, including those on the
PROMIS Oversight Committee. Interestingly, while Department
documents show that "public domain" PROMIS was turned over to
Israel, it is uncertain what version actually was transferred. Department managers believed that all versions of the Enhanced
PROMIS software were the Department's property. The lack of detailed documentation on the transfer, therefore, only creates new
questions surrounding allegations that Enhanced PROMIS may
have been sold or transferred to Israel and other foreign governments. It certainly raises questions, discussed infra, about allegations surrounding Dr. Brian's involvement in the sale of Enhanced
PROMIS to Israel. In particular, it has been asserted by several individuals [112] that the Enhanced PROMIS had been delivered to Dr.
Brian for such a transfer by Mr. Videnieks. Mr. Videnieks was
asked to provide a sworn statement to committee investigators on
this subject, but to date committee attempts to arrange such a
statement have been unsuccessful. [113]

By memorandum dated May 12, 1983, Mr. Rugh turned PROMIS
over to Mr. Brewer for submission to the Government of Israel:

*Enclosed are the PROMIS materials that you asked me
to produce for Dr. Ben Orr of the Government of Israel.*
These materials consist of the LEAA DEC PDP 11/70 version of PROMIS on magnetic tape along with the printed
specifications for that tape, as well as two printed volumes
of PROMIS documentation for the LEAA version of the
system. [114] [Emphasis added.]

In a memoranda to Judge Bua, Elliot Richardson maintains that
documentary evidence such as travel memoranda, reflect a plan by
the U.S. Government for direct accessing of foreign government intelligence and enforcement activity:

One important motive for the theft of Enhanced
PROMIS may have been to use it as a means of penetrat-

---

[111] Mr. Jack S. Rugh, Acting Assistant Director, OMISS, EOUSA, memorandum to file, May 6, 1983.

[112] See section of the report titled, "The Allegators."

[113] Mr. Videnieks provided an initial sworn statement to the committee on November 5, 1990. On March 21, 1991, Michael Riconosciuto provided a sworn affidavit to the Hamiltons in which he described an alleged relationship between Mr. Videnieks and Dr. Brian. On March 22, 1991, committee investigators attempted to schedule a second deposition with Mr. Videnieks through his attorney, Charles Ruff, to discuss these new allegations. On March 25, 1991, Mr. Ruff stated that Mr. Videnieks would not agree to provide a second deposition. Subsequently, Mr. Ruff was contacted on another occasion in which he again stated that Mr. Videnieks would not provide a second deposition. It should also be noted that at the Justice Department's request, Mr. Videnieks testified at the trial of Michael Riconosciuto (see infra).

[114] Mr. Jack S. Rugh, Acting Assistant Director, OMISS, EOUSA, memorandum to C. Madison Brewer, May 12, 1983. Also, note that this action took place after Modification 12 was signed on April 11, 1983, and the Enhanced PROMIS was turned over to the Department.

49

ing the intelligence and law enforcement agencies of other governments. The first step in this scheme was the sale to the foreign government of a computer into which had been inserted a microchip capable of transmitting to a U.S. surveillance system the electronic signals emitted by the computer when in use....Enhanced PROMIS has capabilities that make it ideally suited to tracking the activities of a spy network.

Several INSLAW informants formerly affiliated with United States or Israeli intelligence agencies claim that both the United States and Israel have relied on "cutout" companies to provide ongoing support for the PROMIS software....[115]

In still another departmental memorandum, reference is found to making Enhanced PROMIS available to outside sources after the contracting officer had ruled against INSLAW's claims to the enhancements. As described in Mr. Rugh's August 12, 1983, memorandum:

On Wednesday, August 10, *Don Manson called to inquire about the availability of our Prime [Enhanced] version of PROMIS for distribution to state and local organizations, specifically the Virgin Islands.* I explained to Don that INSLAW had claimed that the U.S. attorneys' version of PROMIS contains proprietary software and cannot be distributed beyond the U.S. attorneys' organization. I told Don that *even though I expected the dispute to be resolved in favor of the Government, we could not supply a copy of the software at this time. Don indicated that he planned to make a formal written request for the software, indicating an urgent need in the U.S. Virgin Islands.* [Emphasis added.] [116]

It is uncertain whether this request was made and, if so, what the outcome was. Several individuals [117] however, have provided sworn statements that Enhanced PROMIS was in fact distributed by the Department or its agents beyond EOUSA.

1. ALLEGATIONS THAT THE JUSTICE DEPARTMENT AND EARL BRIAN CONSPIRED TO DISTRIBUTE PROMIS

Several individuals [118] have stated under oath that the Enhanced PROMIS software was stolen by high level Justice officials and distributed internationally in order to provide financial gain to Dr. Brian and to further intelligence and foreign policy objectives of the United States. While some of this testimony comes from individuals who, given their past activities and associations, might be viewed as less than credible, the committee has uncovered corroborating evidence supporting a number of the aspects of these wit-

---

[115] Memorandum to Judge Nicholas Bua from Mr. Elliot Richardson, p. 34.
[116] Mr. Jack S. Rugh, Acting Assistant Director, OMISS, EOUSA, memorandum to file, August 12, 1983.
[117] These allegations are explored in depth in the section of the report entitled, "The Allegators."
[118] Ibid.

50

nesses' sworn testimony.[119] Although the committee's investigation could not reach a definitive conclusion regarding the motives behind the misappropriation of the Enhanced PROMIS software, the disturbing questions raised, unexplained coincidences and peculiar events that have surfaced throughout the committee's inquiry into the INSLAW case raises the need for further investigation.

Finally, as documented infra, the committee's investigation was unfortunately hampered by numerous obstacles which prevented it from conducting a complete review of several allegations during the investigation of the INSLAW case. This was particularly true of the allegations involving a possible criminal conspiracy by high level Government officials to steal, sell, and disseminate INSLAW's PROMIS software for secret or covert programs domestically and abroad.[120]

Other events—including the arrest and conviction of a key informant and the death of a reporter covering the INSLAW matter—have only generated more questions about the INSLAW matter. Numerous potential witnesses refused to cooperate, for the stated reason that they were fearful for their jobs and retaliation by the Justice Department or that attempts had already been made to intimidate them against cooperating. Other witnesses directly contradicted the statements attributed to them by the Hamiltons and were clearly distressed that their names had been drawn into the web of the INSLAW conspiracy theory. Mr. Riconosciuto and others claimed to have direct knowledge of a conspiracy by high level Department officials to turn INSLAW's PROMIS software over to former Attorney General Meese's friend and former associate, Dr. Earl Brian.[121] Finally, many witnesses have given conflicting and inconsistent testimony which may involve perjury and obstruction. The following is a brief discussion of these issues.

2. SWORN STATEMENT OF MICHAEL RICONOSCIUTO

Mr. Michael Riconosciuto, a self-described computer expert who in the past has been involved with contract computer and munitions work for U.S. intelligence agencies, was brought to the attention of the committee in June 1990. Mr. Riconosciuto alleged that he had access to information that clearly linked Dr. Earl Brian to

---

[119] There is some measure of irony in the reaction of some current and former Department officials in their attempt to discredit automatically these allegations simply because of the past activities of certain witnesses who have worked "both sides" of the enforcement or intelligence communities. The Department showed no similar reluctance or moral fastidiousness in its recent prosecution of Manuel Noriega, which involved the use of over 40 witnesses, the majority of whom were previously convicted drug traffickers. Obviously, a witness' perceived credibility is not always indicative of the accuracy or usability in court of the information provided.

[120] The Department's unwillingness to allow congressional oversight into its affairs, in spite of an alleged coverup of wrongdoing, greatly hindered the committee's investigation of the INSLAW allegations. The Department delayed and hindered congressional inquiries into the INSLAW matter over several years. This committee consumed almost 2 years and had to resort to a subpoena to obtain key information. Even then, key Department files subpoenaed by the committee were reported lost and other key investigative files are still being denied on the basis that these files contain criminal investigative material. The committee also encountered serious problems with obtaining cooperation from U.S. intelligence and law enforcement agencies. While some limited level of assistance was eventually provided from these groups, it often took months to arrange even minimum cooperation. The committee also encountered virtually no cooperation in its investigation of the INSLAW matter beyond U.S. borders. The Government of Canada refused to make its officials available to committee investigators for interviews without strict limitations on the questioning. Also, see discussion in section entitled, "INSLAW Request for Independent Counsel," for greater detail.

[121] See section of report entitled, "The Allegators."

51

the Department's theft of Enhanced PROMIS software. Mr. Riconosciuto alleged that Dr. Brian was given the software as a reward for work he had done for the Reagan Presidential campaign. [122] In a sworn statement to Mr. and Mrs. Hamilton, Mr. Riconosciuto stated that in the early 1980's both he and Dr. Brian were associated with the Wackenhut Corporation [123] to work on a covert project on the Cabazon Indian Reservation located near Indio, California. [124]

On March 21, 1991, Mr. Riconosciuto provided the Hamiltons a sworn affidavit detailing his involvement with Dr. Brian and Peter Videnieks, the Department's contracting official. Mr. Riconosciuto stated that while employed by the Wackenhut Corporation he was involved with the modification of proprietary Enhanced PROMIS software during calendar years 1983 and 1984. Mr. Riconosciuto further stated that the software was provided to him by Dr. Brian, who had obtained it from Mr. Videnieks. Mr. Riconosciuto alleged that the software modifications were made to facilitate implementation of PROMIS software—in particular, porting PROMIS to the systems in two Canadian agencies, the Royal Canadian Mounted Police (RCMP) and the Canadian Security and Intelligence Service (CSIS). According to Mr. Riconosciuto, the modified PROMIS software was implemented by these agencies, and Dr. Brian brokered the sale to the Canadian Government. [125]

In his March 21, 1991, affidavit, Mr. Riconosciuto stated that in February 1991, Peter Videnieks told him in a telephone conversation that it would be beneficial for him to refuse a committee request for an interview. [126]

Despite the alleged interference by the Department, Mr. Riconosciuto provided a sworn statement to committee investigators on April 4, 1991. In his statement, Mr. Riconosciuto directly connected his involvement with modifying PROMIS to Dr. Brian and Mr. Videnieks. Mr. Riconosciuto also provided information concerning the February 1991 telephone conversation with Mr. Videnieks, which he referred to in his March 21, 1991, statement to the Hamiltons. Mr. Riconosciuto further alleged that he had in his possession two copies of the tape recorded conversation at the time of his arrest and that the tapes are currently in the possession of the DEA agents who arrested him. [127]

Mr. Riconosciuto described his role and work with Dr. John Nichols and the Wackenhut/Cabazon joint venture. [128] According to Mr. Riconosciuto, Dr. John Nichols was the director of the Wackenhut/Cabazon joint venture in Indio, CA. [129] Mr. Riconosciuto said that Dr. Nichols and Mr. Brian worked closely on a variety of international projects; and, during the joint venture, Dr. Nichols was

[122] Memorandum to the record, June 21, 1990, prepared by William A. and Nancy B. Hamilton, p. 1.
[123] The Wackenhut Corporation is an investigation and security firm based in Coral Gables, Florida. It has been alleged that Wackenhut has been contracted to conduct covert investigations and other covert projects.
[124] Sworn affidavit of Michael Riconosciuto, March 21, 1991, p. 2 (on file with the committee).
[125] Ibid., p. 1. [Also see section on Canada, p. 109.]
[126] Ibid., p. 3.
[127] Sworn statement of Michael Riconosciuto, April 4, 1991, pp. 59–71.
[128] The Wackenhut-Cabazon joint venture sought to develop and/or manufacture certain materials that are used in military and national security operations, including night vision goggles, machineguns, fuel-air explosives, and biological and chemical warfare weapons.
[129] Sworn statement of Michael Riconosciuto, April 4, 1991, pp. 5–6.

52

constantly being visited by "high profile people currently employed in various agencies of the United States Government...." Mr. Riconosciuto further stated that Dr. Nichols was able to get him into secure areas of military facilities at Picatinny Arsenal during this venture.[130] According to Mr. Riconosciuto, he obtained access to secure areas in connection with the joint venture during 1981 and this was when he first met Mr. Videnieks. Mr. Riconosciuto claimed that he was given a copy of the proprietary version of INSLAW's PROMIS by Mr. Videnieks and Dr. Brian.[131] Mr. Riconosciuto alleged that at that time Dr. Brian was spearheading plans for the worldwide distribution of PROMIS.[132]

Mr. Riconosciuto granted the committee access to storage facilities where computer software[133] and documents were recovered by committee investigators.

Mr. Riconosciuto told committee investigators that Robert Booth Nichols could provide additional information concerning the Cabazon Indian Reservation and the conversion of the PROMIS software.[134] (See page 72.)

Dr. Brian's connection to former Attorney General Meese: Mr. Hamilton alleged in his affidavit and in testimony before this committee that Dr. Brian exploited a friendship with former Attorney General Meese to gain control of INSLAW's Enhanced PROMIS.[135] In their sworn statements to the committee, Mr. Meese and Dr. Brian stated that they had previously worked together as part of Ronald Reagan's cabinet while he was Governor of California, but their contacts since that time have been sporadic, limited, and social. Dr. Brian stated that he neither asked Mr. Meese to intercede on his behalf in any Government contracts nor did he discuss any Government contracts with him. Dr. Brian denied having any

---

[130] Ibid., p. 6.

[131] During the sworn statement of Michael Riconosciuto on April 4, 1991, pp. 41–42, he stated that during a luncheon attended by Earl Brian, Peter Videnieks, James Hughes and Riconosciuto, the Enhanced PROMIS software was loaded into his car.

[132] Ibid., p. 43.

[133] *Analysis of Riconosciuto tapes:* The committee requested that GAO analyze the tapes and disks received from Riconosciuto. On November 12, 1991, GAO reported to the committee that it could recover data from only one of the five magnetic media, which it provided to the committee. The tapes and disks were several years old and had been kept in unsuitable storage facilities. The magnetic media was dirt encrusted and warped possibly from the excessive heat and humidity. The readable media appeared to be a corporate data file of accounts containing primarily individuals' names and addresses and was neither encrypted, as had been alleged by an acquaintance of Riconosciuto, nor did it contain any versions of the PROMIS software. Lacking in-house expertise in repairing severely damaged media, GAO contracted with a professional engineering firm to:

(1) Perform an engineering evaluation of the four remaining media to determine whether they could be repaired to the point that data could be retrieved from them;

(2) repair the media, if possible; and

(3) retrieve any data found on the media.

By letter dated March 23, 1992, GAO reported on its work on the Riconosciuto media. GAO reported that all four of the damaged media were analyzed, but that only one contained readable data. According to GAO the readable media was a tape that contained what seemed to be instructions for installing a modification to what appeared to be a word processing software package. The format and command sequence, according to GAO, resembled those seen on non-IBM minicomputers. One disk appeared to contain some sort of instructions but could not be read.

[134] During a December 1991 telephone conversation with committee investigators, Robert Booth Nichols said that he (Nichols) and Michael Riconosciuto had worked together at the Cabazon Indian Reservation in the early 1980's. Robert Booth Nichols stated that he had been hired by John Phillip Nichols who worked with Mr. Riconosciuto on the joint venture. During this December telephone conversation, Robert Nichols requested that his associate Peter Zokosky, an arms manufacturer, also be present during a future interview with committee investigators. Robert Nichols added that Mr. Zokosky had also known Michael Riconosciuto. (Memorandum of interview on file with committee.)

[135] Affidavit of William A. Hamilton, December 22, 1989, p. 7.

53

awareness of PROMIS during the time alluded to by Mr. Hamilton. Dr. Brian stated—based on advice from his counsel—that after Mr. Meese encountered problems during the 1984 independent counsel inquiry, he had no contact with Mr. Meese until after he resigned under a cloud as Attorney General in 1988. Dr. Brian further stated that he has had only a few conversations with Mr. Meese since then because their relationship had chilled.

There were, however, strong ties between Dr. Brian and Mr. Meese. An independent counsel investigation by Jacob Stein of Mr. Meese, initiated in April 1984, identified certain financial dealings involving Mr. and Mrs. Meese, Dr. Brian, and Mr. Edwin W. Thomas. [136] One major point of the investigation's focus was Mr. Meese's association with Dr. Brian, who was secretary of the agency for health and welfare in Governor Reagan's administration, and Mr. Edwin Thomas, who was a close friend of Dr. Brian and purchased stock in companies in which Dr. Brian was interested. Mr. Thomas loaned Mrs. Meese $15,000 to purchase 2,000 shares of stock in a company called Biotech Capital Corporation, which was a venture capital firm created and controlled by Dr. Brian. [137] Before he actually made the loan, Mr. Thomas was offered a position as Assistant Counselor to the President by Mr. Meese in or about late December 1980 or early January 1981. [138] Mr. Stein concluded that there was substantial uncontradicted evidence that the Counselor position was offered by Mr. Meese to Mr. Thomas based on a longstanding personal and professional relationship between the two men. Following the loan, Mr. Thomas was named chief of the General Service Administration's San Francisco, CA, regional office.

Dr. Brian made a $100,000 loan to Mr. Thomas to fund the purchase of a Virginia townhouse during the same period; however, these funds were mostly used to purchase stock. [139] Mr. Meese stated that he knew Dr. Brian from Reagan's governorship and had seen him perhaps a dozen times from 1974 through 1984. During the first 2 years of the administration of President Reagan, Dr. Brian served as the Chairman of a White House Health Care Cost Reduction Task Force which reported to Mr. Meese. Dr. Brian, at either his or Mr. Thomas' behest, was nominated by the President to the National Science Board based on a recommendation by Mr. Meese. [140]

This nomination was approved by President Reagan, but later withdrawn. In his sworn statement to the committee, Dr. Brian stated that the reason he did not receive the position was due to

---

[136] Report of Independent Counsel Concerning Edwin Meese III, September 20, 1984.

[137] In a March 21, 1984, Washington Post article, it was reported that sources close to Meese said he decided to invest in Biotech because of his confidence in the company's founder, Earl W. Brian. Additionally, in the early months of the Reagan administration, Biotech received a special exemption from the Small Business Administration (SBA) which enabled the firm to obtain $5 million in federally guaranteed financing. The article also reports that this exemption was facilitated by a phone call from an aide of then Vice President Bush to SBA Administrator, Michael Cardenas. According to the March 21, 1984, article, before founding Biotech in 1979, Brian headed a firm called Xonics Inc. In 1977, while Brian was president, the Securities and Exchange Commission (SEC) cited the firm for making false and misleading statements to stockholders, charges that Xonics later settled in an SEC consent decree without admitting or denying the charges. This article also reported that the SEC accused the firm of violating the consent decree.

[138] Report of the Independent Counsel, op. cit., p. 72.

[139] Ibid., pp. 234–235.

[140] Ibid., p. 244. Also, Dr. Brian's application for this position listed Mr. Meese as his supervisor.

54

a personality conflict between himself and the head of the National Science Foundation. Information in the FBI background report and the independent counsel report prepared by Mr. Stein directly contradicted Dr. Brian's statement to the committee about the reason his appointment was withdrawn. According to the report of the independent counsel, Dr. Brian's name was withdrawn from consideration because of issues raised in the background report by the FBI. FBI records also indicate that Dr. Brian was a candidate for a White House position in 1974 and that nomination was withdrawn as well.

During an interview by committee investigators, a confidential law enforcement source,[141] who previously had been a member of Governor Reagan's cabinet, stated that he personally knew Dr. Brian and was aware of his close relationship with Mr. Meese. The source also said that he was aware of a situation in the 1970's in which Dr. Brian was accused of using computer software owned by the State of California for his [Dr. Brian] personal gain.[142] The committee's investigation revealed that in 1974, Dr. Brian was involved in a controversy over the use of 3,000 reels of computer tapes owned by the State of California. According to a news account in the Los Angeles Times,[143] these tapes were transferred to Dr. Brian under questionable circumstances which on the surface share some similarity with certain aspects of the INSLAW affair, as alleged by Mr. Hamilton.

The newspaper report stated that during the final days of Governor Ronald Reagan's administration, computer tapes were given to Dr. Brian under a no-cost contract awarded by then chief deputy director of the State of California Health Department, David Winston. Mr. Winston later became an employee of Dr. Brian's. After Governor Reagan left office, the new health director, Robert Gnaidza, held a news conference and stated he was canceling the contract, which entrusted the computer tapes to Dr. Brian, because the tapes were of incalculable value as a research tool and that handing them to Dr. Brian was, in effect, "a gift of public property for private purposes."[144] Dr. Brian apparently acknowledged having obtained the tapes, but he denied that the tapes were a gift to him. According to the news account, he stated:

> The entire matter is a blatant political ploy intended to obfuscate the abortive Gestapo raid ordered by the [present] health director.[145]

The independent counsel investigation did not include an inquiry into the possible connections between Mr. Meese and Dr. Brian, and the theft of Enhanced PROMIS.[146]

---

[141] Memorandum of interview on file with the committee.
[142] Memorandum of interview on file with committee.
[143] February 14, 1975 edition, Los Angeles Times, "Ex-Health Director Defends Tapes Move," p. 3.
[144] Ibid.
[145] Ibid., p. 3.
[146] Mr. Hamilton, in his affidavit, asserts that had their connection been known at the time, the independent counsel's investigation might well have included the theft of INSLAW's PROMIS software.

55

3. OTHER SOURCES ALLEGE WIDESPREAD DISTRIBUTION OF INSLAW'S ENHANCED PROMIS

Additional allegations of unauthorized distribution of INSLAW's Enhanced PROMIS software have been brought to the committee. Such allegations have been made by Charles Hayes (a surplus computer dealer), Ari Ben-Menashe and Juval Aviv (former Israeli intelligence officers) and Lester Coleman (self-professed writer and security consultant). These sources have stated that PROMIS has been illegally provided or sold to foreign governments including Canada, Israel, Singapore, Iraq, Egypt, and Jordan.[147]

Where possible, the allegations were investigated to the extent possible. Yet, the committee's work was subject to great limitations in attempting to secure cooperation by both private and governmental sources. In some cases, the person or government providing the committee with information abruptly halted such cooperation, which had ostensibly begun in good faith. Such was the case with the Government of Canada. In other cases, individuals appeared to have withheld key documents which allegedly linked the Justice Department and CIA to the sale of the Enhanced PROMIS software internationally. The possible involvement of the CIA and foreign governments presented, in the end, insurmountable obstacles to the committee's attempts to thoroughly investigate the allegations raised in this matter. The CIA was not fully responsive to inquiries from the committee, and would, under no circumstances, provide the committee or GAO with the needed access to its files and personnel. Further, Congress is generally powerless to investigate allegations regarding activities outside the United States without the assistance of the host government. For these reasons, the information presented in the following sections is limited by the restrictive conditions that prevented a fully probative inquiry necessary to resolve a host of still unanswered questions and allegations surrounding INSLAW. Where possible, sworn statements were obtained from individuals alleging information on unauthorized PROMIS software distribution.

4. DOES THE GOVERNMENT OF CANADA HAVE THE PROMIS SOFTWARE?

During November 1990, the Hamiltons informed the committee that they received information from Mr. Marc Valois, a Canadian Government Department of Communications official, that INSLAW's PROMIS software was being used to support 900 locations throughout the Canadian Government.[148] During January 1991, the Hamiltons informed the committee they were told by Mr. Denis LaChance, a Canadian Government Department of Communications official, that the Royal Canadian Mounted Police (RCMP) was using INSLAW's PROMIS to support its field offices.[149]

In a February 26, 1991, letter, the committee requested that the Ambassador of Canada, His Excellency Derek H. Burney, assist the

---

[147] In a sworn affidavit by Mr. Hamilton, allegations of other unauthorized distributions of Enhanced PROMIS have been made by unnamed U.S. Government officials. Mr. Hamilton contends that these sources, who will not come forward for fear of retribution, have alleged that PROMIS has been provided to agencies within and outside the Department of Justice including the Central Intelligence Agency (CIA), DEA and the FBI. Hamilton affidavit, December 22, 1989 (on file with the committee).

[148] Memorandum of interview on file with the committee.

[149] Sworn affidavit of Ms. Patricia C. Hamilton, Feb. 18, 1991, p. 2.

56

committee investigators in contacting knowledgeable Government officials to determine what version of the PROMIS software is being used by the Canadian Government. Subsequently, Mr. Jonathan Fried, Counselor for Congressional and Legal Affairs in the Canadian Embassy (Washington, DC), contacted the committee to express reluctance to fully cooperate with the committee because "Canadians had been burned once before by Congress." Mr. Fried insisted that the following specific conditions be met: (1) that interviews for individuals be conducted only in the presence of both the legal counsel for the Departments involved and their superiors; and (2) that no Canadian public servants would be witnesses in any foreign investigative proceedings. By letter dated March 19, 1991, the committee reluctantly agreed to the Canadian Government's conditions and identified Marc Valois and Denis LaChance as the two Canadian officials the committee wished to interview.

On March 22, 1991, committee investigators interviewed Mr. Valois and Mr. LaChance, the two Canadian officials who had alleged that the Canadian Government was using INSLAW's PROMIS software. Prior to the questioning of the two witnesses, the Government's counsel informed committee investigators that Mr. Valois and Mr. LaChance could only respond to questions specifically addressing the PROMIS software. He further stated that these two officials would not respond to questions concerning any allegation that four software programs that may have been acquired by the Canadian Government may be derivatives of the PROMIS software. The Canadian counsel informed the committee investigators that the committee would have to request in writing any information concerning the Canadian Government's involvement relating to the four software programs alleged to be derivatives of PROMIS.[150]

Mr. Valois and Mr. LaChance stated that they had incorrectly identified INSLAW's PROMIS as the software being used by the Canadian Government. They further stated that, the PROMIS software identified to the Hamiltons as being their product was actually a project management software also named "PROMIS," developed by the Strategic Software Planning Corporation.[151] They also denied any knowledge, or use, of a derivative of INSLAW's PROMIS. Subsequently, the president of the Strategic Software Planning Corporation acknowledged in a sworn statement to committee investigators that his company had sold a few copies of his firm's PROMIS software to the Canadian Government in May 1986.[152]

By letter dated October 23, 1991, to the Canadian Ambassador, the committee again requested full cooperation with the committee's investigation. The Canadian Government was requested to provide information regarding software packages allegedly being used by the RCMP and CSIS identified as derivatives of INSLAW's Enhanced PROMIS by the Hamiltons. Additionally, it was requested that investigators be provided the names of knowledgeable

---

[150] Memorandum of interview on file with committee.
[151] Interviews of Mr. Marc Valois, Mr. Denis LaChance, March 22, 1991, pp. 7 and 4, respectively, and Mr. Ed Bercovitz, March 7, 1991, pp. 4–8.
[152] Sworn statement of Mr. Massimo Grimaldi, president of Strategic Software Planning Corporation, March 19, 1991, pp. 9–10.

57

RCMP and CSIS personnel who could provide insight into the software used by these agencies.

On December 4, 1991, the Ambassador responded by letter that neither the RCMP nor the CSIS were using INSLAW's PROMIS software. He further stated that none of the software packages believed to be derivatives of PROMIS were in use by any branch of the Canadian Government. According to the Ambassador:

> ...The RCMP and CSIS reported...they do not use any case management software....[153]

The Ambassador's conclusory statement did not provide an offer or an opportunity for further verification of the allegations received concerning the Government of Canada.[154] Without direct access to RCMP, CSIS and other Canadian officials, the committee has been effectively thwarted in its attempt to support or reject the contention that INSLAW software was transferred to the Canadian Government.

5. DID THE CIA ASSIST IN THE SALE OF PROMIS?

On November 20, 1990, Chairman Brooks wrote to CIA Director, William H. Webster, requesting that the Agency:

> ...cooperate with the committee by determining whether the CIA has the PROMIS software or any derivative and to have the knowledgeable person or persons available for interviews by committee investigators....

On December 11, 1990, the CIA's Director of Congressional Affairs, Mr. E. Norbert Garrett, responded that:

> We have checked with Agency components that track data processing procurement or that would be likely users of PROMIS, and we have been unable to find any indication that the Agency ever obtained PROMIS software.

The chairman notified the CIA on February 15, 1991, that the committee appreciated the initial inquiry performed by Mr. Garrett. The chairman stated, however, that a more thorough and complete review was needed to determine if the PROMIS software or a derivative is, or has ever been, in the possession or control of the Agency, or any of its contractors, consultants, and operatives.

The chairman advised the Director that the committee received information that, in 1983, the Agency began operating a "floating point system" that operates a "Data Point" software program al-

---

[153] Letter from His Excellency Derek H. Burney, Ambassador of Canada to the Honorable Jack Brooks, December 4, 1991, p. 2.

[154] Although the Canadian Government has continued to deny that it has INSLAW's PROMIS software, information continues to surface indicating the opposite to be true. As recently as April 1992, reports of the use of the PROMIS software by the Canadian Government have been aired through the written and televised media. These media releases include a 1-minute report on CJOH, Ottawa titled, "RCMP Using Stolen INSLAW Software;" an April 16, 1992, article in a Canadian magazine titled "Out of Canada;" an article on March 3, 1992, in a Canadian newspaper titled, "The Globe and Mail;" and a February 28, 1992 article in the Canadian newspaper titled, "The Financial Post."

Of particular interest is a report that Statistics Canada, a Canadian governmental agency, recently admitted previous use of a public domain version of the INSLAW's PROMIS software. According to officials contacted by William Hamilton, the version of the software that had been used was obtained through the LEAA in the late 1970's. (See memorandum of interview on file with the committee). While the use of this version of the PROMIS software would be legal, the Canadian Government had previously denied any knowledge of the use of INSLAW's PROMIS software by any of its agencies.

58

leged to be a derivative of PROMIS.[155] The chairman also informed the Director that it has been alleged that the PROMIS software might also be operating under the name "Data Plus" or "PROMIS Plus" and it might currently be used at military intelligence locations. The chairman stated that the committee had also received information that the CIA may have assisted the Egyptian Government in acquiring this software through the Foreign Military Assistance Program (MAP). Finally, in the letter dated February 15, 1992, the chairman inquired of the Director whether the CIA had awarded several contracts to Dr. Earl Brian, or a company called Hadron, Inc.

Several months after the chairman's February 15, 1991, letter, the committee staff met with CIA representatives. They indicated that after an extensive search within the Agency, no versions of the PROMIS software were found. They also indicated that they checked specifically to see if the software had been supplied to the Government of Egypt and that no evidence of this transaction occurring exist at the Agency.[156]

A letter dated November 18, 1991, was received from the CIA Deputy Director, Richard Kerr, who denied that the Agency had any versions of INSLAW's PROMIS software. He further stated that the PROMIS software currently being used by CIA components was manufactured by Strategic Software Planning Corporation of Cambridge, MA. (This is the same firm that sold its PROMIS software to the Canadian Government, described in a previous section.) Mr. Kerr also stated that the Agency has had some contracts with Hadron, Inc., but they were not related to PROMIS and that the Agency had no record of being in contact with Dr. Earl Brian in connection with any of these contracts.[157] The Deputy Director also denied that the CIA assisted the Egyptian Government in acquiring INSLAW's PROMIS or similar software.[158] He, however, added an important caveat:

> Of course, we have no way of knowing whether any Agency contractors at some point ever acquired PROMIS software, but none did so on behalf of the Agency. Moreover, although we have no indication that any such acquisition took place, we cannot rule out the possibility that an Agency employee acting on his own behalf and without any official authorization or funds acquired PROMIS for his own personal use.[159]

---

[155] In a conversation with committee investigators, William Hamilton provided information he had obtained from Charles Hayes and Juval Aviv, regarding the distribution of the PROMIS software domestically and internationally. (See December 22, 1989, affidavit of William Hamilton, on file with the committee.) In this conversation, Mr. Hamilton stated that the PROMIS software was distributed to the CIA. For greater detail see the section of the report titled, "The Allegators."

[156] In addition, at that meeting, and as a result of information received from several sources (refer to the section of the report titled, "The Allegators") subsequent to the February 15, 1991, letter, committee investigators inquired whether a number of other countries, including Israel, Jordan, Singapore, Canada, Iraq and Iran, had received PROMIS software. To date, no response has been received from the CIA.

[157] Dr. Brian, in his sworn statement of September 20, 1990, described the business relationship between Hadron and the U.S. Navy, the intelligence community, and specifically the CIA. He indicated that Hadron had 30–40 Federal Government contracts with the "intelligence community" (pp. 23–27).

[158] Letter to the Honorable Jack Brooks from Richard J. Kerr, Deputy Director CIA, November 18, 1991, pp. 1, 2, and 3.

[159] Ibid.

59

Thus, the CIA has not fully addressed the questions raised in the chairman's February 15, 1991, letter. While the CIA indicated that they could not locate PROMIS within the Agency, the Agency itself acknowledged that this did not preclude independent contractor usage.

In response to the allegation that the Egyptian Government obtained INSLAW's Enhanced PROMIS software using Foreign Military Assistance Program funds between 1980 and 1990, the committee requested GAO to determine if this fund was used to assist in the purchase of the software.[160] On June 14, 1991, following a study by its National Security, International Affairs Division, GAO advised the committee that their review failed to produce evidence supporting the allegation regarding the purchase of the PROMIS software by the Egyptian Government.[161] During discussions with the GAO evaluators who conducted the study, the committee learned that MAP funds cover broad categories which make it extremely difficult to identify individual purchases.

6. ALLEGATIONS OF PROMIS DISTRIBUTION TO AGENCIES WITHIN THE DEPARTMENT

During this investigation, the committee received allegations that the Drug Enforcement Administration had been mandated to use the PROMIS software. Allegations were also made that the FBI Field Office Information Management System (FOIMS) is based on INSLAW's PROMIS software.

In August 1990, the committee inquired into an allegation that the DEA had been mandated to use PROMIS software. This allegation originated from the former DEA Deputy Assistant Administrator for Planning and Inspections, Carl Jackson, who told committee investigators that, in 1988, Attorney General Richard Thornburgh ordered DEA to install PROMIS software. He stated that he recalled some discussion during a monthly ADP Executive Committee of senior DEA officials in late 1988 or early 1989 concerning the mandate.[162] However, DEA eventually developed a case tracking system called CAST (Case Status System).[163] The committee investigators reviewed the minutes of the ADP Executive Committee monthly meetings conducted in late 1988 and early 1989. The review disclosed no evidence that PROMIS was discussed,[164] but did corroborate DEA's plan to implement CAST.

With regard to the allegations concerning the FBI, committee staff inquired into charges made by Mr. Terry Miller, president of

---

[160] Letter from the Honorable Jack Brooks to Honorable Charles Bowsher, Comptroller General of the United States, January 17, 1991.

[161] Letter report to the Honorable Jack Brooks from Mr. Joseph Kelley, Issue Area Director for Security and International Relations, GAO, June 14, 1991.

[162] Memorandum of interview of Mr. Carl Jackson, August 31, 1990 (on file with the committee).

[163] Ibid.

[164] Copies of minutes of the ADP Executive Committee Meetings, December 1988 through May 1989.

60

government sales, Consultants, Inc. [165] On January 9, 1991, [166] Mr. Miller informed FBI Director William Sessions that he had reason to believe that the software system, FOIMS, used throughout the FBI to track cases, had been stolen from INSLAW. He offered the FBI what he called a simple solution to determine the truth of his allegation—a "code compare" between PROMIS and FOIMS. The FBI's January 25, 1991, response to Miller's allegation was in the nature of an unresponsive form letter. [167] In his February 5, 1991, response to the FBI, Mr. Miller accused the FBI of being very defensive. Mr. Miller further stated that the FBI had requested that he provide, among other things, descriptions of the victim and the thief, if any.

In a February 11, 1991, letter, the FBI's Deputy Assistant Director for the Technical Services Division responded to Mr. Miller. [168] The Deputy Assistant Director stated that he conferred with the Department's attorney handling the INSLAW matter and determined that the Federal courts were the appropriate forum for adjudicating his concerns.

On June 7, 1991, the FBI followed up with another letter to Mr. Miller. [169] In this letter the Assistant Director for the Inspections Division pointed out that they would need additional information before the FBI's OPR could assess the substance of his allegation. On June 13, 1991, Mr. Miller responded that he did not know if FOIMS contained stolen software, but that several people had claimed that FOIMS contains software stolen from INSLAW. [170] Mr. Miller reiterated that it would be rather easy to do a code compare between PROMIS and FOIMS to resolve this issue.

It is the committee's understanding that no code comparison has been made between FOIMS and PROMIS to determine if there is any similarity. [171] FBI officials did inform committee investigators that the Bureau began developing FOIMS in-house around 1978 and that in 1981 the Bureau decided to use the ADABAS [172] data base management system. [173] These officials provided documentation to the committee which indicated that implementation at the first pilot office began during 1979, and that implementation of FOIMS at all FBI field offices began in 1985 and was completed in 1989.

---

[165] Mr. Miller is a 32-year veteran of the computer business. His interest in this matter resulted from his belief that INSLAW was being unfairly treated by the Department. In a series of letters to the FBI, he requested that the FOIMS system be compared to INSLAW's PROMIS software. Additionally, he has requested that he be given permission to perform the comparison. To date, the FBI has failed in his view to satisfactorily answer his questions. Mr. Miller and a INSLAW confidential informant, who is a career official in the Justice Department, have both provided information to the Hamiltons which alleged the use of INSLAW's PROMIS software by the FBI. The Department official alleged he was told by John Otto, former Acting Director of the FBI, that FOIMS is based on INSLAW's PROMIS software.

[166] On file with the committee.

[167] The FBI's January 25, 1991, response to Mr. Miller is on file with the committee.

[168] On file with the committee.

[169] On file with the committee.

[170] On file with the committee.

[171] In a June 23, 1992, letter from FBI Director William Session to Judge Bua, Special Counsel to the Attorney General, the Director stated that a code comparison between FOIMS and PROMIS would be performed by a neutral third party. Since the arrangements for this code comparison are now in progress, no findings have been made.

[172] ADABAS (Adaptable Data Base System) is a relational data base management system with a number of utility programs.

[173] Memorandum of interview on file with the committee.

61

According to the FBI, INSLAW demonstrated its PROMIS software in 1982 and at that time the Bureau's technical support personnel determined that the PROMIS would not meet the agency's requirements. The FBI concluded that, to use INSLAW's PROMIS, the Bureau would need to spend a considerable amount of time and money to modify and/or convert existing systems to accommodate the new software. While there is no specific evidence that PROMIS is being used by the FBI, the matter could be resolved quickly if an independent agency or expert was commissioned to conduct a code comparison of the PROMIS and FOIMS systems. [174]

However, by letter dated July 7, 1992, Judge Bua stated to INSLAW counsel Elliot Richardson that he had decided to "retain my own expert to conduct the examination necessary to compare the software." [175] This action followed the FBI Director's agreement to fully cooperate with a comparison of the FOIMS software to INSLAW's PROMIS, with a number of conditions that included:

> The examiner must advise the FBI of any FOIMS software code which, in his or her judgment, was derived from the enhanced version of PROMIS. This notification will provide the FBI with an opportunity to document the existence of the questioned software code to avoid possible subsequent disputes. [176]

7. RONALD LEGRAND DENIES INSLAW'S ASSERTIONS

The committee received allegations that Ronald LeGrand, former DEA agent, former chief investigator for the Senate Judiciary Committee, and a lawyer, had received crucial information about INSLAW matters from a trusted source who was a senior Department career official "with a title" whom Mr. LeGrand had known for 15 years. [177] In the *Third Supplemental Submission of INSLAW in Support of Its Motion to Take Limited Discovery* (Bankruptcy case No. 85–00070), counsel for INSLAW states:

> INSLAW had sought to depose these officials because of highly specific allegations that Mr. Ronald LeGrand, then Chief Investigator of the Senate Judiciary Committee, had

---

[174] On April 9, 1990, committee investigators requested cooperation and technical assistance in the INSLAW investigation from the General Services Administration's (GSA) Office of Technology Assessment. Although GSA agreed to cooperate with the committee, after 1 year GSA had not provided any assistance to the committee's numerous requests. In an April 11, 1991, letter to committee's chief investigator, Jim Lewin, from Thomas Buckholtz, Commissioner, Information Resource Management Services, GSA, Mr. Buckholtz said that he had consulted with the Department of Justice regarding the committee's request and that Deputy Attorney General Stewart Schiffer informed him that GSA's compliance with the committee's request "would not adversely affect the litigation [with INSLAW] as long as GSA provided Department of Justice with all GSA findings and reports, and any responses GSA received." Mr. Buckholtz added that GSA had decided to provide all information developed by GSA to the Department if the services were provided to the committee. Finally, Mr. Buckholtz said that the committee must pay $150,000 to GSA for supporting the committee's investigation even though in the past GSA has provided such analytical and advisory services to Congress free of charge. Most disturbing and subject to ongoing review is GSA's decision to provide the agency under investigation with confidential information related to the committee's investigation.

[175] Letter from Judge Nicholas J. Bua to Elliot L. Richardson, Esq., dated July 7, 1992.

[176] Letter from FBI Director William S. Sessions to Mr. Nicholas J. Bua, Special Counsel to the Attorney General, dated June 23, 1992, p. 2.

[177] December 22, 1989, affidavit of William Hamilton in *INSLAW, Inc.* v. *Dick Thornburgh, et al.*, pp. 19–20. Mr. LeGrand was chief investigator for the Senate Judiciary Committee at the time it is alleged that his "trusted source" provided him information regarding INSLAW.

62

conveyed to William A. and Nancy B. Hamilton, the principal owners of INSLAW, in May 1988.

According to LeGrand, a trusted source, described to the Hamiltons as a senior DOJ official with a title, had alleged that the two senior Criminal Division officials were witnesses to much greater malfeasance against INSLAW than that already found by the Bankruptcy Court, malfeasance on such a more serious scale than Watergate. LeGrand told the Hamiltons that D. Lowell Jensen did not merely fail to investigate the malfeasance of Videnieks and Brewer but instead had "engineered" the malfeasance "right from the start" so that INSLAW's software business could be made available to political friends of the Reagan/Bush administration. [178]

Because of the seriousness and specificity of the allegations, committee investigators invested considerable effort in obtaining cooperation from Mr. LeGrand. After 5 months of negotiations, Mr. LeGrand was interviewed by committee investigators on May 31, 1990. [179] Mr. LeGrand was asked to identify the "trusted source" so that committee investigators could contact this person to obtain his knowledge of the INSLAW matter. Mr. LeGrand stated that he would contact his source and determine whether he was willing to be interviewed. Mr. LeGrand was also asked if he would provide a sworn statement, and he indicated that he would if the committee made a request to Chairwoman Cardiss Collins of the House Government Operation's Subcommittee on Government Activities and Transportation. [180] Pursuant to Mr. LeGrand's request, Chairman Brooks wrote to Chairwoman Cardiss Collins on July 20, 1990. The chairman requested that committee investigators be allowed to obtain a sworn statement from Mr. LeGrand concerning his knowledge of the INSLAW matter.

After receiving an affirmative response from Chairwoman Collins, committee investigators made numerous attempts to schedule a sworn statement from Mr. LeGrand, to no avail. Mr. LeGrand then left the Washington DC, area without informing the committee. Once Mr. LeGrand was located, the committee wrote to him on November 20, 1990, and renewed its request that he cooperate with the committee by providing a statement under oath. On February 14, 1991, Mr. LeGrand provided a sworn statement to committee investigators. [181] During this statement Mr. LeGrand provided little corroboration of the Hamilton's allegations. According to Mr. LeGrand, the first problem with the remarks attributed to him was the unintentional merging of comments from different persons which the Hamiltons had attributed to Mr. LeGrand's "trusted source." Mr. LeGrand stated that he gathered information from several individuals during his inquiry into the INSLAW matter. However, Mr. Hamilton attributed all the information he had received from Mr. LeGrand as coming from his "trusted source."

---

[178] Third Supplemental Submission of INSLAW in Support of Its Motion to Take Limited Discovery, dated March 23, 1991, p. 2.
[179] Memorandum of interview on file with the committee.
[180] Mr. LeGrand left the Senate Judiciary Committee and joined the House subcommittee in October 1989.
[181] Sworn statement on file with the committee.

63

Mr. LeGrand, however, stated that his trusted source provided the following information pertaining to the INSLAW matter:

> Then Deputy Attorney General Lowell Jensen was going to award the case tracking software business to friends.[182]
>
> Jensen relied on some of the most senior political and career officials in both the Criminal Division and the Justice Management Division to carry out this plan.[183]
>
> Other senior Criminal Division officials not involved in the alleged wrongdoing have knowledge of it and are upset about it but are unwilling to expose themselves to possible reprisals by coming forward with what they know.[184]

Mr. LeGrand was asked whether his source provided the following statement as described by INSLAW counsel in the Bankruptcy Court proceedings:

> Shortly after DOJ's public announcement on May 6, 1988, that DOJ would not seek the appointment of an independent counsel in the INSLAW matter and that it had cleared Mr. Meese of any wrongdoing, the source told Mr. LeGrand that "the INSLAW case is a lot dirtier for the Department of Justice than Watergate was, both in its breadth and in its depth."

Mr. LeGrand responded that his source indicated that there was more to this than people were currently aware of and that there was a comparison to Watergate; however, he did not recall reference to the date or the phrase "both in its breadth and in its depth."[185]

Mr. LeGrand was again asked to provide the name of his source and to date he has refused to do so.[186]

At the Department's request, Mr. LeGrand later submitted an affidavit refuting INSLAW's claim. In the affidavit, Mr. LeGrand stated, "...I did not convey 'highly specific' allegations to Mr. or Mrs. Hamilton. Instead, I told them of general allegations, rumors, I had heard from different sources about various persons within the Department of Justice."[187] After several years of making statements to William Hamilton, the Senate Permanent Subcommittee on Investigations, and this committee, Mr. LeGrand's latest affidavit was striking in its assertion that his source had no personal knowledge of the Department's handling of the INSLAW matter.

8. THE ALLEGATORS

The following is a discussion of the evidence provided by several additional individuals who claim to have detailed and, in some cases, firsthand knowledge of the Justice Department's alleged con-

---

[182] Sworn statement of Ronald LeGrand, February 14, 1991, pp. 20, 46, 52.
[183] Ibid., p. 20.
[184] Ibid., p. 21.
[185] Ibid., p. 41.
[186] Ibid., p. 82.
[187] *INSLAW, Inc.* v. *United States*, Bankruptcy Case No. 85–0070, Declaration of Ronald LeGrand. Mr. Hamilton later alleged to the committee that Roger Pauley was LeGrand's contact and trusted source within the Department. Mr. Pauley is the Director of the Office of Legislation in the Criminal Division. Mr. Pauley denied that he has had contact with Mr. LeGrand while he was with the Senate Judiciary. Mr. Pauley stated that he never told LeGrand that Judge Jensen engineered INSLAW's problems with the Department or any of the other statements attributed to Mr. LeGrand's source.

64

spiracy to steal and to transfer or sell the PROMIS software to foreign intelligence or other parties. Not all individuals would provide sworn testimony regarding their charges. Obviously, greater weight has been given to those who provided sworn statements or affidavits to the committee.

Ari Ben-Menashe Allegations: Mr. Ben-Menashe stated under oath that he is a former Israeli intelligence officer who served in the Israeli Defense Forces and the Israeli Prime Minister's office from August 1977 through November 1989. During an initial interview with committee investigators, in February 1991, Mr. Ben-Menashe stated that he wanted to cooperate but only after the committee agreed to meet certain conditions. Mr. Ben-Menashe explained that he was in the United States by virtue of a visa that was due to expire and he asked that the committee: (1) Arrange for a visa extension and (2) provide him immunity from any prosecution relating to the information and documents he possessed regarding the illegal distribution and/or sale of Enhanced PROMIS by Dr. Earl Brian to the Israeli Government. The request was refused. On May 29, 1991, Ben-Menashe provided a sworn statement without any conditions. [188]

Mr. Ben-Menashe stated that, in 1982, Dr. Earl Brian and Robert McFarland, the former Director of the National Security Council, provided the public domain version of INSLAW's PROMIS software to the Israeli Government's special intelligence operation Defense Forces. [189] Mr. Ben-Menashe stated under oath to committee investigators that he was also present in 1987 when Dr. Brian sold Enhanced PROMIS to the Israeli intelligence community and the Singapore Armed Forces and that, after these sales were completed, approximately $5.5 million was placed in a foreign bank account to which Earl Brian had access. [190] Mr. Ben-Menashe further stated under oath that Earl Brian sold a "public domain" version of the PROMIS software to the military intelligence organizations of Jordan in 1983 and to the Iraqi Government in 1987. [191]

Mr. Ben-Menashe stated during his sworn statement to the committee that he has information about the sale of a "public domain" version of PROMIS by the Israeli Government to the Soviet Union in 1986 and the sale of the enhanced version to the Canadian Government coordinated by Earl Brian. [192] Mr. Ben-Menashe also stated that various unnamed Israeli officials would corroborate his statements. He refused, however, to identify these officials or provide evidence to corroborate his statements unless he was called as an official witness for the committee under a grant of immunity. [193]

Charles Hayes Allegations: Mr. Hayes is a surplus computer dealer with alleged ties to both United States and foreign intelligence communities. Mr. Hayes first came to the attention of the committee during August 1990, following assertions that excess Harris-Lanier word processing equipment he had purchased from the U.S.

---

[188] Interview with Ari Ben-Menashe, February 5, 1991, (on file with the committee).
[189] Sworn statement of Mr. Ben-Menashe, May 29, 1991, pp. 6 and 14, on file with the committee.
[190] Ibid., pp. 3, 8, and 14.
[191] Ibid., pp. 14, 15, and 10. In his sworn statement, Mr. Ben-Menashe stated that the sale of PROMIS to Iraq by Dr. Brian was brokered by an alleged international arms dealer named Carlos Cardoen of Miami, FL, and Chile.
[192] Ibid., pp. 11, 12, and 28.
[193] Ibid., p. 3.

65

attorney's office for the Eastern District of Kentucky, located in Lexington, contained the PROMIS software. [194] Mr. Hayes stated that the U.S. attorney's office had provided him 5¼-inch computer disks when he purchased the excess equipment and that he believed these disks contained INSLAW's Enhanced PROMIS software. [195]

On November 28, 1990, the committee chairman wrote to the Department requesting access to the equipment and documents seized under a search warrant served on Charles Hayes. The chairman also requested files concerning the dispute between Mr. Hayes and the Department from the Civil Division attorney handling the case. On February 12, 1991, W. Lee Rawls, Assistant Attorney General, Office of Legislative Affairs, responded to the chairman that:

> ...we can arrange for the committee staff to see the equipment and examine the manuals and other documents that were retrieved with the equipment pursuant to a civil writ of possession. We cannot, however, either arrange for committee staff to operate the equipment or provide the committee with a print-out of the information contained in the equipment, as informally requested by committee staff on January 31, 1991. We do not yet have a complete print-out of the information contained in the equipment. Moreover, disclosure of this information would compromise an ongoing criminal investigation.

Mr. Rawls also stated that:

> We cannot arrange for committee access to certain documents in the Civil Division files because their disclosure might adversely impact a pending criminal investigation relating to this matter. These include non-public witness statements prepared by the witnesses, portions of Civil Division attorney notes of witness statements, Civil Division attorney notes about conversations with Criminal Division prosecutors, drafts of pleadings and memoranda that would disclose thought processes of the Criminal Division attorneys, and other material that could compromise the pending criminal investigation. We also are unable to disclose the exhibits that were sealed by the court. [196]

On February 13, 1991, Mr. Hayes provided a sworn statement to the committee attesting to his assertions. During the statement Mr. Hayes explained that he believed the PROMIS software had been copied onto the disks from the original PROMIS software by

---

[194] GAO has established that the equipment Mr. Hayes purchased did contain sensitive information. On June 27, 1991, Milton J. Socolar, Special Assistant to the Comptroller General, testified before the Subcommittee on Economic and Commercial Law that:
"We previously testified about a Justice security breach last summer at Lexington, Kentucky. [Justice's Weak ADP Security Compromises Sensitive Data (Public Version) GAO/IMTEC-91-6, Mar. 21, 1991] Computer equipment excessed by the U.S. attorney's office was later found to contain highly sensitive data, including grand jury material and information regarding confidential informants. How this could have happened is disturbing in itself, but even more shocking is that it happened again. As recently as this past February, a different U.S. attorney's office cautioned Federal and local officials that, again, sensitive information that could potentially identify agents and witnesses might have been compromised."
[195] Sworn statement of Mr. Charles Hayes, February 13, 1991, pp. 5 and 23, on file with the committee.
[196] Letter to the Honorable Jack Brooks from Mr. W. Lee Rawls, Assistant Attorney General, Department of Justice, February 12, 1991, pp. 2 and 3.

66

personnel at the U.S. attorney's office. At this time, Mr. Hayes gave the disks and related material to committee investigators. [197] Committee investigators identified the 5¼-inch disks and related materials as nothing more than training programs for the Lanier computers used by the Lexington office. Mr. Hamilton told committee investigators that it was "highly implausible" that the 5¼-inch disks would contain Enhanced PROMIS. Mr. Hamilton further stated that if PROMIS was being used on the Lanier word processing equipment, it would have to be the public domain version which is not the subject of the legal dispute with the Department.

Mr. Hayes continued to have frequent conversations with Mr. Hamilton and his attorneys. Mr. Hamilton provided the committee staff a memorandum, dated October 22, 1990, that memorialized several telephone conversations in which Mr. Hayes allegedly told Mr. Hamilton that: [198]

> He can identify about 300 places where the PROMIS software has been installed illegally by the Federal Government.
>
> Dr. Brian sold PROMIS to the Central Intelligence Agency in 1983 for implementation on computers purchased from Floating Point Systems and what the CIA called PROMIS "Datapoint."
>
> Dr. Brian has sold about $20 million of PROMIS licenses to the Federal Government.
>
> Department officials hinted to CIA officials that they should deny that they are using PROMIS.

In addition, Mr. Hayes repeated to committee investigators on numerous occasions many of the same claims that were contained in Mr. Hamilton's October 22, 1990, memorandum. Mr. Hayes also told committee investigators that he had received information from unnamed sources within the Canadian Government that Dr. Brian sold the PROMIS software to the Canadian Federal Government in 1987. He made numerous promises to committee investigators that the documentation regarding these sales by Dr. Brian would be provided to the committee by the unnamed Canadian officials. However, on August 16, 1991, Mr. Hayes stated that the Canadian officials decided not to cooperate with the committee.

While these allegations are intriguing, Mr. Hayes has not provided any corroborating documentation.

Lester K. Coleman: As part of the bankruptcy proceeding involving INSLAW a sworn affidavit was obtained from Lester K. Coleman. (Adversary Proceeding No. 86–0069.) Mr. Coleman described himself as a freelance writer, editor and security consultant, who, in 1988, was an employee of the Defense Intelligence Agency. Mr. Coleman stated that during April and May 1988, he worked with Eurame Trading Company, Ltd., a DEA proprietary company in Nicosia, Cyprus. Mr. Coleman said that at that time he found that the DEA was using the trading company to sell computer software called "PROMISE" or "PROMIS" to drug abuse control agencies in Cyprus, Pakistan, Syria, Kuwait, and Turkey. Mr. Coleman also said that he witnessed the unpacking of reels of computer tapes

---

[197] Sworn statement of Mr. Charles Hayes provided to committee investigators on February 13, 1991, at Lexington, KY (on file with the committee).

[198] Memorandum from Mr. William Hamilton to Mr. Elliot Richardson, Esq., and Mr. Charles Work, Esq., October 22, 1990, pp. 1–2, on file with the committee.

67

and computer hardware at the Nicosia Police Force Narcotics Squad. The boxes bore the name and red logo of a Canadian corporation with the words "PROMISE" or "PROMIS" and "Ltd." According to Mr. Coleman, the DEA's objective in aiding the implementation of this "PROMIS(E)" system in these Middle East countries' drug abuse control agencies was to augment the United State's ability to access sensitive drug control law enforcement and intelligence files.

Mr. Coleman further stated that a DEA Agent (Country Attaché), was responsible for both the Eurame Trading Company, Ltd., and its initiative to sell "PROMIS(E)" computer systems to Middle East countries for drug abuse control. Mr. Coleman stated to the court under oath that he believed the agent's reassignment in 1990 to a DEA intelligence position in the State of Washington prior to Michael Riconosciuto's March 1991 arrest there on drug charges was more than coincidental. Mr. Coleman stated he believes that the agent was assigned to Riconosciuto's home State to manufacture a case against him. Mr. Coleman stated he believes this was done to prevent Mr. Riconosciuto from becoming a credible witness concerning the U.S. Government's covert sale of PROMIS to foreign governments.

Mr. Coleman stated under oath that he had been contacted by a reporter named Danny Casolaro on August 3, 1991. Mr. Coleman stated that Mr. Casolaro told him that he had leads and hard information about (1) Department of Justice groups operating overseas, (2) the sale of the "PROMIS(E)" software by the U. S. Government to foreign governments, (3) Bank of Credit and Commerce International (BCCI), and (4) the Iran/Contra scandal. [199]

Juval Aviv: Mr. Juval Aviv stated to the committee that he is a former member of the Israeli Mossad who currently serves as president and chief executive officer of Interfor, Inc., a private investigative firm specializing in international investigations. In January 1991, Mr. Aviv told committee investigators that he could provide information that Dr. Brian sold INSLAW's Enhanced PROMIS software to U.S. Government agencies outside the Department, including the CIA, National Security Agency, National Aeronautics and Space Administration, and the National Security Council. Mr. Aviv also stated that Dr. Brian sold the PROMIS software to Interpol in France, the Israeli Mossad, the Israeli Air Force, and the Egyptian Government. [200]

Mr. Aviv stated that Dr. Brian sold the software to Egypt through the use of the foreign military assistance program and that the software was called either Data Plus or PROMIS Plus. He also stated that INSLAW's Enhanced PROMIS software was converted for use by both the United States and British Navy nuclear submarine intelligence data base.

Mr. Aviv stated that there are witnesses and documents to corroborate his allegations. Following Mr. Aviv's meeting with committee investigators in January 1991, he has refused to provide a sworn statement or any further information.

---

[199] Sworn affidavit of Lester K. Coleman, *INSLAW, Inc.* v. *United States et al,* Adversary Proceeding No. 86–0069.

[200] Mr. Aviv met with investigators on January 25, 1991, at Interfor, Inc., offices in New York City. See memorandum of interview on file with the committee.

68

John Schoolmeester: The committee received information from Mr. and Mrs. Hamilton that John Schoolmeester, a former Customs Services program officer, had direct knowledge of ties between Mr. Videnieks and one of Dr. Brian's computer companies called Hadron, Inc., prior to Mr. Videnieks' employment with the Justice Department.[201] Mr. Hamilton asserted that Mr. Videnieks conspired with Dr. Brian and other Hadron, Inc., management to transfer INSLAW's PROMIS software to the company. In two sworn statements provided to the committee, Mr. Schoolmeester stated that Mr. Videnieks, as a contracting officer for the Customs Service, was involved with several Hadron, Inc., contracts, and that Mr. Videnieks would necessarily have met with Dominic Laiti (a former Hadron, Inc., chief executive officer) on a regular basis because that was the way Mr. Laiti conducted business. However, Mr. Videnieks stated under oath that he did not know or have any conversations with Dominic Laiti or Dr. Brian.[202] Mr. Schoolmeester stated that Dr. Brian was "the behind the scenes guy at Hadron, Inc.," but he was not certain whether Mr. Videnieks had met with him.[203] Mr. Schoolmeester also stated that Dr. Brian was well connected in Washington and that he had connections with Mr. Meese and several congressional figures.[204]

Lois Battistoni: The committee also received allegations from Mr. Hamilton that Ms. Lois Battistoni, a former Justice Criminal Division employee, had information which could support the allegation that Dr. Brian had arranged with Justice officials to transfer PROMIS to Hadron, Inc. According to Mr. Hamilton, Ms. Battistoni stated that a Criminal Division employee had told her that there was a company chosen to take over INSLAW's contracts and that this company was connected to a top Department official through a California relationship. Mr. Hamilton stated that she believed that Hadron, Inc., was a possibility because Dr. Brian and Mr. Meese served together in Governor Reagan's administration.[205]

Ms. Battistoni, however, stated under oath to committee investigators that she has little firsthand knowledge of the facts surrounding these allegations, nor did she provide the name of the Criminal Division employee who had provided her with the information about this matter. She indicated that Department employees are afraid to cooperate with Congress for fear of reprisals by the Justice Department.[206]

Ms. Battistoni also raised a number of allegations about the involvement of Department employees in the destruction (shredding) of documents related to the INSLAW matter.[207] While the committee was unable to obtain any direct information about the alleged

---

[201] December 22, 1989, affidavit of William Hamilton in *INSLAW, Inc. v. Dick Thornburgh, et al.*, p. 12.

[202] Sworn statement of Peter Videnieks, November 5, 1990, p. 104 (on file with the committee).

[203] Sworn statement of John Schoolmeester, October 10, 1991, pp. 5–6 (on file with the committee).

[204] Sworn statement of John Schoolmeester, November 6, 1991, p. 17 (on file with the committee).

[205] December 22, 1989, affidavit of William Hamilton, *INSLAW, Inc. v. Dick Thornburgh, et al.*, pp. 18–19.

[206] Sworn statement of Lois Battistoni, October 2, 1991, p. 54. See also numerous memoranda of interview on file with the committee.

[207] Memorandum of interview, February 14, 1992 (on file with the committee).

shredding provided by Ms. Battistoni, the issue stands open and calls for further investigation.

C. Other Important Questions Remain

1. THE DEATH OF DANIEL CASOLARO

On August 10, 1991, the lifeless body of Mr. Daniel Casolaro, an investigative reporter investigating the INSLAW matter, [208] was discovered in a hotel room in Martinsburg, WV. Mr. Casolaro's body was found in the bathtub with both of his wrists slashed several times. There was no sign of forced entry into the hotel room nor of a struggle. A short suicide note was found. Following a brief preliminary investigation by the local authorities, the death was ruled a suicide. [209] The investigation was reopened following numerous inquiries by Mr. Casolaro's brother and others into the suspicious circumstances surrounding his death. On January 25, 1992, after expending over 1,000 man-hours investigating his death, the local authorities again ruled Mr. Casolaro's death a suicide.

The committee did not include the death of Daniel Casolaro as part of its formal investigation of the INSLAW matter. Nevertheless, it is a fair statement to observe that the controversy surrounding the death continues to be discussed in the press and to other figures connected to the INSLAW litigation. These questions appear to be fostered by the suspicious circumstances surrounding his death and the criticism of in the Martinsburg Police Department's investigation. [210]

Other sources have been quoted in the media indicating that Mr. Casolaro did not commit suicide, and that his death was linked to his investigation of INSLAW, Bank of Credit and Commerce International (BCCI), and other matters such as the Iran/Contra af-

---

[208] Daniel Casolaro had indicated to a number of individuals that the INSLAW affair was part of a much deeper tangle of intrigues that he called the Octopus. They included the Iran-Contra arms deals and BCCI.

[209] Telephone interview of Sergeant Swartwood, Martinsburg, West Virginia Police, August 12, 1991. Sergeant Swartwood told committee investigators that Mr. Casolaro's death had been handled as a suicide and that the scene had not been protected.

[210] Elliot Richardson, a former Attorney General, now representing INSLAW, called for a Federal investigation of Mr. Casolaro's death:

"I believe he was murdered, but even if that is no more than a possibility, it is a possibility with such sinister implications as to demand a serious effort to discover the truth." [October 21, 1991, New York Times.]

In a memorandum to Department of Justice Special Counsel Judge Nicholas Bua, Mr. Richardson urges that further investigation of Mr. Casolaro's death is needed. Mr. Richardson stated that:

"During the 3 days preceding his [Mr. Casolaro] death he told four friends in the course of four different telephone conversations that he was about to go to West Virginia to meet someone from whom he was confident of receiving definitive proof of what had happened to the PROMIS software and to INSLAW. There is no apparent reason why Casolaro would have lied to those four friends, nor is there any apparent reason why his friends would deliberately and concertedly misrepresent what he said to him. It is not likely, on the other hand, that Casolaro had unrealistic expectations either toward the significance of the evidence he anticipated receiving or toward the prospect that it would be delivered. He had, after all, been on the INSLAW case for 1 year, and he was bound to know as well as any other of the investigative reporters then pursuing it that promises of hard evidence had often been made and just as often disappointed."

In the light of these facts, the key question is, with whom was Danny Casolaro expecting to meet and with whom did he meet? In our view the answer to that question should be relentlessly pursued.

[Elliot Richardson memorandum to Judge Bua, January 14, 1992, pp. 43–44 (on file with the committee).]

70

fair. [211] It has been reported that Mr. Casolaro had confided to several people that he was receiving death threats because he was getting close to concluding his investigation. Furthermore, he told family and friends not to believe that, if he died, it was by accident. According to his brother, Mr. Casolaro's investigation began to come together during the summer of 1991. Several people indicated he was upbeat and that on the weekend of August 10, 1991, he was in Martinsburg, WV, to receive significant information for his project from a source. [212]

Mr. Casolaro died on August 10, 1991, and his death was officially ruled a suicide on January 25, 1992, over 5 months later. The criticism of the investigation of Casolaro's death by the Martinsburg, WV, police center on the following areas: Prior to any coroners' investigation and before his family was notified, Mr. Casolaro's body was embalmed, which may have limited the effectiveness of autopsies or toxicological examinations. Some evidence has also surfaced indicating that immediately following the discovery of the body, the room was not sealed by the Martinsburg authorities, potentially allowing for the contamination of the possible crime scene. Additionally, it was reported that the room in which Mr. Casolaro was found was cleaned before a thorough criminal investigation could be conducted.

Information received from other sources reveal other curious circumstances surrounding Mr. Casolaro's death that may or may not have been considered by Martinsburg authorities. In a sworn statement to the committee, Richard Stavin (a former Department of Justice Organized Crime Strike Force prosecutor) stated:

> I received a call from Danny Casolaro approximately 1 week before he was found dead.... He spoke to me about INSLAW. He spoke to me about a group he called, the Octopus. I believe he mentioned Robert Nichols, and possibly also John Phillip Nichols, in this conversation, and was extremely interested, intrigued and frustrated in his inability to get a grasp on what he called the Octopus.
>
> He had indicated that he had met with—again I believe it was Robert Nichols on several occasions, that Robert Nichols was extremely talkative to a point, but when Mr. Casolaro would ask specific questions, he [Nichols] would become somewhat evasive. [213]

William Hamilton and Michael Riconosciuto both told committee investigators that Robert Booth Nichols was Danny Casolaro's primary source of information in his investigation into the theft of the

---

[211] Washington Post, January 27, 1992, p. B2.

[212] Telephone interview of Anthony Casolaro, M.D., August 12, 1991. Dr. Casolaro also told committee investigators that on August 5, 1991, Danny Casolaro said to him, "someone else told me I better back off the story." Dr. Casolaro also said that Olga Mokros, Danny Casolaro's housekeeper, received a phone call in which the caller said, "you're dead, you bastard." Olga also told Dr. Casolaro that following Danny Casolaro's death, she noticed that a stack of typed pages that usually sat on top of Danny Casolaro's desk was missing. Dr. Casolaro told the Washington Post (January 27, 1992, p. B2) that it was suspicious that none of Mr. Casolaro's investigative notes or papers were found in his car, hotel room, or at his home after his body was discovered. Mr. Casolaro's brother thought that this was suspicious because all throughout the time that Mr. Casolaro had been conducting his investigation, he always carried his notes with him. Mr. Casolaro's brother said:

"Somebody cleaned out his car and his room. If my brother did that, it seems as though [his papers] should have been found." Washington Post, January 27, 1992, p. B2.

[213] Sworn statement of Richard Stavin, March 13, 1992, pp. 23–24 (on file at committee).

71

PROMIS software system. In a later telephone interview, Mr. Nichols told committee investigators that he was acting as a sounding board for Mr. Casolaro and providing direction and insight for his investigation into the INSLAW matter.[214] Mr. Nichols would not provide a sworn statement to committee investigators.

In addition, the committee was informed by three separate individuals—Mr. Riconosciuto's attorney, a private investigator and a FBI agent—that a current FBI field agent, Thomas Gates, likely had information relating to Danny Casolaro's efforts to investigate the INSLAW matter. At the request of the committee, Director Sessions agreed to allow Special Agent Gates to provide the committee a sworn statement. Though Special Agent Gates' statement covered a broad range of subject matter areas, some speculative and some reflecting first person accounts, he indicated under oath that he had received several calls from Mr. Casolaro, beginning approximately 4 weeks before his death.[215]

Special Agent Gates stated that he was very suspicious about Mr. Casolaro's death for several reasons, including:

In his conversations with Casolaro, even days before the reporter's death, Gates had felt that Casolaro sounded very "upbeat" and not like a person contemplating suicide.

Mr. Casolaro had a phone book which contained his (Special Agent Gates') telephone number. Special Agent Gates said that the phone book had not been located during the police investigation.

The Martinsburg Police Department told him that the wounds to Mr. Casolaro's arms were "hacking" wounds. Special Agent Gates felt that the amount of injury to the arms of Mr. Casolaro were not consistent with injuries inflicted by an individual who had slit his own wrists. Special Agent Gates said he was told by Martinsburg Police investigators that:

> ...he [Mr. Casolaro] hacked his wrists...the wrists were cut, but they were cut almost in a slashing or hacking motion....

An open bottle of wine was allegedly found in the room, but the contents had not been tested at the time of Special Agent Gates' conversation with Martinsburg authorities.

Special Agent Gates said that he made his suspicions known to Martinsburg authorities, and that he called the local FBI office and suggested that they investigate because it was possibly related to criminal activity which falls within the jurisdiction of the FBI.[216]

In his sworn statement, Special Agent Gates concluded that:

> ...based upon my prior testimony concerning my contacts with Casolaro and also with the Captain of the Martinsburg Police Department, there is cause for suspicions to be raised....[217]

---

[214] Memorandum of interview with Robert Booth Nichols, January 21, 1992 (on file with the committee).
[215] Sworn statement of Special Agent Thomas Gates, March 25, 1992, p. 10 (on file with the committee).
[216] Interstate Transportation in Aid of Racketeering (ITAR). Sworn statement of Special Agent Thomas Gates, March 26, 1992, p. 56.
[217] Ibid., p. 61. It should be noted that throughout his deposition, Agent Gates repeatedly connected various strands of his conversations with Casolaro, as well as other aspects of the

Continued

72

2. POSSIBLE CONNECTION BETWEEN EARL BRIAN, MICHAEL RICONOSCIUTO, ROBERT BOOTH NICHOLS AND THE CABAZON INDIAN RESERVATION

Mr. Riconosciuto has alleged in a sworn statement to the committee[218] that Dr. Brian and Mr. Peter Videnieks secretly delivered INSLAW's PROMIS software to the Cabazon Indian Reservation, located in California, for "refitting" for use by intelligence agencies in the United States and abroad. Mr. Riconosciuto could not provide evidence other than his eyewitness account that Dr. Brian was involved in the PROMIS conversion at the reservation. Dr. Brian flatly contradicts Riconosciuto's claims in his own sworn statement to committee investigators.[219] In addition, in a sworn affidavit provided on April 2, 1991, in connection with the INSLAW bankruptcy case, Dr. Brian stated that he had never heard of, or was associated with, the so-called Wackenhut/Cabazon Indian joint venture, nor had he ever met, or had conversations with Peter Videnieks[220]—all in direct opposition to the Riconosciuto deposition as well as to certain law enforcement information on file at the committee.[221] In light of these disputed versions of events, the committee is not in a position to make findings of fact on Dr. Brian's role, but would strongly recommend that further investigation be given to ascertaining the role, if any, of Dr. Brian in INSLAW-related matters including, but not limited to, questions surrounding the Department of Justice's alleged conversion of the PROMIS software and its possible dissemination to other customers beyond the intended usage of the public domain version.[222]

INSLAW investigation, to a single individual, Robert Booth Nichols. In making certain statements, Gates acknowledged that Nichols had filed a law suit against him because of another crime investigation in which he participated which was centered in southern California. Nevertheless, Gates maintained that important and highly pertinent information regarding the past history of Nichols existed in sealed wiretap and confidential grand jury investigations which, by law, Agent Gates is prohibited to disclose in the absence of a subpoena. In this regard, the committee was provided by Richard Stavin with a 72-page affidavit submitted by Special Agent Gates to a Federal court which contained the results of a FBI wiretap on individuals in the entertainment industry suspected of having ties to organized crime. The committee takes no position on any of Gates' assertions or suppositions vis-a-vis Nichols, except to note again that they were duly sworn statements.

[218] Sworn statement of Michael Riconosciuto, April 4, 1991 (on file with the committee); see discussion supra, at pp. 99–102.

[219] Sworn statement of Earl Brian, September 20, 1990 (on file with the committee).

[220] April 2, 1991, affidavit of Earl Brian, *INSLAW, Inc.* v. *United States, et al.*, No. 85–0070, p. 2.

[221] Riverside County District Attorney's Office Special Operations Report, October 10, 1991, pp. 2–4 (on file with the committee).

[222] It should be noted that other information was received by the committee relating to whether Dr. Brian was involved with other individuals in various Wackenhut, Inc./Cabazon Indian Reservation business ventures in California during the early 1980's. While any degree of corroborating evidence on this point does not establish whether Dr. Brian was involved in INSLAW-related matters under investigation, it has been cited by others for the proposition that Dr. Brian, contrary to his sworn affidavit, had indeed heard of Wackenhut/Cabazon enterprise thus casting into doubt other assertions. According to a law enforcement police report on file with the committee, Dr. Brian together with Michael Riconosciuto, among others, attended a weapons demonstration at Lake Cauchilla gun range in Indio, CA, during the evening of September 10, 1981. See Riverside County District Attorney's Office Special Operations Report, October 10, 1991, pp. 2–4 (on file with the committee).

Further, in an article which appeared in the March 30, 1992, edition of the Washington Business Journal, Art Welmas, the former chairman of the Cabazon Tribe stated that Dr. Brian had been seen on the reservation and that his name was frequently mentioned by Mr. Riconosciuto and Dr. John Nichols the manager of the reservation's operations. "Brian must have been involved," Welmas said in the article. "His name was mentioned and discussed on a daily basis." See, Washington Business Journal, March 30, 1992.

Finally, there have been a number of speculative reports and fragmentary records purporting to link Robert Booth Nichols, through a company called Meridian Arms Corporation, and Michael Riconosciuto to certain covert intelligence activities, including a joint venture between the

73

V. ALLEGATIONS OF PERJURY, COVERUP, AND RETRIBUTION: A WEB OF CONTRADICTION AND DECEIT

The committee encountered numerous situations that pointed to a concerted effort by Department officials to manipulate the litigation of the INSLAW bankruptcy, as alleged by the president of INSLAW. For example, there were several possibly perjurious conflicts and contradictions among witnesses of the alleged Department attempt to convert INSLAW from a chapter 11 reorganization to a chapter 7 liquidation.[223] During this controversy, one key Department witness was harassed and, ultimately, fired because the Department decided, based on its own information, that the findings of the Bankruptcy Court were erroneous and the witness' information sharing to INSLAW was a dismissible offense.

On March 17, 1987, William Hamilton and his wife Nancy met with Anthony Pasciuto, then-Deputy Director of the Justice Department's Executive Office for U.S. Trustees (EOUST). Mr. Pasciuto provided them information obtained during a January 12, 1987, conversation with Judge Cornelius Blackshear, the U.S. Bankruptcy Court judge for the Southern District of New York.[224] This conversation led to an allegation that Thomas Stanton, the EOUST Director, sought to have INSLAW's bankruptcy status converted from a chapter 11 reorganization to a chapter 7 liquidation of the company's assets, allegedly through the help of Harry Jones,[225] the Assistant U.S. Trustee for the Southern District of New York and an expert in chapter 11 bankruptcy law.[226] According to Mr. Pasciuto, Judge Blackshear stated that Mr. Stanton had pressured Judge Blackshear to have Mr. Jones sent to Washington to take over the INSLAW case, and that Judge Blackshear didn't like it. During sworn testimony to committee investigators on June 4, 1991, Mr. Pasciuto stated that he attended a January 1987 luncheon meeting with Judge Blackshear, Judge Lawrence Pierce (a U.S. Circuit Court judge and a long time associate of Pasciuto), Mr. Pasciuto, Mr. Jones and Mr. Elliott Lombard (an acquaintance of Pasciuto's). Mr. Pasciuto stated that Judge Blackshear described Mr. Stanton's attempt to pressure him into sending Mr. Jones to work on the INSLAW bankruptcy, and that it was clear in his mind that Judge Blackshear implied that Mr. Stanton wanted INSLAW converted to chapter 7 status and needed Mr. Jones to accomplish this.[227]

Cabazon Indian Reservation and Wackenhut, Inc. The continuing intersection of the names of Michael Riconosciuto, Dr. Earl Brian, Robert Booth Nichols and the Cabazon Indian Reservation are certainly intriguing and curious "associations" but without the requisite degree of causation and factual convergence necessary to draw conclusions at this time into potential wrongdoing in the INSLAW matter.

[223] This allegation is key to INSLAW's claim that the Department attempted to put the company out of business and transfer its principal asset Enhanced PROMIS to Hadron, Inc., a company controlled by Dr. Earl Brian, former Attorney General Meese's friend and associate.

[224] Judge Blackshear was appointed to the bench in November 1985. Prior to this time he was the U.S. Trustee for the Southern District of New York.

[225] Mr. Jones, who has professed ignorance of a possible role in any attempt to convert the company to chapter 7 status, is now a bankruptcy judge.

[226] Sworn statement of Anthony Pasciuto before the House Committee on the Judiciary, June 4, 1991, pp. 18–20, 26–29, 47. Also, Proffer of Anthony Pasciuto provided to the Senate Permanent Subcommittee on Investigations, July 15, 1988, pp. 1–2.

[227] In a sworn statement with committee investigators on April 24, 1991, Mr. Stanton denied that he wanted INSLAW converted, but stated that he called Judge Blackshear to request Mr. Jones about handling the INSLAW bankruptcy because of his experience in bankruptcy cases.

Continued

74

Judge Jane Solomon, a New York City judge, told committee investigators that on March 18, 1987, Judge Blackshear provided her an identical story on the key points of INSLAW's conversion and the Jones transfer to Washington. According to Judge Solomon, Judge Blackshear stated that he had been asked by Mr. Stanton to assign Mr. Jones to the INSLAW case, and he refused without an Attorney General directive. Judge Blackshear also told Judge Solomon that Mr. William White, the U.S. Trustee for the Washington, DC, area, told him that Mr. Stanton pressured Mr. White to move in court to convert the INSLAW bankruptcy from chapter 11 to chapter 7 and steal the PROMIS software.[228] While she was willing to provide a limited and hostile interview to committee investigators, Judge Solomon refused to provide a sworn statement to the committee about Judge Blackshear's discussion with her on the INSLAW matter.

On March 23, 1987, Mr. William White provided his first deposition to INSLAW counsel. Mr. White stated that he received an inquiry from Stanton about the INSLAW case, and he reported back to EOUST on the case's status. Mr. White denied that he was ever directed to take any action regarding INSLAW by the EOUST or anyone else, including filing to convert. Mr. White did state that Judge Blackshear told him that Judge Blackshear's assistant, Harry Jones, was going to be detailed to Washington.[229] Mr. White was involved with the INSLAW case when the company filed a confidentiality motion with the Bankruptcy Court to protect certain proprietary information from public disclosure. INSLAW filed this motion because of allegations that confidential information was being provided to the Department by the EOUST. Mr. White stated that INSLAW's confidentiality motion raised the perception that his office was not independent and, because of this concern, White inserted language in the order that restricted Justice Department access to confidential INSLAW information to his immediate staff. Mr. White also believed this would preclude Mr. Harry Jones from having access to INSLAW materials if he were detailed to Washington.

On March 25, 1987, Judge Blackshear stated, under oath, to INSLAW counsel that Mr. White told him that Mr. Stanton pressured Mr. White to move in court to convert the INSLAW bankruptcy from chapter 11 to chapter 7. Judge Blackshear also stated that Mr. Stanton planned to have Harry Jones loaned to Washington to manage the INSLAW case and to arrange for INSLAW's conversion.[230] As previously indicated, Judge Blackshear spoke with

---

Mr. Stanton stated that, in his view, Judge White and his support staff were relatively inexperienced in bankruptcy matters and Mr. Stanton:

"...was afraid that our staff there was not up to a complex situation if a complex situation developed."

Mr. Stanton stated that Judge Blackshear informed him that he could not spare Mr. Jones from his New York duties, and Mr. Stanton stated the issue went no further.

[228] Staff study, dated September 1989, by the Permanent Subcommittee on Investigations, Senate Committee on Governmental Affairs, on Allegations Pertaining to the Department of Justice's Handling of a Contract with INSLAW, Inc., p. 29.

[229] Sworn statement of William C. White, *In re: INSLAW, Inc.*, Bankruptcy case No. 85–00070, March 23, 1987, pp. 16, 20–23.

[230] Sworn statement of the Honorable Cornelius Blackshear, *In re: INSLAW, Inc.*, Bankruptcy Case No. 85–00070, March 25, 1987, pp. 8–11. Mr. Stanton provided a sworn statement to INSLAW counsel and stated that he had asked Judge Cornelius Blackshear to detail his then First Assistant, Harry Jones to Washington to take over the management of the INSLAW case. Mr. Stanton further stated, however, that he never pressured, directed, or suggested to Mr.

75

Judge Solomon on March 18, providing her an identical story on the key points of INSLAW's conversion and the Jones transfer to Washington.

A. JUDGE BLACKSHEAR'S RECANTATION

Judge Blackshear stated that he called Mr. White immediately after he gave his deposition to INSLAW's attorneys to discuss his statement. At that point, according to Judge Blackshear, Mr. White told Judge Blackshear that he was mistaken because they never discussed converting INSLAW.[231] The next morning, Judge Blackshear's attorney—James Garrity, an assistant U.S. attorney—received a call from Dean Cooper, a trial attorney in the Department's Civil Division. According to Mr. Garrity, Mr. Cooper told him that Judge Blackshear's statement was wrong, and the Department wanted something undertaken (such as a letter) to correct the error. Mr. Garrity spoke with Judge Blackshear by telephone, and Judge Blackshear took the advice of his attorney and decided to correct his alleged errors.[232] It is highly questionable how the Department could ethically represent both itself and Judge Blackshear in the INSLAW litigation. In effect, the Department was a defendant in the case while one of its attorneys (Mr. Garrity) at the same time was representing a key witness (Judge Blackshear) for the plaintiff (INSLAW).

On March 26, 1987, Judge Blackshear submitted an affidavit to the court correcting his previous statement. In this affidavit Judge Blackshear stated that Mr. White never told him that Mr. Stanton was pressuring him to convert INSLAW to a chapter 7 bankruptcy, and that he had confused such an effort with Internal Revenue Service (IRS) pressure on Mr. White to convert United Press International (UPI) to a chapter 7.[233]

B. JUDGE BLACKSHEAR'S STATEMENT TO COMMITTEE LACKS CREDIBILITY

Judge Blackshear provided a sworn statement to committee investigators on January 25, 1991. In contrast to Mr. Stanton's assertion that he contacted Judge Blackshear directly about Mr. Jones,

---

White or anyone else that INSLAW be converted. Sworn statement of Thomas J. Stanton, *In re: INSLAW, Inc.,* Bankruptcy Case No. 85–00070, pp. 26–33.

[231] Record of FBI interview of Cornelius Blackshear, November 10, 1988, p. 3.

[232] Record of FBI interview of James Garrity, assistant U.S. attorney, dated October 26, 1988, p. 2.

[233] In an interview with committee investigators on March 27, 1992, Judge Martin S. Teel, Judge Bason's replacement, said that, prior to his appointment as bankruptcy judge in February 1988, he was the Assistant Chief of the Department's Tax Division. At that time, he supervised the tax portion of both the UPI and INSLAW matter for the Department. Judge Teel refused to provide a sworn statement about his activities with the Tax Division.

Judge Teel said the decision to ask the court to convert INSLAW's bankruptcy status from chapter 11 to chapter 7 in 1987 originated with the IRS—not the Department—and had nothing to do with the Department's conflict over the INSLAW contract. Judge Teel said that, by statute, the Department of Justice is responsible for representing the IRS in tax cases. Judge Teel said that the Department of Justice cannot initiate tax litigation but can only act in response to requests from its client (IRS). Judge Teel said, however, that on occasion, there can be a "backwards flow" in which the Department suggests to the IRS to request filing a conversion but added that this (INSLAW) wasn't one of those times. When asked if there was a conflict of interest when one part of the Department was being sued, and another part of the Department was suing the same business, Judge Teel responded, that it was the policy of the Tax Division to administer tax laws equally. Judge Teel said that no one is insulated from the U.S. Tax Laws and that if INSLAW believed that they were insulated from tax laws they were mistaken. Judge Teel refused to provide a sworn statement on this matter.

76

Judge Blackshear stated that the information he provided in his prior depositions was not based on personal knowledge but on hearsay information provided by other sources.[234] Judge Blackshear attributed much of this information to Mr. Pasciuto, and he stated that he first became aware of the INSLAW case when Mr. Pasciuto told him that Mr. Stanton was attempting to have Mr. Jones assigned to the case.[235]

Judge Blackshear stated that he informed Judge Solomon that he had heard that the Department was attempting to get INSLAW converted and that he gave her most of the information he provided during his March 25, 1987, deposition. He also confirmed that he gave similar information to INSLAW attorneys on separate occasions prior to his March 25 deposition.[236] Judge Blackshear stated that he obtained his ideas about INSLAW from Mr. Pasciuto and the story changed because:

> At the time I was telling the story before the recantation, in my mind, that's the way it had occurred. My mind changed after having talked to Bill White. But my statement [the recantation] did not change the facts of the matter, but just basically changed as to the fact that Bill White did not tell me that. Now I remember that it was Tony Pasciuto that told me those things.[237]

Judge Blackshear stated that he never discussed the INSLAW conversion issue with Mr. White. Judge Blackshear stated, however, that Mr. White discussed with Judge Blackshear how Mr. Stanton attempted to interfere in U.S. Trustee operations managed by Mr. White and several other U.S. Trustees. Judge Blackshear also stated that he had heard that Mr. Stanton had reduced funding for certain U.S. Trustees, but he could not specifically identify the situations or trustees involved.[238]

Judge Blackshear could not explain to committee staff why Mr. White contends that he did not discuss the UPI bankruptcy case with him. Judge Blackshear could not recall who brought up the UPI issue when he contacted Mr. White after the March 25 deposition. He was also confused as to the general timeframe when Mr. White supposedly described the UPI bankruptcy case to him. Judge Blackshear said, however, he was certain that he used UPI as an

---

[234] In a sworn statement provided to committee investigators on April 24, 1991, Mr. Stanton contradicted Judge Blackshear's description of events. Mr. Stanton stated that he called Judge Blackshear to request Harry Jones handling the INSLAW bankruptcy because of his experience in bankruptcy cases. Mr. Stanton stated that, in his view, Mr. White and his support staff were relatively inexperienced in bankruptcy matters and Mr. Stanton:

"...was afraid that our staff there was not up to a complex situation if a complex situation developed."

Mr. Stanton stated that Judge Blackshear informed him that he could not spare Mr. Jones from his New York duties, and Mr. Stanton stated the issue went no further. Mr. Stanton stated that he spoke with Mr. White once about the INSLAW bankruptcy and this involved a request for INSLAW's bankruptcy petitions and schedules. Mr. Stanton stated that he had no conversations with Mr. White or Mr. Brewer regarding conversion of INSLAW from chapter 11 to chapter 7.

Mr. Stanton stated that he could not explain the discrepancy between his recollection about the Jones detail and what Judge Blackshear indicated in his sworn statements. Mr. Stanton maintained that he specifically talked to Judge Blackshear about assigning Mr. Jones to work on the case.

[235] Sworn statement of Judge Cornelius Blackshear, January 25, 1991, pp. 2, 59–60, 69–73, 86–88.

[236] Ibid., pp. 50–51.

[237] Ibid., p. 157.

[238] Ibid., pp. 73–76.

77

example at the ABA [American Bar Association] conference and on several other occasions (although he could not specifically recall these other occasions).[239] Judge Blackshear, in discussing the PSI findings[240] regarding Judge Blackshear's "implausible" statements, told committee investigators:

> ...my statement concerning INSLAW was probably consistent with Tony's [Pasciuto] because Tony advised me as to what was going on with INSLAW. As far as the statement concerning the UPI case, all I can say is that I was told that by Bill White. It may have come up at the ABA meeting, and it may have been informal as opposed to [being] formally on the record.[241]

Judge Blackshear stated under oath to committee investigators that Mr. White became extremely upset when Judge Blackshear described what he had said about converting INSLAW. Mr. White responded that they never had a conversation about an INSLAW conversion and told Judge Blackshear that his (White's) deposition indicated that Mr. Stanton never pressured him to convert INSLAW. Mr. White then asked Judge Blackshear to remember when they discussed INSLAW, and Judge Blackshear could not pinpoint such a conversation. It was at this point that Judge Blackshear says he recalled some discussions with Mr. White about the UPI case and, with Mr. White's prompting, decided that he had confused INSLAW with UPI.[242]

Judge Blackshear also indicated to committee investigators that the opposing statements raised difficult questions in his mind about whether his story would be perceived as more credible than Mr. White's in court. The judge stated:

> ...I knew that if we had to go to court, and he [Mr. White] was saying that Tom Stanton did not pressure him, and I was saying that he told me that he did, that it would become a credibility question. They would probably give my story more credibility than his. I did not wish to put it at a place where they would be judging our credibility and taking mine over his.[243]

C. COMMITTEE ANALYSIS OF ATTEMPT TO ASSIGN HARRY JONES TO THE INSLAW CASE

Numerous witnesses involved in the Jones reassignment issue provided conflicting sworn statements; however, Judge Blackshear is clearly at odds with everyone on this allegation. Judge Blackshear maintains that (1) Mr. White had contacted him to advise that Mr. Stanton was going to ask that Mr. Jones be sent to Washington, (2) he spoke only with Mr. White and Mr. Jones and (3) he never talked to Mr. Stanton about the Jones issue. Judge

---

[239] Ibid., pp. 109–120.
[240] PSI staff found Blackshear's recantation to be "implausible" and inconsistent with their investigative findings. For example, the staff determined that Blackshear provided information on four separate occasions that was consistent with the story Pasciuto told the Hamiltons at their breakfast meeting; furthermore, facts the staff uncovered did not support Blackshear's recantation statements that he confused INSLAW with UPI.
[241] Sworn statement of Cornelius Blackshear, op cit., p. 156.
[242] Ibid., pp. 106–109.
[243] Ibid., pp. 78–79.

78

Blackshear stated that he told Mr. Jones that if he were contacted regarding an assignment to the Washington office for handling INSLAW, he was to decline and refer the matter to Judge Blackshear.

In contrast to Judge Blackshear's statements, Mr. Stanton stated under oath that he called Judge Blackshear regarding the Jones detail, and he is sure that he told Judge Blackshear why he wanted Mr. Jones assigned. Also, Mr. White stated that Judge Blackshear called him about Mr. Stanton's request, and he had no knowledge of this request before his discussion with Judge Blackshear. Mr. White stated that Judge Blackshear told him that the call had been made by Mr. Stanton directly to Mr. Jones, which would fit Judge Blackshear's pattern of denying any firsthand knowledge of INSLAW matters.

In contrast to Judge Blackshear's and Mr. White's statements, Mr. Jones claims in his sworn statements that *he could not recall any discussions regarding his possible assignment to the INSLAW case.* Mr. Jones denies having been contacted by either Mr. Stanton, Judge Blackshear or Mr. White regarding an assignment to the INSLAW case, or being aware that such a request had been made. Judge Solomon also provided a recollection that indicates that Judge Blackshear was contacted by Mr. Stanton to request Mr. Jones. However, as mentioned earlier, she has refused to provide a statement under oath.

D. Bason Allegations Against Blackshear Not Adequately Considered

Bankruptcy Judge Bason ruled that he believed INSLAW's witnesses had told the truth, while the Department's witnesses had not. The judge thought that the witnesses' stories ranged from intentionally lying to failure of recollection. According to Judge Bason, Judge Blackshear in particular had conducted himself in a way that called for strong action. On January 2, 1991, Judge Bason filed a complaint to the Judicial Council of the Second Circuit U.S. Court of Appeals against Judge Blackshear. In the statement of facts accompanying the complaint, the judge stated that:[244]

> I have now regretfully concluded that Judge Blackshear recanted not because of an honest mistake but because he made a conscious choice to testify falsely....
> Nor can I now escape the conclusion that Judge Blackshear attempted by his deliberately false testimony to prejudice and obstruct the administration of justice in the INSLAW bankruptcy-court proceeding.[245]

Judge Bason added in his complaint that:

> As the presiding trial judge in INSLAW I was outraged at Department of Justice employees' attempts to obstruct justice by deliberately giving false testimony. That this

---

[244] On October 24, 1991, at the request of the committee, Judge Bason provided a copy of his complaint.
[245] Judicial Council of the Second Circuit, Complaint Against Judicial Officer Under 28 U.S.C. 372 (c), filed by George F. Bason, Jr., former U.S. bankruptcy judge for the District of Columbia, Statement of Facts, pp. 1–2.

79

charge can now legitimately be made against a sitting judge is even more disturbing.[246]

Unfortunately, there was no meaningful investigation of Bason's allegations. The Judicial Council of the Second Circuit appointed a special committee consisting of several judges to consider Judge Bason's allegation and provide a comprehensive written report. However, both groups refused to address Judge Bason's complaint because Judge Blackshear's alleged perjury dealt with matters outside of his judicial activities. On that basis Judge Bason's complaint was dismissed in its entirety on October 3, 1991.

Mr. Pasciuto's Firing: Mr. Anthony Pasciuto was the Deputy Director for Administration in the Justice Department's Executive Office for U.S. Trustees. As discussed previously, prior to the bankruptcy trial, Mr. Pasciuto told the Hamiltons at a March 17, 1987, breakfast meeting that Judge Blackshear had told him that Mr. Stanton had pressured Mr. White to convert INSLAW to chapter 7 liquidation, and had retaliated against Mr. White for refusing to do so. However, under strong pressure from senior Department officials, Mr. Pasciuto recanted his statement at the trial to say that neither Mr. White, Judge Blackshear nor anyone else from the Department had told him that Mr. Stanton had pressured Mr. White to convert the case to a chapter 7.[247]

In a March 17, 1988, letter, Mr. Pasciuto's attorney asserted that what Mr. Pasciuto had told the Hamiltons was true. The attorney stated that Mr. Pasciuto had backed away from his original statements at the trial because Judge Blackshear and Mr. White would not acknowledge the truth and because Mr. Stanton was putting pressure on Mr. Pasciuto to cooperate if he wanted to receive his appointment as an Assistant U.S. Trustee.

Mr. Pasciuto's sworn statement to committee investigators on June 4, 1991, was consistent with his previous statements to the Hamiltons. Mr. Pasciuto stated that at the January 1987 luncheon meeting, Judge Blackshear described Mr. Stanton's attempt to pressure him into sending Mr. Jones to work on the INSLAW bankruptcy, and that Judge Blackshear definitely implied that Mr. Stanton wanted INSLAW converted to chapter 7 status and needed Mr. Jones to accomplish this.[248] Mr. Pasciuto also told committee investigators under oath that, prior to the January luncheon meeting, Mr. White told him Mr. Stanton was putting pressure on him regarding the INSLAW bankruptcy.

Mr. Pasciuto stated that he believed that the process to approve his Albany, NY, appointment was manipulated to influence his statement at the bankruptcy trial.[249] He cited as support his ap-

---

[246] Ibid., pp. 4–5.
[247] Letter from Gary Howard Simpson, Pasciuto's attorney, to Mr. Arnold I. Burns, Deputy Attorney General, Department of Justice, March 17, 1988.
[248] Sworn statement of Anthony Pasciuto, June 4, 1991, pp. 18–20, 26–29.
[249] Mr. Stanton stated under oath that he recommended Mr. Pasciuto for the Assistant Trustee position in Albany, NY. The Deputy Attorney General, Arnold Burns, was required to sign as the approving official. Mr. Stanton, however, stated that, after Mr. Pasciuto provided his statement, the appointment paperwork was returned to Mr. Stanton, unsigned, from Mr. Burns' office with no explanation. Mr. Stanton claims he never received an explanation from Mr. Burns about why Mr. Pasciuto's appointment was not approved. However, he inferred that discrepancies between Mr. Pasciuto's depositions and his statement at the June 1987 bankruptcy trial

Continued

pointment which was held up for months but was signed by Mr. Stanton and given to him 2 days before he was to testify. It was then made clear to him that Mr. Burns would have final approval of his appointment; however, after Mr. Pasciuto provided his statement, Mr. Burns did not provide this approval and Mr. Pasciuto was eventually forced out of the Department as a result of an OPR investigation.[250]

Mr. Pasciuto now regrets being coerced by the Department into recanting his original statements to the Hamiltons, and has stated under oath to committee investigators that he stands by his original statements made to the Hamiltons that Judge Blackshear had informed him that the Department wanted to force INSLAW out of business.

OPR Investigation of Mr. Pasciuto: In July 1987, the Department's Office of Professional Responsibility (OPR) received a referral from Deputy Attorney General Arnold Burns to begin an investigation into allegations of misconduct by Anthony Pasciuto, then Deputy Director of the EOUST. On December 18, 1987, OPR, based on its inquiry, recommended that Mr. Pasciuto be terminated from his position in the Department.[251]

On January 20, 1988, Boykin Rose, the Associate Deputy Attorney General, sent a notice to Mr. Pasciuto proposing his removal from the Department. On March 17, 1988, Mr. Pasciuto's attorney wrote to the Department on Mr. Pasciuto's behalf, reaffirming Mr. Pasciuto's allegations to the Hamiltons about the Jones transfer and INSLAW conversion.[252] On March 23, 1988, Mr. Pasciuto's attorney also provided an oral reply to Mr. Pasciuto's proposed termination.[253] After the brief oral hearing, the Department position remained unchanged, and Mr. Pasciuto, who was actively looking for alternative employment, agreed to leave the Department on April 1, 1988.[254]

The Department fired Mr. Pasciuto based on its internal analyses and conclusions drawn from evidence presented in the INSLAW litigation. Significantly, the Department ignored evidence that may have resulted in a less harsh course of action. OPR unilaterally concluded that:

> Based on the interviews during our inquiry, and on our review of the Civil Division's June 18 memorandum addressing the June 12 ruling, we conclude that the bankruptcy court's remarks were unsubstantiated and unfair. Although the blame for this injudicious result appears to rest squarely on the court's shoulders, it is clear that the environment for his ruling was created largely because of

---

may have been factors in the decision to decline Mr. Pasciuto's appointment. Sworn statement of Thomas Stanton, April 24, 1991.

[250] Sworn statement of Anthony Pasciuto, op. cit. pp. 4–69.

[251] Memorandum from the Office of Professional Responsibility to the Deputy Attorney General regarding allegations of misconduct by Anthony Pasciuto, dated December 18, 1987, p. 9.

[252] Letter from Gary Howard Simpson to Arnold Burns, Deputy Attorney General in response to the Department's termination notice to Anthony Pasciuto.

[253] Department officials attending the oral reply proceedings included Deputy Attorney General Burns and two officials from the Justice Management Division.

[254] Settlement agreement and mutual release between the Department and Mr. Pasciuto. Mr. Pasciuto's attorney, Gary Simpson, in an oral reply to the Department stated that he would advise Mr. Pasciuto that he ought not to remain employed by the Department and that Mr. Pasciuto would best be served by going to work elsewhere.

81

Pasciuto's own totally irresponsible statements and actions. [255]

OPR came much closer to describing the real basis for Mr. Pasciuto's termination when it concluded that:

> In our view, but for Mr. Pasciuto's highly irresponsible actions, the department would be in a much better litigation posture than it presently finds itself. Mr. Pasciuto has wholly failed to comport himself in accordance with the standard of conduct expected of an official of his position. [256]

The Department's conclusion that Mr. Pasciuto's statements on the INSLAW case, which he believed to be accurate, were "irresponsible" because it hurt the litigation posture of the Department is highly questionable. [257] Mr. Pasciuto's statements held considerable credibility with the court. Further, there is significant evidence indicating that Mr. Pasciuto was telling the truth when he told the Hamiltons about a high level effort within the Department to force INSLAW into chapter 7 liquidation. This is particularly evident given the contradictory statements made under oath by Judge Blackshear and other key witnesses regarding this matter. Unfortunately, the Department decided to fire Mr. Pasciuto rather than conduct an independent investigation of the matter.

Mr. Pasciuto's firing undoubtedly sent a chilling message to Justice employees that the Department reserved the right to ignore court rulings and arrive at its own conclusions about the credibility of witnesses' statements. Further, it was apparent from this case that the Department planned to administer the harshest possible punishment to those it perceived were disloyal while it conveniently overlooked inconsistent and possibly perjurious statements made by witnesses that supported the Department's position. As stated during the oral hearing, Mr. Pasciuto's attorney, who had considerable expertise in personnel law, concluded that:

> ...I could certainly understand a reprimand for what he did specifically. That would be comprehendible [sic]; that would be in some way humanly understandable....I would understand that in a way that I would not understand a

---

[255] Memorandum from the Department's Office of Professional Responsibility to the Deputy Attorney General regarding allegations of misconduct by Anthony Pasciuto, dated December 18, 1987, p. 8.

[256] Ibid., p. 9.

[257] On February 26, 1988, INSLAW filed a complaint with the Department's Public Integrity Section (PIS), alleging that Judge Blackshear and Trustee White had committed perjury. On May 2, 1988, Acting Assistant Attorney General John C. Keeney, of the Department's Criminal Division, requested that the FBI open a criminal investigation into allegations of perjury by Judge Blackshear and Trustee White.

The FBI investigation included statements from Mr. White, Judge Blackshear, Mr. Stanton and Mr. Jones. The FBI decided to limit the scope of its investigation because supposedly there were no witnesses with firsthand knowledge to refute the sworn statements of these witnesses.

The FBI concluded that the description of events by Judge Blackshear, Mr. White, and Mr. Stanton were consistent in every important respect, and that it could not use the information suggested by INSLAW to prosecute any persons for perjury.

The FBI, however, felt that it was possible that it could prove that Mr. Pasciuto perjured himself, relying on the statements of Mr. White, Mr. Stanton and Judge Blackshear. The Department decided not to pursue Mr. Pasciuto because:

"...Pasciuto seems to have been punished adequately for his role in this case. He lost his job and endangered his career."

82

removal. I think the removal is punitive... I cannot understand somebody firing Mr. Pasciuto for this. [258]

Fundamentally, the Department held Mr. Pasciuto very accountable for his discussion with the Hamiltons—which was corroborated by other witnesses, including Judge Blackshear—while Judge Blackshear was excused for making identical statements to Judge Solomon and, under oath, to INSLAW attorneys. The Department concluded that no perjury charge could be brought against Judge Blackshear and Mr. White because it could not find evidence that their statements were false. [259]

VI. THE DEPARTMENT HAS PROVEN TO BE INCAPABLE OF A FORTHRIGHT INVESTIGATION OF THE INSLAW MATTER

Several requests were made to the Department to investigate the INSLAW matter. However, the Department focused its investigations on defending its supporters and either ignoring or attacking whistleblowers. Further, the Department's review of the need for an independent counsel investigation appears to have been deliberately shallow, which allowed the Department to conclude that it lacked sufficient evidence to warrant even a preliminary investigation of wrongdoing by the Department officials.

The Department also did little to resolve numerous conflicts and contradictions that arose during INSLAW's investigation of an alleged Department effort to liquidate INSLAW. A more thorough study would have revealed a troubling pattern of incomplete, contradictory, and possibly perjured testimony of key Government witnesses. A more indepth investigation of Department witness statements is clearly warranted to determine who lied and who told the truth. Also, in a show of extraordinary force, the Department fired an employee who merely relayed information to the Hamiltons from what should have been a highly credible source. This action no doubt had a chilling effect on other potential Department witnesses.

A. JENSEN FAILED TO ADEQUATELY INVESTIGATE INSLAW'S CONCERNS

On March 13, 1985, Elliot Richardson and Donald Santarelli, the former Administrator of LEAA, met with Acting Deputy Attorney General D. Lowell Jensen and requested that: (1) He authorize immediate, fair, and expedited negotiations between the Department and INSLAW to resolve the disputes that caused the withholding of moneys and INSLAW's bankruptcy, (2) the Department give immediate consideration to a new INSLAW proposal, and (3) he appoint someone to investigate INSLAW's repeated assertions that

---

[258] Written proceedings of the Oral Reply to Proposed Removal Action in the Matter of Anthony Pasciuto, Deputy Director for Administration, EOUST, dated March 23, 1988.

[259] "To be sure, the United States need not prove motive to make out a perjury case. The United States must, however, present a jury with a realistic fact situation in order to have any chance to convince a jury that the defendant lied. While INSLAW may have convinced Judge Bason that the truth was completely diametrical to the testimony, I believe it highly unlikely we could ever convince a rational jury of this beyond a reasonable doubt." [Memorandum from David Green, Trail Attorney, Public Integrity Section to Gerald McDowell, Chief, Public Integrity Section, June 14, 1989, p. 18.]

83

Department officials—particularly C. Madison Brewer—were biased against INSLAW.[260]

Judge Jensen stated in a June 1987 deposition that he appointed Jay Stephens, a Deputy Associate Attorney General, to conduct an investigation of the bias allegations, and he recalled discussing the results of Mr. Stephens' review. He added that, based on Mr. Stephens' investigation, he did not consider that an investigation by OPR was warranted. Judge Jensen stated that he wanted to be sure that the Department's actions were not driven by personal considerations or bias but were based on the merits of INSLAW's concerns. On the point of Mr. Brewer's alleged bias, Judge Jensen stated that:

> I would think that the better path of wisdom is not to [hire an alleged fired employee to monitor the contract of his former employer] do that if that's possible to do....I think that it's better to have these kinds of issues undertaken by people who...don't have questions raised...whether they are not biased in favor of or against the people they deal with.[261]

However, Judge Jensen concluded that, based on Mr. Stephens' investigation, he was satisfied that decisions were made on their merits and were justified, and Department officials did not intend any personal animosity.[262] It is also interesting, in light of Mr. Meese's denials that he was ever involved in the details of the INSLAW matter,[263] that Judge Jensen stated that:

> I have had conversations with the Attorney General [Meese] about the whole INSLAW matter...as to what had taken place in the PROMIS development and what had taken place with the contract and what decisions had been made by the department with reference to that.[264]

Mr. Stephens stated under oath that, in March 1985, Judge Jensen handed him an INSLAW proposal[265] and asked him to check out INSLAW's proposal for new business and determine if there was anything the Department could do with it. Mr. Stephens stated under oath in direct contradiction of Judge Jensen's statement that he was never asked to investigate the bias issue.[266]

Mr. Stephens stated that, after Judge Jensen asked him to review the INSLAW new business proposal, he received several telephone calls from both Charles Work and Elliot Richardson, who are attorneys for INSLAW. He felt that they were lobbying the Department very hard because they believed that INSLAW had some special relationship with the Department. He added that they attempted to convey that based on a longstanding relationship be-

[260] Deposition of Judge D. Lowell Jensen, June 19, 1987, pp. 23–25.
[261] Ibid., p. 34.
[262] Ibid.
[263] Meese stated in his interview with this committee that he could not recall any discussions with Jensen about office automation or case tracking at the Department; he stated that if he did, it would have been casual conversation. Interview of Edwin Meese III, July 12, 1990, p. 23.
[264] Deposition of Lowell Jense, op. cit., pp. 35–36.
[265] INSLAW submitted a proposal suggesting an approach for implementing PROMIS in the smaller U.S. attorneys' offices, since the Department terminated INSLAW's involvement in the word processing portion of the contract.
[266] Sworn statement of Jay Stephens, July 12, 1991, pp. 14–17, 42.

84

tween the Department and INSLAW, the Department should look favorably on INSLAW's new business proposal. [267]

Mr. Stephens stated he reported to Judge Jensen that the need for INSLAW's business proposal was questionable and that it was the Department's position that INSLAW's new business proposal could be done in-house. Judge Jensen informed Mr. Richardson by letter stating that the Department reviewed the proposal but it didn't have an immediate need and would not act on the proposal. [268]

Because the Department did not adequately investigate INSLAW's allegations, the company was forced into expensive, time-consuming litigation as the only means by which the Department's misappropriation of INSLAW's Enhanced PROMIS could be exposed. During an interview with the committee, Judge Jensen was asked if he agreed with Judge Bason's ruling pertaining to allegations of bias by the Department (which the Hamiltons claim is an indication of misbehavior by the Department). Judge Jensen stated that just because the Judge [Bason] made a ruling, he didn't automatically agree that the allegations of bias were correct; however, the decision does raise concerns that there may have been more bias toward INSLAW than he was aware of. [269] The Bankruptcy Court found that he "had a previously developed negative attitude about PROMIS and INSLAW" from the beginning (Finding No. 307–309) because he had been associated with the development of a rival case management system while he was a district attorney in California, and that this affected his judgment throughout his oversight of the contract.

B. OPR's INSLAW INVESTIGATIONS ARE DEFICIENT

As early as June 1986, OPR [270] was aware of the allegations of bias by senior Department officials—including then Deputy Attorney General Jensen. These allegations included a claim that Judge Jensen had encouraged INSLAW's bankruptcy and disliked PROMIS. [271] In spite of a number of inquiries from Congress and the issue being raised in both Judge Jensen's and Mr. Arnold Burns' 1986 confirmation hearings, OPR did not begin to investigate the matter until November 1987. [272]

---

[267] Ibid., pp. 12–14–16–17.
[268] Ibid., pp. 21–33.
[269] Jensen interview with committee investigators, dated April 1990.
[270] OPR reports directly to the Attorney General and is responsible for investigating allegations of criminal or ethical misconduct by employees of the Justice Department. OPR's role is to ensure that Department employees continue to perform their duties in accordance with the high professional standards expected of the Nation's principal law enforcement agency. Source: U.S. Government Manual for 1989/90, p. 375.
[271] On June 16, 1986, OPR received a letter from Laurie A Westly, chief counsel to Senator Paul Simon, asking OPR's view of allegations made by INSLAW against the Department, specifically Lowell Jensen, then nominee to the U.S. District Court. Ms. Westly referred to the litigation initiated by INSLAW on June 10, 1986, specifically the claim that Jensen contributed to the bankruptcy of INSLAW and had a negative bias toward INSLAW's software. In addition, she asked whether Jensen had breached any ethical or legal responsibility as a Department employee. Jensen was confirmed by the Senate as a U.S. District Court Judge on June 24, 1986.
[272] On October 14, 1987, Deputy Attorney General Arnold Burns requested that OPR "conduct a complete and thorough investigation into the allegation of bias and misconduct by various Justice Department officials against INSLAW." This referral was based on the allegations raised by the Bankruptcy Court ruling in the INSLAW case. On November 10, 1987, OPR notified Burns that it would proceed with the investigation of his referral. Source: March 31, 1989, Report of the Investigation by OPR in the INSLAW Matter.

85

Ironically, in 1986 OPR delayed investigating the INSLAW bias issue because it planned to rely on the judgment of the Bankruptcy Court.[273] Robert Lyons, acting counsel for OPR, stated that the bias allegation was not an issue OPR would normally review and that it would be more appropriate for the Bankruptcy Court to resolve the issue.[274] OPR changed its position after the Bankruptcy Court concluded that there was serious bias up to Judge Jensen's level. During its investigation OPR chose to ignore the court's findings and conclusions that there was bias against INSLAW at the Department. Instead, OPR stated in its March 31, 1989, report that it agreed with the Department's brief on appeal to the District Court that:

> The bankruptcy court's credibility determinations are unbalanced, inexplicably savage, and based on unreasonable inferences. They amount to nothing more than...attacks on virtually every person who testified for DOJ....

OPR concluded that the court's findings of misconduct on the part of specified Department employees, and of the Department generally, were wholly erroneous. Instead of investigating the possibility of Department collusion to misrepresent witnesses' sworn statements, OPR attacked the Bankruptcy Court position concluding that it mistrusted the Department's witnesses.[275] OPR concluded in its report that:

> ...based on our review of the record, this finding, [of the Bankruptcy Court] and the subsidiary findings on which it is based, are clearly erroneous.[276]

OPR also concluded that the allegations of misconduct on the part of Mr. Meese, Judge Jensen, and Mr. Burns were unsubstantiated. OPR limited its investigation to the allegations of misconduct and, incredibly, it excluded any consideration of the merits of the contract disputes (such as the data rights issue and possible misappropriation of the PROMIS software).[277] Although it did not investigate such issues, OPR gratuitously stated that:

> There is no credible evidence that the Department took, or stole INSLAW's Enhanced PROMIS by trickery, fraud and deceit. Additionally, we have found no credible evidence that there existed in the Department a plot to move to convert INSLAW's Chapter 11 bankruptcy to one under Chapter 7 of the Bankruptcy Code.[278]

District Judge Bryant's November 22, 1989, memorandum in favor of INSLAW contradicted the conclusions reached by OPR. Judge Bryant stated that Judge Bason's record was clear and that:

[273] OPR conducted an initial review of the bias issues in 1986 and concluded that there was no misconduct by Judge Jensen. Source: March 31, 1989, Report of the Investigation by OPR in the INSLAW matter, p. 7.
[274] Interview of Robert Lyon, acting counsel OPR and David Bobzien, assistant counsel OPR with committee investigators, dated May 18, 1990.
[275] March 31, 1989, Report of the Investigation by the Office of Professional Responsibility in the INSLAW Matter, pp. 63–64.
[276] Ibid., p. 48.
[277] May 18, 1990, interview of Robert Lyons and David Bobzien, OPR.
[278] March 31, 1989, Report of the Investigation by the Office of Professional Responsibility in the INSLAW Matter, pp. 89–91.

86

...the Department violated the automatic stay when it claimed Enhanced PROMIS to be its property and installed it in at least 45 offices throughout the United States. [279]

Even Department management recognized that the Enhanced version of PROMIS was INSLAW's property. Mr. Burns stated in his OPR deposition that the Department's attorneys involved in the INSLAW case were (sometime in 1986):

...satisfied that INSLAW could sustain the [data rights] claim in court, that we had waived those rights.... [280]

Committee investigators were informed that Michael Shaheen and Richard M. Rogers, Counsel and Deputy Counsel for OPR, respectively, recused themselves from the INSLAW investigation because of their association with Deputy Attorney General Burns, who was named in the allegations. [281] However, Mr. Rogers was present during a sworn statement provided by then-Attorney General Meese, which contradicts his claim that he had recused himself from the investigation.

C. GAO STUDY OF THE OFFICE OF PROFESSIONAL RESPONSIBILITY

The type of problems the committee found with OPR's investigation of the INSLAW matter were illustrated in a 1992 GAO study of the Office. GAO reviewed OPR's operations, [282] and several of its findings paralleled the one-dimensional nature of the OPR investigation of INSLAW. GAO found that:

OPR operated informally, did not routinely document key aspects of its investigations, and provided little background information in its case documentation.

OPR generally did not record the complete scope of and rationale behind the investigations or of the decisions reached in the course of the investigations.

OPR's conclusions that allegations were or were not substantiated were generally not explained.

In many instances, OPR did not pursue all available avenues of inquiry.

OPR counsel relied on the attorney's judgment and informal consulting among attorneys within OPR as the basis for making decisions and reaching conclusions about specific investigations. [283]

GAO concluded that OPR's informal approach to investigations, the limited scope of many of its investigations, and the minimal documentation contained in its files expose it and the Department to a range of risks, including: [284]

---

[279] November 22, 1989, memorandum on appeal before Judge Bryant, U.S. District Court for the District of Columbia, p. 38.

[280] March 30, 1988, interview of Deputy Attorney General Arnold Burns by OPR, p.12.

[281] May 18, 1990, interview of Robert Lyons and David Bobzien, OPR.

[282] "Employee Misconduct: Justice Should Clearly Document Investigative Actions," Report to the chairman, Government Information, Justice, and Agriculture Subcommittee on Government Operations, House of Representatives, GAO/GGD–92–31, dated February 7, 1992.

[283] Ibid.

[284] Ibid.

87

If OPR's informality were to lead it to conclude an investigation prematurely, the integrity of the Department could be compromised.

If asked to defend an investigation against a charge that it was not aggressively pursued, OPR probably would not have sufficient documentation to defend its efforts. A review of the quality of an investigation based on the documentation would yield little information.

GAO recommended, among other matters, that OPR:

Establish basic standards for conducting its investigations, which could be obtained from other Department components.

Establish case documentation standards.

Follow up more consistently on the results of misconduct investigations done by other units and what disciplinary actions, if any, were taken as a result of all misconduct investigations.

The Department, INSLAW and others would have been better served had OPR conducted a full and complete investigation of the INSLAW bias allegations rather than the cursory review it conducted. Instead, OPR chose to attack the credibility of the Bankruptcy Court rather than investigate wrongdoing by high level Justice officials.

D. THE DEPARTMENT DID NOT SERIOUSLY CONSIDER THE NEED FOR AN INDEPENDENT COUNSEL

On December 5, 1990, in testimony before the Subcommittee on Economic and Commercial Law of the Committee on the Judiciary, former Attorney General Elliot Richardson, representing INSLAW, stated that he believed that "these attempts to acquire control of PROMIS were linked by a conspiracy among friends of Attorney General Edwin Meese to take advantage of their relationship with him for the purpose of obtaining a lucrative contract for the automation of all the Department's litigation divisions." As a result of this belief, Mr. Richardson advised his client, INSLAW, to contact the Department in an attempt to obtain a fair and complete investigation of the matter.

Mr. Richardson stated that INSLAW's attempts included (1) a referral to the Public Integrity Section of the Department's Criminal Division; (2) a referral to the Office of Independent Counsel McKay; (3) an appeal to the U.S. Court of Appeals to request an independent counsel; (4) letters to the Attorney General; and, as a last resort, (5) a petition for a writ of mandamus.

In February 1988, INSLAW submitted allegations raised from the Bankruptcy Court's January 1988 Findings of Facts and Conclusions of Law and other information developed by INSLAW to the Public Integrity Section. In its complaint, INSLAW charged the Department with (1) procurement fraud, (2) violation of the automatic stay invoked by the Bankruptcy Court and (3) Department attempts to change INSLAW's chapter 11 (reorganization) to a chapter 7 (liquidation).

Procurement Fraud: INSLAW alleged that the Department's acts criticized by Judge Bason were part of a larger "procurement

88

fraud" perpetrated by the Department.[285] INSLAW alleged that Attorney General Meese and D. Lowell Jensen schemed to ensure that INSLAW's proprietary enhancements to PROMIS be obtained by the Department without payment and be made available to Dr. Earl Brian, a businessman and entrepreneur who owns and controls several businesses including Hadron, Inc., a software company which has contracts with the Justice Department and other agencies.

Violation of the Automatic Stay: INSLAW further alleged that the Department violated the automatic stay under Federal bankruptcy law by using INSLAW's proprietary enhancements to PROMIS after the bankruptcy case was filed. Judge Bason's opinion found that the Department violated the automatic stay under Federal bankruptcy law, an act that could constitute an obstruction of the bankruptcy proceedings. Although Judge Bason's ruling was upheld by the District Court, it was ultimately overruled by the Circuit Court. (See infra.)

INSLAW's Conversion: INSLAW also alleged that the Department unsuccessfully attempted to have Harry Jones detailed from the U.S. Trustee's office in New York to Washington to take over the INSLAW bankruptcy for the purpose of causing INSLAW's liquidation. INSLAW's proof of this claim consisted of:

The sworn statement (later recanted) of Judge Blackshear that he was pressured to detail Harry Jones to Washington to convert INSLAW's bankruptcy status, and

Director Stanton's alleged unsuccessful pressure on U.S. Trustee William White to convert the bankruptcy case into a chapter 7 liquidation.

The Public Integrity Section (the Section) notified INSLAW that it would investigate some of the allegations made by the Hamiltons. Subsequently, the Department reviewed INSLAW's allegations under the independent counsel statute to determine whether the information provided was sufficient to trigger a preliminary investigation of any person covered by the statute,[286] including Edwin Meese, Arnold Burns, and Lowell Jensen. By memorandum dated February 29, 1988, William Weld, the Department's Criminal Division Assistant Attorney General, stated that the Section concluded that INSLAW did not provide specific information sufficient to constitute grounds to begin a preliminary investigation of the need for an independent counsel.[287] The Department stated that the facts presented were essentially unsupported speculation that

---

[285] The bankruptcy judge, George Bason, ruled in INSLAW's favor, and in a scathing opinion found that the Department "acted in bad faith, vexatiously, wantonly, and for oppressive reasons." (Judge Bason's opinion of September 2, 1987 [Opinion], at p. 215.) The judge further found that the Department "fraudulently" induced INSLAW into agreeing to provide the proprietary enhancements to the Department. (Opinion at p. 206, 53.)

[286] The independent counsel statute, 28 U.S.C. §§591–99, provides that, upon receipt of information regarding the commission of a crime by a person covered by the statute, the Department must conduct a preliminary investigation if the information is sufficient to constitute grounds to investigate; i.e., whether any of these persons "may have violated" any Federal criminal law. The preliminary investigation is limited to a determination of the credibility of the source (the Department determined that INSLAW was a credible source) and the specificity of the information. 28 U.S.C. §591(d)(1). The Attorney General is a covered person under the independent counsel statute. 28 U.S.C. §591(b)(2). The Deputy Attorney General is a covered person under the statute. 28 U.S.C. §591(b)(3). D. Lowell Jensen is a covered person under 28 U.S.C. §591(b)(4) and (6) because of his former positions with the Justice Department.

[287] Memorandum of William F. Weld, Assistant Attorney General, Criminal Division, February 29, 1988. p. 1.

89

persons covered by the independent counsel statute were involved in a scheme to defraud. The Assistant Attorney General concurred with a recommendation that the review be closed "due to lack of evidence of criminality."

The Department's investigation of these charges was shallow and incomplete. Further, it appeared to have been more interested in constructing legal defenses for its managerial actions rather than investigating claims of wrongdoing which, if proved, could undermine or weaken its litigating posture. Mr. Richardson also stated that the Section had not, in fact, conducted a comprehensive, thorough, or credible investigation, and that the investigation was a cursory review of INSLAW's charges. In a May 11, 1989, letter to Attorney General Thornburgh, Richardson repeated those concerns. He stated he believed that there was a conflict of interest arising from the Department defending itself against a civil suit brought by INSLAW while at the same time dealing with allegations of criminal conduct by top management that would, if proven, destroy the Department's defense. He also stated that it was apparent that the Department's all-out, no-holds-barred defense in INSLAW's civil suit had been given priority over the criminal investigation.

Mr. Richardson noted in this letter that no one from the Section contacted him or Mr. Charles Work, INSLAW's counsel, nor did they seek information from the Hamiltons. In addition, they failed to contact witnesses who had provided information to INSLAW. In fact, in December 1988 the Hamiltons provided the Section with the names of thirty individuals who could provide information pertinent to this investigation. In his letter, Mr. Richardson concluded that the only solution would be the appointment of an independent counsel. On August 10, 1989, Mr. Work also wrote to the Department, calling attention to the inadequacies of the Section's purported investigation, but the Department did not reopen the matter.

E. DEPARTMENT'S RESPONSE TO COURT FINDINGS OF POSSIBLE PERJURY

In a parallel initiative, Judge Bason recommended on July 17, 1987, to Attorney General Meese that he designate an appropriate official outside the Department to review the disputes between INSLAW and the Department and to give the Attorney General independent advice on this matter.[288]

Judge Bason stated in his Findings of Facts and Conclusions of Law that during the trial he observed the witnesses very closely and reached certain "definite and firm convictions" based on their demeanor, as well as on an analysis of the inherent probability or improbability of their testimony. On pages 172 through 177 of his Findings of Facts, Judge Bason commented on the credibility of the Department's witnesses and pointed strongly to a pattern of deception and coverup by Department employees. This pattern of deception suggests the possibility of perjury and coverup that can only be completely investigated by someone who is independent of the Department of Justice.

The following are extracts from Judge Bason's statements:

---

[288] July 17, 1987, letter from Judge George Bason to Attorney General Edwin Meese.

90

Lawrence McWhorter, Deputy Director for the Executive Office for U.S. Attorneys (EOUSA) was "totally unbelievable."

Jack Rugh, Assistant Director, Information Systems Staff for EOUSA was "also not believable."

William Tyson's (Director EOUSA), statement that Mr. Brewer's attitude toward INSLAW was positive, constructive and favorable "...is so ludicrous in light of the evidence taken as a whole it is difficult for this court to believe any of Mr. Tyson's testimony."

C. Madison Brewer, Director, Office of Management Information Systems & Support, EOUSA "...was most unreliable, and entirely colored by his intense bias and prejudice against Hamilton and INSLAW."

Peter Videnieks, Contracting Officer, Justice Management Division was "...substantially unreliable. Videnieks was under Brewer's domination and was thoroughly affected by Brewer's bias."

The testimony of *Janis Sposato,* Administrative Counsel, Justice Management Division, "is to be viewed with considerable skepticism. Given Sposato's position as a DOJ ethics officer, her casual treatment of repeated serious allegations of outrageous misconduct by Brewer can only be described, even charitably, as willful blindness to the obvious."

Judge Bason concluded his comments by stating that:

The acts of DOJ as described in the foregoing findings of fact were done in bad faith, vexatiously, in wanton disregard of the law and the facts, and for oppressive reasons—to drive INSLAW out of business and to convert, by trickery, fraud and deceit, INSLAW's PROMIS software.

Apparently in response to Judge Bason's charges as well as INSLAW's request for the appointment of an independent counsel, Arnold Burns, the Deputy Attorney General, asked the Civil Division for advice on the question of the appointment of an outside party to review the INSLAW matter. The Deputy Assistant Attorney General of the Civil Division, Stuart Schiffer, wrote to Richard Willard, Assistant Attorney General, Civil Division, that the idea "would not achieve productive results." Both Mr. Schiffer and Mr. Willard agreed that taking this "extraordinary step" would only serve to highlight the matter and give those criticizing the Department an opportunity to argue that resorting to this remedy proved by inference that events warranted an investigation.

Mr. Schiffer crystallized the Department's defensive posture on this matter when he wrote that his reasons for supporting the denial of an outside investigation were founded on whether the Department could achieve any benefit from such a study. According to Mr. Schiffer:

I remain convinced that this idea would not achieve productive results.... I have serious doubts whether we could achieve any benefit from the outside person's study.... [T]he outside person might find instances in

91

which the Department could have better handled the contract (with 20/20 hindsight this is not unlikely). These deficiencies, no matter how minor, would be seized upon and magnified by the court as admissions "at last" of the Government's wrongdoing. [289]

Mr. Schiffer concluded that the use of an outside person to investigate and report on the Department's handling of the INSLAW contract was, a "no-win" option and the leadership of the Civil Division passed this recommendation on to Deputy Attorney General Burns. [290]

F. INSLAW REQUEST FOR INDEPENDENT COUNSEL

INSLAW filed a Petition for Writ of Mandamus on December 20, 1989, requesting that the District Court order a full and thorough investigation of the INSLAW allegations and direct the Attorney General to appoint an independent counsel. The petition asserted that the Department had not made a serious effort to determine whether or not INSLAW's allegations, which were supported in court, were true. The Department moved to dismiss the petition.

A thorough investigation of the Department's handling of the PROMIS contract was again denied INSLAW on September 8, 1989, when the D.C. Court of Appeals turned down INSLAW's request for an independent counsel to investigate alleged misconduct by top Department management. This request was an appeal of the Department's May 4, 1988, determination that the appointment of an independent counsel was not warranted. The court denied the request because the Attorney General had not applied to the court for the appointment of an independent counsel as required by law. Therefore, the court concluded that it had no jurisdiction in the matter.

On September 27, 1990, the court denied the petition. The court added in a footnote that:

> ...the House Judiciary Committee is presently investigating the activities of the Department and its then-officials, employees, and friends as to the extent of a conspiracy of the type and magnitude alleged by INSLAW. The Washington Post reports that "[a]fter months of negotiations, Attorney General Dick Thornburgh has now assured the Judiciary Committee Chairman Jack Brooks (D-Tex.) that his inquiry will have the full cooperation of the department. Committee investigators will have direct access to department personnel and documents, and employees will be assured that they can testify without fear of retribution.... Clearly, this house committee is a body far better placed in the governmental scheme of things than the court (with resources unmatched in the judiciary) to undertake such an evaluation." [291]

---

[289] Memorandum from Stuart E. Schiffer, Deputy Assistant Attorney General, Civil Division, to Richard K. Willard, Assistant Attorney General, Civil Division, July 7, 1987, p. 1–2.

[290] July 7, 1987, memorandum from Stewart Schiffer, Deputy Assistant Attorney General, Civil Division, to Richard Willard, Assistant Attorney General, Civil Division titled: "INSLAW."

[291] Unfortunately, the cooperation suggested by the District Court never occurred. Almost 1 year after the ruling, the committee was forced to issue a subpoena for the documents on July

Continued

92

Sadly, such cooperation with this committee never materialized. In fact, the committee remains embroiled in a conflict with the Department over full access to information. As stated earlier in this report, in July 1991 a subpoena even had to be issued to compel the production of key Justice Department documents and files related to INSLAW. This occurred 2 full years after the initial request to Attorney General Thornburgh to cooperate with the committee's INSLAW investigation. Even today, sensitive documents are missing and certain files which the Department claims are related to ongoing criminal investigations and to sensitive law enforcement matters are still being denied the committee.

VII. TOP DEPARTMENT OFFICIALS FRUSTRATED COMMITTEE'S INVESTIGATION

The committee's investigation often encountered Department barriers to documents and agency personnel. While the committee could not prove that the Department deliberately conspired to conceal evidence of criminal wrongdoing, serious questions have been raised about the possible: obstruction of a congressional investigation; destruction of Department documents; and, witness tampering by Department officials. The following discussion demonstrates the considerable effort by the Department to delay and deter this committee from conducting a complete and thorough investigation of the INSLAW matter. Furthermore, it appears that these are similar to barriers faced by the Senate Permanent Subcommittee on Investigations when it attempted to conduct its investigation into the INSLAW allegation. [292]

The committee eventually overcame many of the obstacles put in its path by the Department and established several important precedents. First, committee investigators were ultimately given unrestricted access to all contract, personnel and administrative files of the agency, which consisted, in the INSLAW case, of several thousand documents. Second, access was given to the sensitive files of the Office of Professional Responsibility (OPR) which included not only the reports of that Office but individual interviews and sworn statements conducted during OPR investigation. Third, for the first time known to the committee, the FBI agreed to permit one of its field agents, Special Agent Thomas Gates, to give a sworn statement to committee investigators and to otherwise cooperate with the committee. Fourth, the Department agreed to allow Justice officials and employees to give sworn statements

---

25, 1991. See section II, entitled "Committee Investigation, Prior Studies, Hearings and Subcommittee Proceedings."

[292] During April 1988, the Department began to hinder the investigation of the INSLAW matter by PSI. After failing to convince PSI not to conduct an inquiry, the Department not only failed to cooperate with PSI, but also raised barriers to restrict subcommittee access to information and to influence witnesses not to cooperate with the investigation (p. 46 of PSI report). The Department: (1) demanded that members of its INSLAW litigation team be present during interviews with Department personnel and (2) provided only limited information about the scope and results of its investigations on the conduct of Department personnel.

PSI concluded that the Department's roadblocks to the subcommittee's investigation:

"...resulted in substantial delays and seriously undercut the subcommittee's ability to interview, in an open, candid, and timely manner, all those Department employees who may have had knowledge of the INSLAW matter....[I]n requiring departmental attorneys to simultaneously represent both the Department and individual Department employees in this investigation, the Department violated basic principles of conflict of interest and the attorney-client relationship."

93

without a Department attorney present. Finally, under the force of a subpoena issued by the subcommittee, the Department provided more than 400 documents, which it had identified as related to on-going litigation and other highly sensitive matters and "protected" under the claims of attorney-client and attorney work product privileges.

A. DEPARTMENT ATTEMPTS TO THWART COMMITTEE INQUIRY

The committee's investigation began with an August 1989 letter from Chairman Brooks to Attorney General Thornburgh initiating an investigation into a number of serious allegations regarding the Department of Justice's (DOJ) handling of a contract with INSLAW, Inc., and asked for the Department's full cooperation with committee investigators.

Attorney General Thornburgh responded on August 21, 1989; and while seriously questioning the need for a comprehensive investigation, he stated:

> Nevertheless, I can pledge this Department's full cooperation with the committee in this matter, and I have so instructed all concerned agency employees, with the understanding that we will have to make arrangements to protect any information, documents, or testimony that we may proffer to the committee from interested vendors and litigants, including INSLAW. [293]

Armed with the Attorney General's pledge of cooperation, the committee nevertheless immediately encountered severe resistance by Justice officials when they were asked to provide access to agency files and personnel. On September 29, 1989, Department officials told committee investigators that they would not be given full and unrestricted access to agency files and individuals associated with the INSLAW contract. The Department insisted that committee investigators instead go through the cumbersome and lengthy process of putting all requests for documents, interviews and other materials in writing. [294] Initially, even INSLAW's contract files, which were readily accessible to the General Accounting Office (GAO), were denied to the committee. The Department also insisted that a Department attorney be present during any interviews of Department employees. During this time even individuals who had left the Department refused to be interviewed. This refusal possibly stems from pressure exerted by the Department which strongly believed that: "Justice has to speak through one voice," regarding the INSLAW matter. [295]

As part of these negotiations the Department's Office of Legislative Affairs (OLA) informed committee investigators that some of the requested information would be made available, but because of Privacy Act and trade secret concerns the Department wanted the chairman to put each request in writing. The alternative was for

---

[293] Letter from Attorney General Richard Thornburgh to the Honorable Jack Brooks, chairman, Committee on the Judiciary, August 21, 1989. pp. 1–2.
[294] Letter from Carol T. Crawford, Assistant Attorney General to the Honorable Jack Brooks, chairman, Committee on the Judiciary, September 29, 1989, p. 1.
[295] Memorandum to file, October 16, 1989, documenting a telephone conversation with Jim Cole, Deputy Chief of the Department's Public Integrity Section. Also see January 9, 1990, letter from the Honorable Jack Brooks to Attorney General Richard Thornburgh.

94

the committee to obtain individual releases from as many as 50 individuals. The committee's request for access to the Public Integrity Section files was also denied. OLA also stated that the Office of Professional Responsibility was concerned with the Privacy Act and regarded its files "as highly sensitive, potentially hurtful, and is concerned that the information could be misused."

As a result of the Department's position, the chairman stated in a January 9, 1990, letter to the Attorney General that he could not devise any better way to preclude an investigative body from obtaining objective and candid information, on any matter, than by intimidating employees who otherwise may cooperate with an investigation.[296] He added that the presence of a Department attorney would undercut the committee's ability to interview persons in an open, candid, and timely manner, and he was deeply troubled by the continued lack of cooperation by Department employees. The chairman again personally informed the Attorney General of his concerns about the continued delays and resistance to providing needed information when they met on January 29, 1990.

The chairman requested immediate, full and unrestricted access to Department employees and documents.[297] In a February 1990, response the Department agreed to allow its employees to be interviewed without Department counsel present. However, the Department delayed access to numerous files and negotiated for several months about the confidentiality of a variety of documents requested for the investigation.

The Attorney General and the chairman reached another agreement in April 1990 on access to information. At this time, the Department agreed to provide free and unrestricted access to INSLAW files and Department employees. At the Department's fiscal year 1991 authorization hearings on May 16, 1990, Attorney General Thornburgh again indicated that the Department had decided to provide access to the committee for the INSLAW investigation:

> ...I have discussed with you and other members of this and other committees, our willingness to examine on a case-by-case basis any request that comes from the Congress....But rather than lay down a bunch of reasons why we can't release materials I prefer...to discuss ways and means in which we can work with you and your staff to figure out ways that we can produce materials as I think we have accomplished in your request regarding INSLAW and Project Eagle.[298]

The Attorney General's statement clearly indicated a willingness to supply the requested materials to the committee as long as some agreement was reached to protect this material from being improperly released. Unfortunately, the Department's ability to abide with its agreement was short lived.

On June 15, 1990, the Department informed committee investigators that there were 64 boxes of INSLAW litigation files which

---

[296] Letter from the Honorable Jack Brooks to Attorney General Richard Thornburgh, January 9, 1990, pp. 1–2.
[297] Ibid., p. 2.
[298] Committee on the Judiciary hearing, Department of Justice Authorization for Appropriations for Fiscal Year 1991, May 16, 1990, Serial No. 94, p. 48.

95

they listed on a 422-page index. At this time, Department officials refused to give committee investigators the index because it included "privileged" information that the Department was concerned would be made available to INSLAW. [299] Finally, on June 28, 1990, the Department's Acting Assistant Attorney General for Legislative Affairs agreed to provide the litigation file indices on the condition that they not be released to the public by the committee. [300] However, Department officials refused to identify what documents were privileged or available. At the same time numerous interviews and sworn statements were being taken by committee investigators; however, these interviews were impaired by the lack of documentation from which to draw investigation-related questions.

By letter dated September 6, 1990, the OLA Deputy Assistant Attorney General again refused to permit committee staff access to what he declared were "privileged" work-product and attorney/client documents. [301] This judgment originated from Ms. Sandra Spooner, lead Department counsel on INSLAW'S litigation, who reviewed each file and removed those she believed to be "privileged" attorney/client or work product documents. Committee investigators finally gained access to the Department's "INSLAW Files" in late October 1990. However, soon thereafter the Department increased the number of documents and/or files withheld from an initial 175 to 190. On November 19, 1990, the Department again increased the number of documents and/or files withheld from the committee to 193. [302]

The chairman protested the additional obstacles raised by the Department. The Attorney General responded that his pledge of free and unrestricted access did not include, "privileged" attorney-client or work product documents. [303] This posture became the focus of a hearing on December 5, 1990.

The Judiciary Committee's Subcommittee on Economic and Commercial Law convened on December 5, 1990, to address the Department's refusal to provide access to "privileged" INSLAW documents. During this hearing Steven R. Ross, General Counsel to the House Clerk, stated that:

> ...the Attorney General's claimed basis for this withholding of documents is an attempt to create for himself and his functionaries within the Department an exemption from the constitutional principle that all executive officials, no matter how high or low, exercise their authority pursuant to law and that all such public officials are accountable to legislative oversight aimed at ferreting out waste, fraud, and abuse. [304]

Mr. Ross added that the Department was attempting to redefine committee investigations to mean that congressional investigations

---

[299] House Judiciary Committee interview of Sandra Spooner, Department of Justice official on June 15, 1990.
[300] House Judiciary Committee hearing, December 5, 1990, Serial No. 114, pp. 195–197.
[301] Ibid., pp. 203–204.
[302] The amount of material included approximately 970 files/documents.
[303] Letter from Attorney General Thornburgh to the Honorable Jack Brooks, chairman, Committee on the Judiciary, September 26, 1990.
[304] House Judiciary Committee hearing, December 5, 1990, Serial No. 114, p. 78.

96

are justifiable only as a means of facilitating the task of passing legislation. Mr. Ross stated:[305]

> What that proposed standard would do would be to eradicate the time-honored role of Congress of providing oversight, which is a means that has been upheld by the Supreme Court on a number of occasions, by which the Congress can assure itself that previously passed laws are being properly implemented.

After providing several examples of Department attempts to withhold information by claiming attorney/client privilege, including Watergate, Ross concluded by stating:[306]

> It is thus clear, in light of history of claims by the Department that it may be excused from providing the Congress in general and this committee in particular with documents that it deems litigation sensitive, that Congress' broad power of investigation overcomes those litigative concerns.[307]

After the December 1990 hearings, Attorney General Thornburgh once again agreed to provide the committee full and unrestricted access to all INSLAW-related documents.[308] Both sides agreed to a two-step procedure in which documents would be reviewed first by committee investigators followed by a written request for copies of a specific item.[309] Access was given for the first time in May 1991, to the files of the Civil Division's Chief Litigating Attorney, Ms. Sandra Spooner. These files consisted of documents and information which had been consolidated from various quarters of Justice's office complex, located at 550 11th Street, N.W., Washington, DC. During the review of these files, committee investigators were informed that Ms. Spooner had self-selected and removed approximately 450 documents on the purported basis of various asserted "privileges," including "attorney work product" and "attorney client" despite the agreement between the Branches and despite the confidentiality safeguards established to protect just such documents. She also removed all documents related to communications between the Department and Congress, as well as those related to the Department of Transportation Board of Contract Appeals proceedings. Ms. Spooner also informed the investigators for the first time that an indeterminate number of documents—and possibly entire file folders—were missing.

---

[305] Ibid.

[306] In the case of *McGain* v. *Daugherty*, the Supreme Court focused specifically on Congress' authority to study "charges of misfeasance and nonfeasance in the Department of Justice." The court noted with approval the subject to be investigated by the congressional committee was the administration of the Department, whether its functions were being properly discharged or being neglected or misdirected. In its decision, the Supreme Court sustained the contempt arrest of the Attorney General's brother for withholding information from Congress, since Congress "would be materially aided by the information which the investigation was calculated to elicit." Thus the Supreme Court itself has declared null any attempt at pretensions that oversight could be barred regarding "whether the Attorney General and his assistant were performing or neglecting their duties in respect of the institution and prosecution of proceedings."

[307] Committee on the Judiciary hearing, op cit., p. 81.

[308] Letter from Attorney General Richard Thornburgh to the Honorable Jack Brooks, chairman, dated April 23, 1991.

[309] Letter from the Honorable Jack Brooks to Attorney General Richard Thornburgh, dated April 23, 1991.

97

On May 29, 1991, committee staff requested that the Department abide by the Attorney General's April 23 agreement and provide copies of all documents contained in the INSLAW index. The Department was also requested to explain why some of Ms. Spooner's files could not be found. [310]

The Assistant Attorney General for Legislative Affairs wrote on May 29, 1991, that the Attorney General's April 23 agreement did not include documents related to: (1) matters pending before the District Court, (2) appellate litigation, or (3) matters pending before the DOTBCA. [311] Consequently, the committee was denied over 400 documents and files. The Assistant Attorney General made no mention of the missing files in his letter.

B. AUTHORIZATION AND OVERSIGHT HEARINGS

On July 8, 1991, the committee chairman announced his plans to hold authorization and oversight hearings on July 11 and 18 to discuss the Department's fiscal year 1992 budget request. The chairman indicated that as part of these hearings, he would be asking, among other things, Attorney General Thornburgh about his failure to live up to the several previous commitments he had made to the committee to provide full and open access to the Department's INSLAW files. Chairman Brooks opened the July 11, 1991, hearing by noting that oversight of executive branch policy and activity is at the heart of the congressional mandate as an integral component of the checks and balances architecture of constitutional government. He further noted that Department officials had continued to resist meaningful outside review of their activities by refusing to cooperate with GAO and congressional investigations. Chairman Brooks expressed grave concern that the Department seemed increasingly bent on pursuing controversial theories of executive privilege and power at the expense of removing government from the sunshine of public scrutiny and accountability. [312] This tendency appeared to be an increasing problem under the stewardship of Attorney General Thornburgh and had seriously hindered and delayed several congressional investigations, including the INSLAW case. [313]

The chairman concluded the hearing by stating that the Judiciary Committee must carefully consider the actions needed to be taken to require production of documents requested from the Department and urged that all committee members attend the July

---

[310] Letter from chief investigator of the House Judiciary Committee to Assistant Attorney General J. Michael Luttig, dated May 29, 1991.

[311] Letter from Assistant Attorney General W. Lee Rawls to the chief investigator of the House Judiciary Committee, dated May 29, 1991.

[312] House Judiciary Committee hearing, July 11, 1991, Serial No. 12, p. 1.

[313] During the hearing, the chairman indicated that the Attorney General, who was scheduled to appear before the subcommittee on July 18, 1991, was asked to be prepared to provide his reasoning behind the interbranch conflicts over GAO and congressional access to Justice documents, including those related to INSLAW. Steven Ross testified that the Department's actions concerning the release of documents in the INSLAW matter were yet another instance in which the Department has attempted to thwart a congressional inquiry into possible executive branch wrongdoing. Mr. Ross noted that "8 months had lapsed since the last hearing on access to records problems at Justice, and that committee investigators were still being refused access to, let alone copies of, hundreds of INSLAW related documents." Mr. Ross also stated that "the same baseless arguments raised and rejected" at the subcommittee's December 5, 1990, hearing held to discuss this issue were again being trotted out by the Department.

98

18, 1991, hearing, during which Attorney General Thornburgh would be asked to respond to these issues.[314]

On July 18, 1991, the committee reconvened to review the Justice Department's fiscal year 1992 authorization request for appropriations and to hear the testimony of Attorney General Thornburgh. Unfortunately, the Attorney General decided at 7 p.m. the night before to refuse to appear.[315]

Committee Chairman Brooks responded to the Attorney General's unprecedented nonappearance to a duly noticed hearing:

> In light of the extreme importance of this proceeding, it is particularly unfortunate and deeply disturbing that the Attorney General notified us last night, late last night, that he would refuse to appear before us this morning. He refuses to attend for a myriad of reasons—even though his appearance was duly scheduled for 1 full month.[316]

The chairman noted the seriousness of the issues facing the Department and the need to resolve them as quickly as possible. He was particularly concerned with the Department's lack of cooperation with the committee on the INSLAW investigation. He concluded by expressing concern over the "great damage" that had been done to the relationship between the Judiciary Committee and the Justice Department stating:

> I am shocked and saddened by the appearance of the empty chair before us and all the other chairs that he asked to be reserved for his people. The unanswered request and the delayed response are becoming the symbols of an increasingly remote and self-centered Justice Department that seems bent on expanding the accepted boundaries of executive branch power and prerogatives.[317]

C. THE DEPARTMENT REPORTS KEY SUBPOENAED DOCUMENTS MISSING

On July 25, 1991, the Subcommittee on Economic and Commercial Law issued a subpoena to the Attorney General requiring that he provide all documents within the scope of the committee investigation listed in the subpoena.[318] On July 29, the Attorney General provided as many subpoenaed documents as possible, but stated that some documents were lost—including, but not necessarily limited to, many documents from Ms. Spooner's files, such as:[319]

> A memorandum to Ms. Spooner which allegedly involved a discussion and chronology of INSLAW's data rights claim.

---

[314] Ibid., p. 134.

[315] Attorney General Thornburgh stated: "I would also like to express my personal appreciation for the courtesy you have extended to me, Mr. Chairman, throughout my tenure as Attorney General. It is my impression that this committee has established a positive working relationship with both my office and the many components of the Department." Statement of Attorney General Richard Thornburgh before the House Committee on the Judiciary, regarding Department of Justice Authorizations for fiscal year 1992, July 18, 1991.

[316] House Judiciary Committee hearing, July 18, 1991, Serial No. 12, p. 137.

[317] Ibid., pp. 137, 139.

[318] The chairman's July 31, 1991, statement before the House Subcommittee on Economic and Commercial Law.

[319] A total of 64 sensitive Justice documents and 14 files pertaining to INSLAW are still missing or incomplete.

99

Ms. Sandra Spooner's notes to file concerning the transcript of Peter Videnieks' PSI deposition.

An August 10, 1989, facsimile with attachment from Ms. Janis Sposato to Ms. Sandra Spooner concerning a response to Chairman Brooks.

A May 28, 1989, routing slip from Elizabeth Woodruff to Ms. Spooner concerning the whistle-blower protection statute.

Ms. Spooner's notes described as numerous attorney notes.

An August 4, 1988, memorandum from Stuart Schiffer to John Bolton transmitting a memorandum from Stuart Schiffer to Thomas Stanton.

A September 21, 1989, memorandum from Roger Tweed to Ms. Spooner regarding facilities for use by the INSLAW case auditors.

Patricia Bryan's notebook of outlines, notes, and documents prepared by counsel to facilitate compromise discussions.

Also, many documents that were provided were incomplete (i.e., missing pages or attachments), or were of such poor quality that they could not be read. Because Ms. Spooner's files lacked an index, it was also impossible to ascertain whether other documents or files were missing as well. Based on the numbering system used by the Department, however, it appears numerous additional documents are missing.

On July 30, 1991, Mr. W. Lee Rawls, Assistant Attorney General, stated that Ms. Spooner's documents not provided to the committee:

> ...ha[ve] not yet been found and neither Ms. Spooner nor any other employee who would normally have access to it knows how it may have been lost....Under these circumstances, the litigation team under Ms. Spooner's direction has endeavored to reconstruct the missing volume from other files containing the same documents. We are now providing the committee with a reconstructed volume that contains all but eight of the fifty-one documents that were contained in the original file. [320]

It is unclear whether the Department formally investigated why these documents disappeared, as the committee requested in June 1991.

During a July 31, 1991, subcommittee meeting convened to discuss the Attorney General's noncompliance with the subpoena, Chairman Brooks concluded:

> My concern with the missing documents flows from the fact that our investigation is looking into allegations by those who claim that high level Department officials criminally conspired to force INSLAW into bankruptcy and steal its software. It is alleged this was done to benefit friends of then Attorney General Edwin Meese. Under these circumstances, I fully expected that the department would take great care in protecting all these documents. Unfortunately, the fact of missing documents will now

---

[320] Letter from Assistant Attorney General W. Lee Rawls to the chairman, dated July 30, 1991.

100

leave lingering questions in the minds of some who have closely followed the investigation about whether documents may have been destroyed.[321]

The question of unauthorized destruction of Government documents again came up recently when the committee received information from Ms. Lois Battistoni, a former Justice Department employee, that Department employees were involved in the illegal destruction (shredding) of documents related to the INSLAW case. This matter has not been investigated by the committee.[322]

D. DEPARTMENT INTERFERES WITH MICHAEL RICONOSCIUTO'S SWORN STATEMENT TO THE COMMITTEE—REFUSES REQUEST TO INTERVIEW DEA AGENTS

On March 29, 1991, Mr. Riconosciuto was arrested by DEA special agents for possession and distribution of a controlled substance. It is important to stress that Riconosciuto began cooperating with the Hamiltons and provided the committee with information about the alleged conspiracy by the Justice Department to steal INSLAW's PROMIS software well before the time of his arrest.

The Department interfered with committee attempts to obtain information from Mr. Riconosciuto. Following Mr. Riconosciuto's arrest, the committee contacted his attorney, John Rosellini, to request that the committee be given permission to interview his client. On April 1, 1991, arrangements were made to conduct the interview with Mr. Riconosciuto. Facilities for a private interview were made available by the Kitsap County chief jailer, Larry Bertholf, for the committee interview of Mr. Riconosciuto, which was to be conducted on April 4, 1991.

During the negotiations with Mr. Riconosciuto's attorney, the Department called the committee and advised that, if the interview was to be conducted at all, it would be held at the U.S. Court House in Seattle, WA. Prior to commencing the interview of Mr. Riconosciuto, the Department attorney handling Mr. Riconosciuto's prosecution was asked by committee investigators to provide a sworn statement that the committee's interview of Riconosciuto would not be monitored or recorded by the Department. The Department attorney refused to provide the statement, advising that he would not under any circumstances agree to such a request. He stated that it was not Department policy to record private conversations held between clients and their attorney, and he considered the committee as being in the same category.

Following Mr. Riconosciuto's sworn statement, the committee asked for permission from the Department to interview the DEA arresting agents. This request was critical because Mr. Riconosciuto had alleged that a tape recording of a conservation between him and a Justice Official (Mr. Peter Videnieks) was confiscated by DEA agents at the time of his arrest. This tape allegedly shows that Mr. Videnieks threatened Mr. Riconosciuto with

---

[321] The chairman's July 31, 1991, statement before the House Subcommittee on Economic and Commercial Law.
[322] As mentioned before, Lois Battistoni is a former Department of Justice Criminal Division employee.

101

retribution if he talked to the Judiciary Committee investigators. As has been the practice throughout this investigation the Department refused to cooperate with the committee's request, using the justification that Mr. Riconosciuto's prosecution was an ongoing investigation. The Department has also refused to allow the committee access to its investigative files on Mr. Riconosciuto.

Since his arrest, Mr. Riconosciuto has been convicted of the drug related charges, and he is currently imprisoned. Although this incident diminishes his credibility as a witness, the timing of the arrest, coupled with Mr. Riconosciuto's allegations that tapes of a telephone conversation he had with Mr. Videnieks were confiscated by DEA agents, raises serious questions concerning whether the Department's prosecution of Mr. Riconosciuto was related to his cooperation with the committee. As described in other sections of this report, the committee received sworn testimony and recovered documents which support aspects of Mr. Riconosciuto's story, and ties Mr. Riconosciuto, Dr. Brian, and an individual named Robert Booth Nichols to U.S. intelligence agencies and in the case of Mr. Nichols, possibly, organized crime.

E. DEPARTMENT OFFICIAL MAY HAVE ATTEMPTED TO INFLUENCE A KEY WITNESS

During the sworn statement of FBI Special Agent Thomas Gates on March 25, 1992, he and his attorney, Richard Bauer, stated that Ms. Faith Burton from the Department's Office of Congressional Affairs had told them that the committee, as a matter of policy, provided the Department with copies of all depositions taken in the INSLAW investigation. The clear implication was that the Department would know everything that had been said by Special Agent Gates in his sworn testimony. It was apparent that this lack of confidentiality concerned Special Agent Gates' attorney and this may have had a chilling effect on Special Agent Gate's testimony to the committee. Special Agent Gates and his attorney were informed that the committee policy in fact prohibited giving copies of the confidential sworn statements to anyone but the person who gave the statement or to that person's attorney. [323]

On March 26, 1992, committee investigators met with Ms. Burton to discuss this issue. Ms. Burton stated that the allegations made by Special Agent Gates and his attorney were "totally false," and that it didn't make any sense because she "knew the policy that the Department didn't get the transcripts." Ms. Burton stated Special Agent Gates and his attorney must have misunderstood her and attributed the misunderstanding to their long flight. Committee investigators asked Ms. Burton if she said anything to imply directly or indirectly that the Department received or reviewed copies of the committee's sworn statements, she responded "absolutely not."

On March 26, 1992, Special Agent Gates and his attorney were informed of Ms. Burton's response and Special Agent Gates was

---

[323] Confidential statements such as Special Agent Gates' are not made available or released in any manner. However, other types of sworn statements may be included in the printed record.

102

asked if it was possible that he misunderstood what Ms. Burton had said. Special Agent Gates responded:

> Its always possible, but it was fairly clear to me, what she said.

Mr. Bauer further stated that there was:

> ...a clear indication that there was a receipt of transcripts and a review of transcripts.

In fact, Mr. Bauer and Special Agent Gates stated that Ms. Burton had told them before their meeting with committee investigators that, *"to date, the Department has reviewed all transcripts and no wrongdoing has been found."* [Emphasis added.]

VIII. JUDGE BASON'S ALLEGATIONS OF JUSTICE DEPARTMENT'S IMPROPER INFLUENCE ON THE JUDICIAL SELECTION PROCESS

In February 1984, Judge Bason was appointed to fill the unexpired term of Judge Roger Whalen who voluntarily resigned as the bankruptcy judge for the District of Columbia. Judge Bason was the sole bankruptcy judge for the District of Columbia from February 1984 through February 1988. As a result, he personally heard the sworn statements and observed the witnesses during the INSLAW litigation.

In 1987, Judge Bason sought reappointment pursuant to the bankruptcy amendments and Federal Judgeship Act of 1984. Judge Bason, however, lost his reappointment bid and was replaced by S. Martin Teel, Jr., a Department attorney who had represented the Government and who had appeared before Judge Bason in the INSLAW bankruptcy case. According to Judge Bason, Martin Teel was appointed to the judgeship through his primary expertise focused on tax law with extremely limited bankruptcy litigation experience.[324]

---

[324] By letter dated January 12, 1988 (on file with committee), to the Honorable Patricia M. Wald, Chief Judge, U.S. Court of Appeals, Judge George Francis Bason, Jr., U.S. bankruptcy judge, requested a hearing before the Judicial Council of the District of Columbia Circuit because, among other reasons:

"As to the criterion of 'substantial legal experience,' the other candidate [Judge Teel] has had a considerably shorter total period of legal experience. He started as a trial attorney in the Justice Department's Tax Division, and remained such for approximately 10 years. He then became a reviewer for another period of years. For the past 7 years he has been a regional assistant section chief. As a reviewer and as an assistant section chief his duties have largely involved reviewing other people's work, not producing his own independent work, and not appearing in court. He has appeared in the court over which I preside [Bankruptcy Court] no more than two or three times in the last 4 years. When he has appeared he has remained mostly silent and has left it to his subordinates to argue the matter before the court. To my knowledge...the other candidate [Judge Teel] has never appeared before the appellate court." [January 12, 1988, letter from George Francis Bason, Jr., U.S. bankruptcy judge, to the Honorable Patricia M. Wald, Chief Judge, U.S. Court of Appeals, p. 6.]

In an interview of Judge Teel conducted by the committee on February 28, 1992, Judge Teel indicated that of the six cases he had listed on his application as representing the most important litigation in which he had been involved, all six had nothing to do with bankruptcy law. In a second interview conducted on March 27, 1992, Judge Teel was asked about his experience. Judge Teel stated that he was qualified for the position because: He had 6 years of fairly extensive bankruptcy experience; he was a legal scholar; he had worked on collection matters; as a result of his experience as a tax litigator for the Department of Justice, he was able to understand and effectively handle complicated cases; he had broad experience as a litigator and that this litigation had been exclusively civil in nature; he had dealt with bankruptcy lien priority issues; that he had extensive knowledge and grasp of the Rules of Evidence and Procedure. Judge Teel provided committee investigators with a letter outlining his qualifications to be a bankruptcy judge (on file with committee).

103

After learning that his bid for reappointment failed, Judge Bason alleged that the Department had influenced the selection process resulting in his removal from the bench. [325]

On December 5, 1990, Judge George F. Bason, Jr., testified before the subcommittee under oath that his failed bid for reappointment as a bankruptcy judge was the result of improper influence from within the Department. Judge Bason also stated that new information came to his attention that in his opinion leaves no doubt that the Department manipulated the process before the panel:

> One of the Justice Department's lawyers was heard saying to another, "We've got to get rid of that judge."
>
> Judge Bason also stated that in May 1988, a news reporter—who allegedly had excellent contacts and sources in the Department—suggested to him that the Department could have procured his removal from the bench by the following means:
>
> "The district judge chairperson of the Merit Selection Panel [Judge Norma Johnson] could have been approached privately and informally by one of her old and trusted friends from her days in the Justice Department. He could have told her that I was mentally unbalanced, as evidenced by my unusually forceful 'anti-government' opinions. Her persuasive powers coupled with the fact that other members of the Panel or their law firms might appear before her as litigating attorneys could cause them to vote with her." [326]

This reporter also told Bason that a high level Department official had boasted to him that Bason's removal was because of his INSLAW rulings. Judge Bason added that there is every reason to believe that Department officials would not hesitate to do whatever was necessary and possible to remove from office the judge who first exposed their wrongdoing, and that he would not have lost his job as bankruptcy judge but for his rulings in the INSLAW case. [327]

The committee could not substantiate Judge Bason's allegations. If the Department of Justice had influence over the process, it was subtle, to say the least. The judges who provided interviews to the committee investigators all agreed that they had little firsthand knowledge of the experience or performance of the candidates, including the incumbent judge. As a result, the members of the Council had to rely on the findings of the Merit Selection Panel (MSP). The MSP's findings were provided to the Council by Judge Norma Johnson, whose oral presentation played a large role in the selection. The other members of the MSP said that Judge Johnson firmly ran the MSP in these matters and that they relied on her judgment. [328] Judge Bason asserts that Judge Johnson was easily accessible to the Department because she had previously worked with Stuart Schiffer, the Department of Justice official who led the

[325] House Judiciary Committee hearing, December 5, 1990, Serial No. 114, pp. 53–55.
[326] Ibid., p. 55.
[327] Ibid.
[328] Interview of Jerome Barron, December 4, 1989 (on file with committee).

104

move to have Judge Bason removed from the INSLAW case. [329] The committee has no information that Judge Johnson talked to Mr. Schiffer about INSLAW, Judge Bason or the bankruptcy judge selection process.

A. CONFIDENTIAL MEMORANDUM

During the committee's investigation, one of the judges provided an apparently unofficial document that had been given to several Appeals Court judges when Judge Bason requested that the decision of the Circuit Court regarding his nonreappointment be reconsidered. The document was a December 8, 1987, "confidential memorandum" to Judge Johnson. The memorandum was unsigned (though the judge who provided the document and a member of the MSP identified the author of the memorandum as another member of the MSP, that individual denied that he had written the memorandum) and was marked at the top "read and destroy." The memorandum states that "its purpose is to 'help' elucidate in particular our reasoning in ranking the candidates as we did." [330]

The memorandum describes each of the four final candidates for the position of bankruptcy judge. What is striking about the memorandum is that the description of each candidate except Judge Bason begins with positive commentary about the individual. The section describing Judge Bason begins "I could not conclude that Judge Bason was incompetent." Other phrases used to describe Judge Bason include "he is inclined to make mountains out of molehills," "Judge Bason seems to have developed a pronounced and unrelenting reputation for favoring debtors," and finally, "Judge Bason evidenced no inclination to come to grips personally with the management challenge posed by the terrible shortcomings of the Office of the Clerk of our Bankruptcy Court." [331]

The written report of the MSP, which was very brief (consisting of less than 2 pages and dated November 24, 1987), did not include any of the observations included in the confidential memorandum. [332] The Judicial Council met on December 15, 1987. The unofficial confidential memorandum to Judge Johnson was dated on December 8, 1987. When the committee interviewed several of the members of the MSP and the Council, they were shown a copy of the memorandum but did not recognize it. When asked why the memorandum was not destroyed as it indicated on the top of the document, the judge who provided the committee with the memorandum stated that it was an important document and that it would be improper to destroy it.

B. CONDITION OF THE CLERK'S OFFICE UNDER JUDGE BASON

According to Judge Robinson, Judge George Bason inherited a mess (administratively) in the clerk's office when he took over for former Judge Roger Whalen. However, several of the judges inter-

---

[329] In a committee review conducted on July 22, 1992, Judge Bason also pointed out that Judge Tim Murphy worked with Judge Johnson at the D.C. Superior Court from 1970 to 1980. Judge Murphy left the bench on April 15, 1985, and worked for Mr. Brewer as his Assistant Director on the Justice Department's PROMIS implementation.
[330] Confidential memorandum to Judge Johnson, December 8, 1987, p. 1.
[331] Ibid., p. 2
[332] Report of the Merit Selection Panel, November 24, 1987.

105

viewed believed Judge Bason was responsible for the deficiencies in the Bankruptcy Court.[333] Committee interviews with members of the MSP and several members of the Council echo the sentiments that Judge Bason's nonreappointment was heavily influenced by the poor administration of the clerk's office. Yet most of the district and circuit judges interviewed said that they had little or no contact with Judge Bason and were not in a position to have firsthand knowledge of the condition of his court. Nonjudicial members of the MSP said that: (1) No statistics were examined to determine the condition of the court, (2) Judge Bason was not interviewed regarding the condition of the court, and (3) neither the clerk of the Bankruptcy Court, nor any members of Judge Bason's staff were interviewed regarding the condition of the court. In fact, the determination that the administrative condition of the court was "poor" was based solely on the comments of "a couple" of lawyers, one female member of the clerk's office and two people who might have been associated with the Administrative Office of the U.S. Court who apparently were interviewed during the selection process.

Judge Bason stated that the only explanation ever offered him regarding the reason behind his failed bid for reappointment was related to inefficiency in the District of Columbia's Bankruptcy Clerk's Office. It has also been reported that Judge Bason inherited a Bankruptcy Court which was in an administrative shambles.[334] By May 1986, however, Judge Robinson said Judge Bason was getting the system under control, which was reported in the Judicial Conference report for the D.C. Circuit that year. Judge Robinson also stated, in defense of Judge Bason, that "very few judges have any knowledge of how to administer a court" and once the new clerk was hired there was a vast improvement in the court's operation.[335]

Committee investigators interviewed Judge Bason, the current bankruptcy clerk, and the former bankruptcy clerk. None of these individuals were ever questioned during the 1987 bankruptcy judge selection process about the administration of the Bankruptcy Court. Judge Bason stated that there was no mechanism in place for Circuit or District Court judges to personally evaluate the administrative condition of the Bankruptcy Court.[336] According to Judge Bason, there were no other judges, besides Judge Robinson, in the D.C. Circuit or District Courts who were in a position to personally evaluate the operation of his court.[337]

Considering that poor administrative controls seemed to be one of the primary reasons for Judge Bason's failed attempt at reappointment, it is unusual that neither Judge Bason nor the other individuals most responsible for the administration of the court were interviewed by the Panel. Judge Robinson made a telling comment to committee investigators when he said it is unfortunate

---

[333] House Judiciary Committee interviews of Judge Johnson, dated November 15, 1989, and Judges Wald and Mikva, dated October 16, 1989.
[334] Memorandum of interview of Judge Aubrey Robinson, March 9, 1992.
[335] Ibid.
[336] Sworn statement of George F. Bason, March 20, 1992, p. 8.
[337] Ibid.

106

bankruptcy judges are selected by judges furthest removed from the Bankruptcy Court. [338]

Mr. Martin Bloom, clerk of the Bankruptcy Court, told committee investigators that "there were difficulties in many areas" when he began employment with the D.C. Circuit Bankruptcy Court in 1986. He said the "financial books and records did not balance..." and "there were some critical areas in management, both in personnel resources and equipment resources, that were lacking." According to Mr. Bloom, the relationship between Judge Bason and the previous clerk had broken down, resulting in a decline in office procedures. [339]

Mr. Bloom added that problems may have existed in the clerk's office "because the office was not managed efficiently or effectively" due to a lack of management capabilities and a lack of staff. When asked if the Bankruptcy Court judge was responsible for this lack of management capabilities he responded that "I can only relate to the responsibilities in the clerk's office. In no way or in any way will I look towards the judge," implying that the office had not been managed properly by the previous clerk. [340] He added that when he reported to the court "it seemed that no one... had any understanding of closing [cases]." [341] Mr. Bloom stated, however, that by "the latter part of 1987, administratively, I think the court was up to par." [342] Mr. Bloom further stated that Judge Bason took an active role in providing whatever assistance he could in improving the administrative condition of the court.

C. DEPARTMENT'S ATTEMPTS TO HAVE BASON REMOVED FROM INSLAW CASE FAIL

Internal Department of Justice documents indicate that Justice officials were concerned about Judge Bason's handling of the INSLAW case very early in the litigation. They believed that the judge was not sympathetic to the Department's position and that he tended to believe INSLAW's assertions. Those concerns increased throughout the litigation to the point where, by the summer of 1987, the Department was actively seeking ways to remove Judge Bason from the case.

Richard Willard, the Assistant Attorney General of the Civil Division, in a June 1987 letter to Deputy Attorney General Arnold Burns, wrote that "Judge Bason's conduct in this case was so extraordinary that it warranted reassignment to another judge." [343]

The Department believed that Judge Bason disregarded the sworn statements of Department witnesses. The Department also believed that Judge Bason made lengthy observations regarding

---

[338] Memorandum of interview of Judge Aubrey Robinson, March 9, 1992 (on file with the committee).

[339] Sworn statement of Martin Bloom, March 4, 1992, p. 4.

[340] Ibid., p. 11.

[341] Ibid., p. 20.

[342] Ibid., p. 5.

[343] Memorandum from Richard K. Willard, Assistant Attorney General, Civil Division to Arnold I. Burns, Deputy Attorney General, entitled: "Judge Bason's Adverse Decision in INSLAW," June 19, 1987.

Apparently Department officials attempted to discredit Judge Bason by questioning his judgment and judicial temperament. In his sworn statement to the committee, former Attorney General Edwin Meese said he was told by his staff that Judge Bason was "off his rocker." Sworn statement of Edwin Meese III, July 12, 1990, p. 46.

107

the credibility of its witnesses and that Judge Bason's uniformly negative conclusions were based on inferences not supported by the record. [344]

Mr. Burns asked the Civil Division to "consider initiatives for achieving a more favorable disposition of this matter." [345] In response to this Stuart Schiffer, the Deputy Assistant Attorney General of the Civil Division, asked Michael Hertz, Director, Commercial Litigation Branch, Civil Division, to investigate the possibility of having Judge Bason disqualified from the INSLAW case on the grounds of bias. [346] The Department hoped to challenge the judge's findings of fact by claiming them to be unsupported by the evidence and reflecting a justification to reach a preordained conclusion. This position was founded primarily on the Department's observations that some of Judge Bason's findings of fact were "rambling and based on deductions that are both strained and have flimsy support." [347]

Mr. Hertz informed Mr. Schiffer that the facts simply did not support a legally sufficient case of bias to disqualify Judge Bason from the remainder of the INSLAW case. Mr. Hertz also stated that he was "fairly confident" that any motion to dismiss Judge Bason would not succeed and the denial of any such motion could not be successfully challenged on appeal. He cited the following reasons: (1) The Department had no evidence that what they viewed as "Judge Bason's incredible factual conclusions or alleged bias," actually stemmed from an extrajudicial source, as the case law required; (2) the research revealed that adverse factual findings and inferences against the Government are insufficient to support a claim of bias; and (3) even adverse credibility rulings about some of the Government's witnesses in the prior phase of the INSLAW proceedings were not on their own sufficient to disqualify Judge Bason from the remainder of the proceedings. [348]

Mr. Hertz advised that attempting to demonstrate bias by Judge Bason could adversely affect any future appeal by the Department on the Findings of Fact. He also advised Mr. Schiffer that as much as the Department may disagree with Judge Bason's findings:

> ...they are not mere conclusory statements. Instead they reflect a relatively detailed judicial analysis of the evidence, including reasons for believing certain witnesses and disbelieving others, as well as consideration of what inferences might or might not be drawn from the evidence. [349]

During August 1987, Assistant Attorney General Willard reported to Mr. Burns that the Department:

---

[344] Ibid.

[345] Memorandum from Stuart Schiffer, Deputy Assistant Attorney General, Civil Division to Richard K. Willard, Assistant Attorney General, Civil Division, entitled: "INSLAW," July 7, 1987.

[346] Memorandum from Michael F. Hertz, Director of the Commercial Litigation Branch, Department of Justice, to Stuart E. Schiffer, Deputy Assistant Attorney General, Civil Division, Department of Justice, entitled: "Feasibility of Motion to Disqualify the Judge in INSLAW," July 6, 1987.

[347] Ibid.

[348] Ibid.

[349] Ibid.

108

...developed a good trial record; however, there is virtually no reason for optimism about the judge's ruling.
Even though our witnesses performed admirably and we
believe we clearly have the better case, Judge Bason made
it apparent in a number of ways that he is not favorably
disposed to our position. [350]

On September 28, 1987, Judge Bason removed any doubt when
he ruled that the Department violated the automatic stay by using
"trickery, fraud and deceit" to steal INSLAW's proprietary computer software.

On October 29, 1987, Mr. Schiffer wrote in a memorandum to the
Chief of the Civil Division that:

Bason has scheduled the next [INSLAW] trial for February 2 [1988]. Coincidentally, it has been my understanding that February 1 [1988] is the date on which he [Bason]
will either be reappointed or replaced. [351]

Judge Bason learned from Chief Judge Patricia Wald, U.S. Court
of Appeals, that he would not be reappointed to the bankruptcy
bench on December 28, 1987. [352]

On January 19, 1988, the Department filed a motion that Judge
Bason recuse himself from further participation in the case, citing
that he was biased against the Department. This motion was filed
even though Michael Hertz had previously advised against such a
move. Following a hearing on January 22, 1988, the Bankruptcy
Court denied the Department's motion. On January 25, 1988, the
Department argued a motion before Chief Judge of the District
Court Aubrey Robinson for a writ of mandamus directing Judge
Bason to recuse himself. Chief Judge Robinson denied the Department's writ ruling:

I can't see anything in this record that measures up to
the standards that would be applicable to force another
judge to take over this case. There isn't any doubt in my
mind, for example, that the Declaration filed [by the Justice Department] in support of the original motion is inad-
equate. [353]

The Department again raised the issue of Judge Bason's recusal in
its appeal to the District Court. District Court Judge William Bryant upheld the two previous court rulings stating:

This court like the courts before it can find no basis in
fact to support a motion for recusal. [354]

---

[350] Memorandum from Richard K. Willard, Assistant Attorney General, Civil Division to Arnold I. Burns, Deputy Attorney General, entitled: *"INSLAW, Inc. v. Department of Justice,"* un-
dated.
[351] Memorandum from Stuart Schiffer, Deputy Assistant Attorney General, Civil Division to
Richard Willard, Assistant Attorney General, Civil Division, entitled: "INSLAW," October 29,
1987.
[352] Memorandum from Stuart Schiffer, Deputy Assistant Attorney General, Civil Division to
Arnold Burns, Deputy Attorney General, entitled: "Recent Developments in *INSLAW v. DOJ,*"
February 12, 1988,
[353] *U.S. et al,* v. *INSLAW, Inc.,* Advisory Proceeding 86–0009, opinion of Judge William Bryant. See p. 48a.
[354] Ibid., see 49a.

109

IX. CONCLUSION

Based on the committee's investigation and two separate court rulings, it is clear that high level Department of Justice officials deliberately ignored INSLAW's proprietary rights in the enhanced version of PROMIS and misappropriated this software for use at locations not covered under contract with the company. Justice then proceeded to challenge INSLAW's claims in court even though it knew that these claims were valid and that the Department would most likely lose in court on this issue. After almost 7 years of litigation and $1 million in cost, the Department is still denying its culpability in this matter. Instead of conducting an investigation into INSLAW's claims that criminal wrongdoing by high level Government officials had occurred, Attorney Generals Meese and Thornburgh blocked or restricted congressional inquiries into the matter, ignored the findings of two courts and refused to ask for the appointment of an independent counsel. These actions were taken in the face of a growing body of evidence that serious wrongdoing had occurred which reached to the highest levels of the Department. The evidence received by the committee during its investigation clearly raises serious concerns about the possibility that a high level conspiracy against INSLAW did exist and that great efforts have been expended by the Department to block any outside investigation into the matter.

Based on the evidence presented in this report, the committee believes that extraordinary steps are required to resolve the INSLAW issue. The Attorney General should take immediate steps to remunerate INSLAW for the harm the Department has egregiously caused the company. The amount determined should include all reasonable legal expenses and other costs to the Hamiltons not directly related to the contract but caused by the actions taken by the Department to harm the company or its employees. To avoid further retaliation against the company, the Attorney General should prohibit Department personnel who participated in any way in the litigation of the INSLAW matter from further involvement in this case. In the event that the Attorney General does not move expeditiously to remunerate INSLAW, then Congress should move quickly under the congressional reference provisions of the Court of Claims Act to initiate a review of this matter by that court.

Finally, the committee believes that the only way the INSLAW allegations can be adequately and fully investigated is by the appointment of an independent counsel. The committee is aware that on November 13, 1991, newly confirmed Attorney General Barr finally appointed Nicholas Bua, a retired Federal judge from Chicago, as his special counsel to investigate and advise him on the INSLAW controversy. However, at that time the Attorney General had not empowered Judge Bua to subpoena witnesses, convene a grand jury or compel the Department to produce key documents.

INSLAW officials have voiced concerns that Judge Bua, lacking independent counsel status, would not be able to entice Department employees who were knowledgeable of the INSLAW matter to come forward and assist Judge Bua in bringing this matter to closure. Consequently, they are concerned that Judge Bua will not be

110

able to get to the bottom of the matter, and they believe his investigation will end up being subverted by the Department.

The inability to subpoena and/or to convene a grand jury was apparently of concern to Judge Bua and, after a meeting on January 28, 1992, the Attorney General granted Judge Bua broad investigative authority which included the power to subpoena witnesses and to convene special grand juries. However because of the actions by the Department regarding potential whistleblowers such as Anthony Pasciuto, it is very likely witnesses will still feel intimidated by the Department. This problem was present throughout the committee's investigation and remains a potential problem today.

Without independent counsel status, Judge Bua remains an employee of the Department of Justice. The image problem is illustrated in a recent interview with Roger M. Cooper, Deputy Assistant Attorney General for Administration. In an interview with the Government Computer News, Mr. Cooper stated that:

> The judge (Bua) will do as the attorney general wants him to do, and that's fine. I think all of us in the department would like to get it [the INSLAW matter] behind us. It's sort of an albatross.

Mr. Cooper may have meant that Attorney General Barr wants Judge Bua to conduct a thorough investigation. The committee has no reason to doubt the commitment of Judge Bua or Attorney General Barr to do a thorough investigation of this matter—the problem rests with the fact that, as long as the investigation of wrongdoing by former and current high level Justice officials remains under the control of the Department, there will always be serious doubt about the objectivity and thoroughness of the work.

This matter has caused great harm to several individuals involved and has severely undermined the Department's credibility and reputation. Congress and the executive branch must take immediate and forceful steps to restore the public confidence and faith in our system of justice which has been severely eroded by this painful and unfortunate affair. As such, the independent counsel should be appointed with full and broad powers to investigate all matters related to the allegations of wrongdoing in the INSLAW matter, including Mr. Casolaro's death and its possible link to individuals associated with organized crime.

X. FINDINGS

1. The Department, in an attempt to implement a standardized case management system, ignored advice from vendors—including INSLAW—that PROMIS should not be adapted to word processing equipment. As predicted, problems arose with adapting PROMIS to word processing equipment. The Department immediately set out to terminate that portion of the contract and blamed INSLAW for its failure.

2. The Department exhibited extremely poor judgment by assigning C. Madison Brewer to manage the PROMIS implementation contract. Mr. Brewer had been asked to leave his position as general counsel of INSLAW under strained relations with INSLAW's owner, Mr. William Hamilton. INSLAW's problems with the Department, which started almost immediately after the award of the

111

contract in March 1982, were generated in large part by Mr. Brewer, with the support and direction of high level Department officials. The potential conflict of interest in the hiring of Mr. Brewer was not considered by Department officials. However, Mr. Brewer's past strained relationship with Mr. Hamilton, and the fact that he lacked experience in ADP management and understanding of Federal procurement laws, raises serious questions about why he was selected as the PROMIS project manager.

3. Mr. Brewer's attitude toward INSLAW, combined with Mr. Videnieks' harsh contract philosophy, led to the rapid deterioration of relations between the Department and INSLAW. Any semblance of fairness by key Department officials toward INSLAW quickly evaporated when Mr. Hamilton attempted to protect his companies' proprietary rights to a privately funded enhanced version of the PROMIS software. In a highly unusual move, Mr. Brewer recommended just 1 month after the contract was signed that INSLAW be terminated for convenience of the Government even though INSLAW was performing under the contract. From that point forward there is no indication that Mr. Brewer or Mr. Videnieks ever deviated from their plan to harm INSLAW. The actions taken by Messrs. Brewer and Videnieks were done with the full knowledge and support of high level Department officials.

4. Peter Videnieks, the Department's contracting officer, negotiated Modification 12 of the contract which resulted in INSLAW agreeing to provide its proprietary Enhanced PROMIS software for the Department's use. This negotiation was conducted in bad faith because Justice later refused to recognize INSLAW's rights to privately financed PROMIS enhancements. Mr. Videnieks and Mr. Brewer, supported by Deputy Attorney General Jensen and other high level officials, unilaterally concluded that the Department was not bound by the property laws that applied to privately developed and financed software.

5. Thereafter, the Department ignored INSLAW's data rights to its enhanced version of its PROMIS software and misused its prosecutorial and litigative resources to legitimize and coverup its misdeeds. This resulted in extremely protracted litigation and an immense waste of resources both for the Government and INSLAW. These actions were taken even though the Department had already determined that INSLAW's claim was probably justified and that the Department would lose in court. In fact, Deputy Attorney General Burns acknowledged this fact to OPR investigators.

6. Department of Justice documents show that a "public domain" version of the PROMIS software was sent to domestic and international entities including Israel. Given the Department's position regarding its ownership of all versions of PROMIS, questions remain whether INSLAW's Enhanced PROMIS was distributed by Department officials to numerous sources outside the Department, including foreign governments.

7. Several witnesses, including former Attorney General Elliot Richardson, have provided testimony, sworn statements or affidavits linking high level Department officials to a conspiracy to steal INSLAW's PROMIS software and secretly transfer PROMIS to Dr. Brian. According to these witnesses, the PROMIS software was subsequently converted for use by domestic and foreign intelligence

112

services. This testimony was provided by individuals who knew that the Justice Department would be inclined to prosecute them for perjury if they lied under oath. No such prosecutions have occurred.

8. Justice had made little effort to resolve conflicting and possibly perjurious sworn statements by key departmental witnesses about the alleged attempt by high level Department officials to liquidate INSLAW and steal its software. It is very possible that Judge Blackshear may have perjured himself and even today his explanations for his recantation of his sworn statement provided to INSLAW are highly suspicious. The investigation of this matter by the Department's Office of Professional Responsibility was superficial.

9. The Department's response to INSLAW's requests for investigations by an independent counsel and the Public Integrity Section was cursory and incomplete.

10. The reviews of the INSLAW matter by Congress were hampered by Department tactics designed to conceal many significant documents and otherwise interfere with an independent review. The Department actions appear to have been motivated more by an intense desire to defend itself from INSLAW's charges of misconduct rather than investigating possible violations of the law.

11. Justice officials have asserted that, as a result of the recent ruling by the Appeals Court and the refusal of the Supreme Court to hear INSLAW's appeal, the Findings and Conclusions of Bankruptcy Judge George Bason and senior Judge William Bryant of the District Court are no longer relevant. The Appeals Court decision, in fact, did not dispute the Bankruptcy Court's ruling that the Department "stole...through trickery, fraud and deceit" INSLAW's PROMIS software. Its decision was based primarily on the narrow question of whether the Bankruptcy Court had jurisdiction; the Appeals Court ruled that it did not. This decision in no way vindicates the Department nor should it be used to insulate Justice from the criticism it deserves over the mishandling of the INSLAW contract.

12. The Justice Department continues to improperly use INSLAW's proprietary software in blatant disregard of the findings of two courts and well established property law. This fact coupled with the general lack of fairness exhibited by Justice officials throughout this affair is unbefitting of the agency entrusted with enforcing our Nation's laws.

13. Further investigation into the circumstances surrounding Daniel Casolaro's death is needed.

14. The following criminal statutes may have been violated by certain high level Justice officials and private individuals:

18 U.S.C. § 371—Conspiracy to commit an offense.

18 U.S.C. § 654—Officer or employee of the United States converting the property of another.

18 U.S.C. § 1341—Fraud.

18 U.S.C. § 1343—Wire fraud.

18 U.S.C. § 1505—Obstruction of proceedings before departments, agencies and committees.

18 U.S.C. § 1512—Tampering with a witness.

18 U.S.C. § 1513—Retaliation against a witness.

18 U.S.C. § 1621—Perjury.

113

18 U.S.C. § 1951—Interference with commerce by threats or violence (RICO).

18 U.S.C. § 1961 et seq.—Racketeer Influenced and Corrupt Organizations.

18 U.S.C. § 2314—Transportation of stolen goods, securities, moneys.

18 U.S.C. § 2315—Receiving stolen goods.

15. Several key documents subpoenaed by the committee on July 25, 1991, were reported missing or lost by the Department. While Justice officials have indicated that this involves only a limited number of documents, it was impossible to ascertain how many documents or files were missing because the Department did not have a complete index of the INSLAW materials. The Department failed to conduct a formal investigation to determine whether the subpoenaed documents were stolen or illegally destroyed.

XI. RECOMMENDATIONS

1. The committee recommends that Attorney General Barr immediately settle INSLAW's claims in a fair and equitable manner.

These payments should account for the Department's continued unauthorized use of INSLAW's Enhanced PROMIS and other costs attributed to INSLAW's ongoing attempt to obtain a just settlement for its struggle with the Department, including all reasonable attorneys' fees. If there continue to be efforts to delay a fair and equitable result, the committee should determine whether legislation is required to authorize a claim by INSLAW against the United States, pursuant to 28 U.S.C. § 1492.

2. The Attorney General should require that any person in the Department that participated in any way in the litigation of the INSLAW matter be excluded from further involvement in this case, with the exception of supplying information, as needed, to support future investigations by a independent counsel or litigation, as appropriate.

3. The committee strongly recommends that the Department appoint an independent counsel to conduct a full, open investigation of the INSLAW allegations of a high level conspiracy within the Department to steal Enhanced PROMIS software to benefit friends and associates of former Attorney General Meese, including Dr. Earl Brian, as discussed in this report. Among other matters, the investigation should also:

Ascertain whether there was a strategy by former Attorneys General and other Department officials to obstruct this and other investigations through employee harassment and denial of access to Department records.

Investigate Mr. Casolaro's death.

Determine whether current and former Justice Department officials and others involved in the INSLAW affair resorted to perjury and obstruction in order to coverup their misdeeds.

Determine whether the documents subpoenaed by the Committee and reported missing by the Department were stolen or illegally destroyed.

Determine if private sector individuals participated in (1) the alleged conspiracy to steal INSLAW's PROMIS software and distribute it to various locations domestically and overseas,

114

and (2) the alleged coverup of this conspiracy through perjury and obstruction.

Determine if other criminal violations occurred involving:

18 U.S.C. § 371—Conspiracy to commit an offense.

18 U.S.C. § 654—Officer or employee of the United States converting the property of another.

18 U.S.C. § 1341—Fraud.

18 U.S.C. § 1343—Wire fraud.

18 U.S.C. § 1505—Obstruction of proceedings before departments, agencies and committees.

18 U.S.C. § 1512—Tampering with a witness.

18 U.S.C. § 1513—Retaliation against a witness.

18 U.S.C. § 1621—Perjury.

18 U.S.C. § 1951—Interference with commerce by threats or violence (RICO).

18 U.S.C. § 1961 et seq.—Racketeer Influenced and Corrupt Organizations.

18 U.S.C. § 2314—Transportation of stolen goods, securities, moneys.

18 U.S.C. § 2315—Receiving stolen goods.

115

DISSENTING VIEWS OF HON. HAMILTON FISH, JR., HON. CARLOS J. MOORHEAD, HON. HENRY J. HYDE, HON. F. JAMES SENSENBRENNER, JR., HON. BILL McCOLLUM, HON. GEORGE W. GEKAS, HON. HOWARD COBLE, HON. LAMAR S. SMITH, HON. CRAIG T. JAMES, HON. TOM CAMPBELL, HON. STEVEN SCHIFF, HON. JIM RAMSTAD, AND HON. GEORGE ALLEN

We are unable to support this Investigative Report because it injects the Committee into judicial functions, publicizes unproven allegations, and recommends inappropriate United States Claims Court and Independent Counsel involvement. The Committee endorses findings by a bankruptcy judge in the INSLAW case without the benefit of Committee or subcommittee hearings on the contract dispute that is the focus of the litigation. The Report repeats, and thus disseminates, charges of wrongdoing that can damage reputations even though the Committee itself generally cannot arrive at conclusions on whether various alleged activities—going beyond bankruptcy judge findings—actually occurred. The Committee calls for expeditious governmental remuneration of INSLAW, although those entrusted with the enforcement of our laws in the Executive Branch are better qualified than Members of Congress to assess the utility of settling a legal controversy on terms favorable to a private litigant. A congressional reference of this matter to the Claims Court is unjustified; INSLAW has not been prevented from adjudicating its claims before an appropriate tribunal in a timely fashion, and proceedings remain pending before the Department of Transportation Board of Contract Appeals. An appointment pursuant to the Independent Counsel statute is unnecessary and potentially disruptive of a criminal investigation currently in progress.

The recitation in an official Committee document of accusations of wrongdoing—in the absence of proof satisfactory to the Committee—is an unfortunate and harmful feature of the Report. This practice makes it imperative to note initially in our dissent that the Report does not reach conclusions about the truth of many allegations. The Report, for example, describes allegations of a high-level Department of Justice conspiracy involving INSLAW's software but does not purport to determine whether such a conspiracy existed. Elsewhere, the Report describes former Bankruptcy Judge George Bason, Jr.'s suggestions of Department of Justice impropriety in connection with his failure to gain reappointment, a process controlled by the Federal Judiciary. The Report points out, however, that "[t]he Committee was unable to substantiate Judge Bason's charges."

INSLAW, a computer software company, had contracted with the Department of Justice in March 1982 to supply case management software for U.S. Attorneys' offices. Contract disputes arose between INSLAW and DOJ relating to the incorporation into the software of enhancements INSLAW claimed were privately funded. Although the parties executed a contract modification in 1983 that facilitated software delivery to the Department of Justice, they never reached agreement on the identification of any non-government funded enhancements. INSLAW eventually filed for bankruptcy protection, and Bankruptcy Judge Bason concluded in an adversary

116

proceeding that the Department of Justice had engaged in improper conduct.

The Report expresses basic agreement with Judge Bason's view of the evidence, although Members of the Committee on the Judiciary are not in a position to conclude one way or the other whether Judge Bason's findings—hotly contested by the Department of Justice—accurately reflect what actually transpired. Members of the Committee—other than possibly the Chairman—did not participate in this long investigation conducted by Majority investigative staff with the substantial assistance of GAO detailees. The testimony the Subcommittee on Economic and Commercial Law received from a few people involved in INSLAW litigation during a December 5, 1990, hearing on access to certain INSLAW documents is no substitute for direct familiarity with the voluminous record. We cannot assess the credibility of the many government witnesses who testified in the bankruptcy court without the benefit of hearing from them ourselves.

Although the district court affirmed the bankruptcy court's order in most respects, the United States Court of Appeals for the District of Columbia concluded that the bankruptcy court lacked jurisdiction and therefore reversed the district court and directed the dismissal of INSLAW's complaint. The United States Court of Appeals for the District of Columbia—after noting that "[t]he bankruptcy and district courts here both concluded that the Department 'fraudulently obtained and then converted enhanced PROMIS [software] to its own use'"—commented that "[s]uch conduct, if it occurred, is inexcusable." [Opinion, p. 15.] We find ourselves in the similar position of criticizing the conduct described by lower courts "if it occurred."

The Report erroneously claims that DOJ litigated the INSLAW matter "even though it knew in 1986 that it did not have a chance to win the case on merits"—and observes that "[t]his clearly raises the specter that the Department actions taken against INSLAW in this matter represent an abuse of power of shameful proportions." The only support for these sweeping statements, however, appears to be a misconstruction of a 1988 DOJ Office of Professional Responsibility interview with Deputy Attorney General Arnold Burns. In that interview, Mr. Burns recounted that "I wanted to know, as a lawyer, why we didn't make a claim against INSLAW for the royalties on the theory that we were the proprietary owners." [OPR Interview, p. 12.]

This context relating to a possible DOJ counterclaim is critical to understanding Mr. Burns' comment that DOJ lawyers were "satisfied that INSLAW could sustain the claim in court, that we had waived those rights...." Mr. Burns goes on to point out in the Office of Professional Responsibility interview that he "had concluded in good faith...that unless there was movement on their [INSLAW's] part on that [proprietary rights] issue, not having anything to do with our counterclaim then, just a question of whether they have the right to collect royalties from us, that this was not susceptible of settlement and I so advised Mr. Ratiner [INSLAW's attorney] on August 28, 1986." [OPR Interview, p. 13.] Mr. Burns apparently learned that DOJ had waived its rights to seek royalties from INSLAW (by way of a counterclaim) for making the PROMIS

117

software available to others but never suggested that INSLAW had a legitimate claim against the Department or that the Department had waived its right to oppose such a claim. The August 28, 1986, letter Mr. Burns refers to states explicitly: "We believe that Inslaw's claim for license fees is wholly without merit, and that your client's expectations with respect to compensation in this regard are entirely unjustified and unjustifiable."

The unidentified correspondence that Mr. Burns refers to as waiving rights[1] may be a subject of some discussion in the Report itself. The Report points out that INSLAW's attorney, in a May 26, 1982, letter to Associate Deputy Attorney General Stanley E. Morris, "provided a detailed description of what the company planned to do to market the software commercially...." Mr. Morris' response can be viewed as acquiescing to sales by INSLAW to third parties.

In view of the Report's heavy reliance on its construction of a small part of a single interview with the Office of Professional Responsibility, it seems unusual that the Report cites no effort to question Mr. Burns in the course of the Committee's investigation. This omission appears particularly glaring in view of other evidence contradicting the Report's perception of how DOJ viewed the merits of its case. Justice Management Division General Counsel Janis Sposato, for example, "concluded [in 1985] that INSLAW's claim to its privately financed enhancements had no merit." [83 B.R. 89 at 154 (Bkrtcy. D. Dist. Col. 1988).] Although the Report claims that DOJ "fought two judgments that it believed were in error based on technical, legal issues rather than on the merits of the case," DOJ's appellate brief in the district court contains 65 pages devoted to arguing that various factual findings by Judge Bason are clearly erroneous.

The Report's repeated references to the Department of Justice's violation of the automatic stay are confusing in view of the ruling on this point by the United States Court of Appeals for the District of Columbia in the INSLAW litigation. Circuit Judge Williams' opinion for the Court states:

> Inslaw claimed that the Department had violated the stay provision by continuing, and expanding, its use of the software program in its U.S. Attorneys' offices. The bankruptcy court found a willful violation..., and the district court affirmed on appeal.... Because we find that the automatic stay does not reach the Department's use of property in its possession under a claim of right at the time of the bankruptcy filing, even if that use may ultimately prove to violate the bankrupt's rights, we reverse. [Court of Appeals opinion, p. 3.]

The lower courts erroneously construed Bankruptcy Code Section 362 [automatic stay]—and the Report perpetuates that misconstruction in spite of the appellate decision.

Judge Bason's opinion is particularly critical of the PROMIS Project Manager in the Executive Office of U.S. Attorneys. At an earlier point in his career, C. Madison Brewer had served as gen-

[1] "...that somebody in the Department of Justice, in a letter or letters, as I say in this back and forthing [sic], had, in effect, waived those rights." [OPR Interview, p. 12.]

118

eral counsel for INSLAW's predecessor corporation. Although we do not endorse DOJ's decision over ten years ago to select Mr. Brewer as Project Manager—in view of his former association with INSLAW's predecessor—fairness to DOJ requires noting that the earlier employment had terminated more than five years before Mr. Brewer's selection, DOJ did not know at the time of his selection that he apparently had been encouraged to leave his former employment, and INSLAW waited until Mr. Brewer expressed views it regarded as unfavorable before complaining to DOJ about his service as Project Manager.

The Report is highly critical of DOJ's response to allegations of wrongdoing relating to INSLAW. In that connection, the Report does not give appropriate credit to the Department for promptly initiating an Office of Professional Responsibility investigation following Bankruptcy Judge Bason's September 28, 1987, oral ruling in which he said "the Department of Justice took, converted, stole, Inslaw's enhanced PROMIS by trickery, fraud, and deceit...." [P. 9 of transcript.] Deputy Attorney General Arnold Burns asked OPR to "conduct a complete and thorough investigation into the allegations of bias and misconduct by various Justice Department officials against Inslaw" in an October 14, 1987, memorandum [quoted on p. 4 of OPR report]—preceding by over three months the filing of formal findings of fact and conclusions of law (on January 25, 1988), in the INSLAW case. OPR, in a detailed 91-page report, ultimately concluded that the allegations relating to a number of individuals were unsubstantiated.

After reviewing February 1988 allegations from INSLAW's President William Hamilton against high level Department of Justice officials, the Public Integrity Section of the Criminal Division concluded that "[t]he facts submitted by Hamilton are not sufficiently specific to constitute grounds to investigate whether any person covered by the Independent Counsel statute committed a crime." A Special Division of the United States Court of Appeals for the District of Columbia recounts in a per curiam opinion:

> Upon receiving the INSLAW material...the Department of Justice had promptly conducted a thorough review of the allegations in conformance with the Independent Counsel Act, determined that they were insufficient to warrant a preliminary investigation under the standards of 28 U.S.C. 591(d) [footnote omitted], and accordingly closed the matter. [In Re: INSLAW, INC. at p. 4 (September 8, 1989).]

The Report describes at great length a series of allegations of wrongdoing—going beyond Judge Bason's findings in the INSLAW litigation—about which the Report does not reach conclusions. The propriety of reciting such allegations in a public report—in the absence of sufficient evidence to reach conclusions—is questionable. The release of such raw data may cause needless injury to reputations. This modus operandi is antithetical to the criminal process model in which the government does not disseminate allegations unless the evidence justifies a criminal prosecution. Some of the allegations, in addition, relate to the conduct of foreign governments—and dissemination of such material may have potential im-

119

pacts on our foreign relations. There are major problems also with the credibility of some of the individuals whose allegations are aired. One individual making allegations is referred to in the Report itself as "a shady character...recently convicted on drug charges."

The Report erroneously attributes the fact that "the Committee could not reach any definitive conclusion about INSLAW's allegations of a high criminal conspiracy" in part to "the lack of cooperation from the Department." In reality, however, the Department provided the investigators access to voluminous records and facilitated extensive interviews with its employees. The Report itself delineates various "important precedents" that were established in terms of access—an acknowledgment that clearly contradicts an argument that DOJ frustrated the investigation.

The Report concludes that "[i]n the event that the Attorney General does not move expeditiously to remunerate INSLAW, then Congress should move quickly under the congressional reference provisions of the Court of Claims Act to initiate a review of this matter by that Court." INSLAW, however, still has the opportunity to appear before the Department of Transportation Board of Contract Appeals. No conduct by the government has prevented INSLAW from litigating this matter in a proper forum within the period of the statute of limitations. It clearly is not the fault of the United States that INSLAW and its attorneys decided to initiate a proceeding in a court that lacked jurisdiction.

Strong policy reasons oppose permitting litigants against the government to avoid the strictures of statutes of limitation. Designed to bar stale claims, statutes of limitation are predicated both on the evidentiary problems involved in arriving at the truth many years after events and on the potential injustice of greatly protracted legal proceedings. We simply do not have equities justifying extraordinary relief in the INSLAW matter in view of the fact that sweeping allegations remain unproven by the Report's own acknowledgment.

The Report recommends the appointment of an Independent Counsel in spite of the fact that a former federal judge [Nicholas Bua of Chicago, a President Carter judicial appointee] is actively investigating INSLAW and is subpoenaing witnesses to testify before a federal grand jury. There appears to be every indication that Judge Bua and his staff are operating with complete independence in the Department of Justice. An appointment pursuant to the Independent Counsel statute is superfluous at this point however one views the evidence—and is likely to result in unnecessary delay, expense, and duplication of effort. Judge Bua's investigation must be permitted to go forward and reach a conclusion if we hope to dispose of lingering allegations as expeditiously as possible. He has the authority to get to the bottom of this matter—and his efforts must be facilitated rather than circumvented.

120

All Committee Republicans voted against the adoption of the Investigative Report.

HAMILTON FISH, JR.
CARLOS J. MOORHEAD.
HENRY J. HYDE.
F. JAMES SENSENBRENNER, JR.
BILL MCCOLLUM.
GEORGE W. GEKAS.
HOWARD COBLE.
LAMAR S. SMITH.
CRAIG T. JAMES.
TOM CAMPBELL.
STEVEN SCHIFF.
JIM RAMSTAD.
GEORGE ALLEN.

121

SEPARATE DISSENTING VIEWS OF HON. TOM CAMPBELL

I concur in the dissenting views but write separately to add emphasis to three points.

First, the Majority Report places a great deal of reliance on the findings of the Bankruptcy Judge and refers to those findings as having been upheld by the Federal District Judge as well. The Majority Report accepts those findings as fact.

But our committee does not know if they are fact or not. The Bankruptcy Judge lacked jurisdiction to enter the findings that he did, as the Majority Report acknowledges. The Majority Report claims as a result that the factual findings of the Bankruptcy Judge were not cast in any doubt, since the reversal of his judgment was on jurisdictional grounds—what the Majority Report terms a legal technicality.

Legal technicalities are what you call holdings of law that devastate your case. You call them unassailably learned conclusions of law if they support your case.

The reason the U.S. Court of Appeals' finding of no jurisdiction devastates the Majority's case is that this decision renders the Bankruptcy Judge's findings of no effect. The key point is this: if the Bankruptcy Judge *had* jurisdiction, then the three judges of the U.S. Court of Appeals on review would have had to consider whether to uphold those findings or not. But we'll never know what they would have done with those findings.

The Department of Justice makes a strong case the findings were not substantiated by the evidence. It is wrong to say that the findings were left untouched on appeal—the U.S. Court of Appeals simply never got to them because they didn't have to. To hold that they retain any significance at all would require reviewing courts, having already found a lower court's decision to be without jurisdiction, to proceed nonetheless to review each and every finding by that court, lest someone subsequently says those findings were "left untouched" on appeal. It is axiomatic in our legal system that when a court is found to lack jurisdiction on appeal, all of its findings of fact and conclusions of law are from that moment without the slightest weight.

The Federal *District* Judge *did* uphold the findings of the Bankruptcy Judge, prior to the Court of Appeals holding they both lacked jurisdiction. The Majority Report tries to make this sound as though two completely separate decisionmakers passed on the facts and law presented. In reality, however, a federal district judge will affirm the findings of a bankruptcy judge unless they are clearly erroneous. So all that can be concluded is that one bankruptcy judge found as the Majority Report states, and one federal district judge could not call those findings clearly erroneous.

Hence, the tendency of the Majority should be resisted to intimate that the "score" is somehow 2 to 0. If anything, it might be 1+ to 0, since the Federal District Judge's finding of no clear error does not constitute a separate analysis of the facts except on the most generous of review standards.

But, once again, we have no idea how the three federal appeals court judges would have ruled. They may well have found the Bankruptcy Judge's conclusions to be clearly erroneous. If they did,

122

the "score" would have been 1+ to 3, even adopting the somewhat bizarre assumption that one federal judge's opinion is entitled to the same weight as any other's, though some sit on a higher court.

But we don't know, because the U.S. Court of Appeals judges found the conclusions to have been without jurisdiction. In reality, therefore, the only meaningful score is 0 to 3; since the unanimous opinion of the three reviewing judges was that the findings of fact below should have no legal effect.

Secondly, the Majority Report, and some Majority Members at the Committee Markup, suggested that the involvement of Judge Nicholas Bua made the case for an Independent Counsel stronger. It is argued that the Attorney General has, by appointing Judge Bua to conduct an outside investigation, admitted that the Department of Justice is incapable of proceeding in this matter in a fair way.

This is a dangerously erroneous position to maintain. Its logical conclusion is that the Attorney General never appoint an outsider to assist him, except through the mechanisms of the Independent Counsel statute. This would be regrettable. The Attorney General should remain free in those cases where an Independent Counsel is not appropriate nevertheless to seek a report from an outside source. To hold otherwise will discourage future Attorneys General from seeking the judgment of outsiders. There is no knife-edge between Justice Department proceeding entirely internally and the appointing of an Independent Counsel—middle courses are still available, and in this case, may well be useful.

Third, and last, much was made at the Committee Markup of statements made under oath by the Honorable Elliot Richardson, who is counsel for one of the parties in this matter.

I cannot name a public figure for whom I have higher regard than Mr. Richardson.

However, it remains that his views are not evidence. He was not a party to any of the contract negotiations at issue in this case. His conclusions are entitled only to the weight they deserve as arguments offered by counsel for a very interested party.

Cogent argument by a very respected attorney representing one side in a lawsuit is valuable to a court; it is not dispositive. That we accord it more weight than that shows how different we are, in fact, from a court.

The Inslaw matter is proceeding properly through the route of administrative remedy, with subsequent judicial review awaiting. This Committee errs in deciding factual matters in dispute on behalf of one side, errs in effectively awarding that side damages, and errs most fundamentally in taking a judicial and administrative matter into the legislative branch.

TOM CAMPBELL.

O

8
Espionage

Introduction

While espionage against the government may decline somewhat because of recent world events, industrial espionage may fill the void. I personally have not encountered any instances of espionage against the government. However, I have had encounters with industrial espionage. One case that I was personally involved in will be presented in Case 16 in this chapter.

Mr. Howard W. Timm, Ph.D., is a program manager at the Defense Personnel Security Research and Educational Center (PERSEC) in Monterey, California. He was previously an associate professor at Southern Illinois University's Center for the Study of Crime, Delinquency, and Corrections. An article recently written by him titled "Who Will Spy?" was published in *Security Management* magazine. Material is presented from that article to provide the reader with some insight as to what kind of individuals may be at risk. The views expressed by Mr. Timm are his and do not reflect the official policy or position of the Department of Defense or the United States government.[1]

Mr. Timm writes:

> Espionage is a major problem for both industry and the government. During the last decade the number of incidents reported has grown dramatically. A data base maintained at the Defense Personnel Security Research and Education Center contains information on more than 60 Americans who committed espionage against the United States since 1981. This figure does not include a much larger number of industrial espionage cases that also occurred during that same period.

The problem of espionage is likely to get much worse over the next few years. On the supply side, numerous Americans with access to classified information and industrial secrets may suffer from industrial, military, and civil reductions in force. Many of them will have acquired life-styles and statuses that depend on their comparatively high-paying and important positions as well as on the high levels of credit they have been granted. After being laid off, they may face a depressed job market with little demand for their skills, a depressed housing market that is further glutted by the homes of their laid-off coworkers, and reduced levels of available credit and government services.

On the demand side, fierce competition among companies and nations for technological advantages will be compounded by reductions in money available for research and development. The fall of the Iron Curtain will reduce the travel restrictions that have impeded the East's efforts at technological espionage.

Having a human intelligence structure already in place and facing desperate economic conditions at home could further increase espionage activity by former east bloc countries. In addition, there will always be companies and countries that feel threatened, seek revenge, or covet the property of others and are willing to engage in espionage to gain an edge.

Industrial Espionage

Recently *InformationWeek* published a story titled "Do You Know Where Your Laptop Is?" by Rob Kelly. Mr. Kelly writes:

According to news reports, and independently confirmed by *InformationWeek,* visiting executives from NCR Corp. learned that reality the hard way recently when they returned to their rooms after dinner at Tony Nikko Hotel in Paris to find the doors removed from their hinges. The rooms were ransacked, turned upside down, but the thieves found what they were looking for. All that was taken were two laptops containing valuable corporate secrets. Paul Joyal, president of the Silver Spring Md., Security firm Integer and a former director of security for the Senate Intelligence Committee, says he learned from insiders close to the incident that French intelligence agents, who are known for being chummy with domestic corporations, stole the machines.

Joyal suspects they were working for a local high-tech company. An NCR spokesman denies knowledge of the incident, but adds that "with 50,000" employees, it would be impossible to confirm." Similar thefts, sources say, have occurred in Japan, Iraq, and Libya.

Thieves are not only taking laptops to get at data stored in the disk drives, but also to dial in to company mainframes. And sometimes these thieves are people the victims would least suspect. One security expert tells of "the wife of a salesman for a Fortune 500 manufacturing firm who worked for a direct competitor." While her husband slept, she used his laptop to log on to a mainframe at his company and down load confidential sales data and profiles of current and potential customers. "The husband's job," says the security expert, "not the wife's, was terminated."[2]

I am going to divulge the circumstances of one particular instance and present appropriate analysis. The primary reason for this type of activity is pure and simple greed. One unique aspect of industrial espionage is that individuals that participate in the activity are not subject to the same laws that govern espionage that is perpetrated on the United States government or any other government for that matter. If participants are caught, usually little more is done than dismissal from their position. The employees or participants involved in espionage against a company are usually paid or promised gifts by an agent of a competitor to provide information on various operational aspects of the company in which they work.

Investigation of suspected industrial espionage must be conducted by trained professionals—professionals who will protect the interests of their clients within the limits of civil and criminal law. Computer-related consulting firms are not prepared for the industrial espionage environment. This work should be left to companies that specialize in private investigations.

In this country there is one company that was established some 140 years ago that can be contacted to perform these investigations—its name is Pinkerton. Pinkerton can provide investigative services globally, and conducts undercover investigations in all kinds of business settings. Regular operational status reports are given to clients and on completion, they receive a thorough report with notarized statements to document the case or facilitate prosecution and other legal options.

Pinkerton is ideally suited to help any company design and implement computer security. Pinkerton also offers employee assessment programs which enable management to hire honest and dependable employees. Certainly, the one thing Pinkerton should be considered to perform is continuing evaluations of employees in sensitive areas, specifically employees involved in maintaining computer systems and networks.

Law enforcement officials will only become involved when it is substantiated that laws have been broken within their jurisdiction. Appropriate law enforcement agencies should be notified and appraised of suspected or substantiated instances of industrial espionage. Apprehension of individuals that participate in industrial espionage is the responsibility of appropriate law enforcement agencies. These law enforcement agencies primarily include local and state agencies, the Federal Bureau of Investigation, and the Justice Department.

Case 16

In Chapter 1, Case 2 and in Chapter 3, Case 7, I reveal the details of a wholesaler's unfortunate dealings with a systems vendor. The wholesaler in this case had weekly sales amounting to millions of dollars. Information regarding sales and financial status of the wholesale company in a competitor's hands could impair the profitability of the company.

One of the owners of the wholesale company severed their relationship with the wholesale company through civil litigation and received appropriate compensation. This particular individual had a personal and professional relationship with the systems vendor previously mentioned in Cases 2 and 7. It was this previous owner that originally endorsed using the systems vendor that was later replaced by the wholesale company. The relationship between the systems vendor and the remaining management at the wholesale company disintegrated at an accelerated rate after the elimination of one of the owners. I was retained after it was discovered that the systems vendor had offered pricing information to a competitor of the wholesale company.

The systems vendor had been backing up the database that belonged to the wholesaler over a modem connection apparently for some months. Modems at the wholesaler's business remained unplugged from the first day that I began helping that company. Modem connections were not reconnected until proper security measures had been put in place, thus protecting the wholesale company data from further intrusions.

After consulting at the wholesale company for approximately 2 months, I was informed by its management that a number of employees were hired by the systems vendor that had been on site. These employees hired by the systems vendor were aware of confidential information pertaining to the wholesale company's day-to-day operations.

The other consultant and I were involved in transmitting wholesale and retail pricing information to clients of the wholesale company. These faxes were coordinated with client representatives to ensure that the proper information was transmitted. Additionally, tapes that contained pricing information were also supplied to clients in the form of nine-track, 1600-bpi magnetic media. This was a function previously handled by the systems vendor that had been on site. Hundreds of magnetic tapes had been mailed out and were routinely returned by the clients. No time limit for return of tapes had been imposed on clients. The clients were provided with the proper return address and all tapes were mailed with a label designating the wholesale company as owner of the information.

The systems vendor knew the clients of the wholesaler and could easily communicate with representatives of these companies. One of the clients of the wholesale company had been receiving tapes but had not placed orders. Now the revelation—a disgruntled employee of the systems vendor contacted the management at the wholesale company and informed them that some tapes sent to clients within the last month were in the possession of the systems vendor. This employee provided evidence that conclusively proved that tapes belonging to the wholesale company were in the hands of the systems vendor. Photographs of nine-track, 1600-bpi magnetic media tapes sitting on a desk at the systems vendor's place of business were obtained. On looking at the photographs, I noticed my handwriting on one of the labels. Approximately 20 other tapes all belonging to the wholesale company were photographed hanging in a tape rack at the system vendor's place of business. The tapes had definitely been created after the relationship between the wholesale company and the systems vendor had been formally severed. The systems vendor had been previously requested by legal counsel representing the wholesale company to return all confidential materials and not to withhold any information belonging to the wholesale company. Each magnetic tape cost about $15, therefore for 20 tapes that equals about $300 worth of tapes that were now in the possession of the systems vendor. The systems vendor had been receiving these tapes from a client of the wholesale company.

Magnetic media provided to clients were numbered and logged out to clients after the revelation from the former employee of the systems vendor. Letters were sent to all clients that received tapes requesting that they be returned to the address of the wholesale company that was provided on the label of the tape.

Analysis

This case is unique in my entire career. I have never seen so little regard for business ethics and possible criminal acts. Employees of the wholesale company were compromised by the systems vendor. The systems vendor was not a wholesaler and did not have products provided by the wholesale company. Who was the recipient of the illicitly received information? While greed may have been the motivation in this case you cannot rule out the possibility of someone deliberately attempting to seek revenge against a former employer or business associate. The actual advantage for the competitor was to undercut prices for clients of the wholesale company. Cutting wholesale or retail prices a few cents would be sufficient on the part of a competitor to obtain sales that might otherwise have been given to the wholesale company. The wholesale products distribution business is obviously competitive, but no excuse could condone the actions of the systems vendor. It is also obvious that the systems vendor may have been acting as agent for another wholesale company.

Possession of the tapes by the systems vendor was a civil matter, even though the tapes were clearly labeled with the name of the wholesaler and their address. The Confidential Information label was also on the tapes. Wrongful taking of the tapes would have to be proved to make possession of the tapes by the systems vendor a criminal issue.

Discontented employees are easily compromised and are usually targets for agents involved in industrial espionage. However, the offer of gifts or gratuities to employees of any company may ultimately achieve the desired results by agents acting for a competitor. Certainly the morale of company employees is also a factor.

After seeing the photographs of the tapes and listening to management at the wholesale company, I recommended that they obtain the services of a private investigation company. Pinkerton investigation services were recommended by me in this particular case.

Counterindustrial Espionage

There is nothing illegal or unethical that would prevent a company from using a counterespionage strategy. This may be accomplished by allowing individuals that are suspected of working with agents of a competitor access to information that is misleading or incorrect. Potential repercussions to agents or their clients is dependent on how blindly they follow the illicit information they received. At best, you may discredit agents of a competitor who are involved in industrial espionage.

Employees that are suspected of supplying confidential information should be observed if possible to establish allegations against them and to identify possible associates that are assisting them. Care should be taken that the employees' rights are observed and not disregarded.

Counterindustrial espionage should only be conducted by trained professionals. It should only be considered viable when more time is needed to determine if a single individual or multiple individuals are involved internally in victimizing a company. Once data illicitly received becomes suspect or is determined to be of no real value, agents involved in perpetrating industrial espionage will move on to easier targets.

Audit Strategy

Audits and covert audits are discussed in Chapter 10. I recommend regular audits of computer systems and networks to which they are attached. Additionally, I advocate covert audits of computer systems.

These audits are conducted on site during normal business hours. In the event that industrial espionage is suspected or discovered, a covert audit is recommended. The covert audit should be coordinated with a private investigation services company. The covert audit can be conducted by a computer consulting firm that has conducted this type of audit previously. The covert audit should be directed at security procedures safeguarding confidential information and employees who have access to confidential information. The last or previous audit should be reviewed, and the next regularly scheduled audit of the computer system or network should be moved up.

Espionage Against the Government

I have worked at several defense sites in this country as a consultant. Security meetings at these sites continually made everyone aware of a clear and present danger of espionage being perpetrated. We were always advised to contact security representatives immediately in the event we suspected espionage. Also, we were instructed to contact security if anyone attempted to compromise us personally or elicit information about our workplace.

While we are entering a new peaceful era in Europe, we should not ignore the fact that countries in other parts of the world will continue to be a threat. Security of computer systems and networks supporting businesses and our government requires our continued vigilance.

Cognitive Factors Affecting Whether a Person Commits Espionage (Figure 8-1) and Characteristics to Look for Before Granting Access to Sensitive Material (Figure 8-2, p. 196) were presented in an article titled "Who Will Spy?" by Howard W. Timm, in *Security Management Magazine*, July 1991.

Figure 8-1 Cognitive Factors Affecting Whether a Person Commits Espionage (From Howard W. Timm, "Who Will Spy," *Security Management*, July 1991, p.9. American Society for Industrial Security, 1655 North Fort Myer Drive, Suite 1200, Arlington, VA 22209. *Reprinted by permission.*)

1. Perceived opportunity? (yes or no)

2. Contemplation of act? (yes or no)

3. Strong desire to obtain one or more likely positive outcomes or avoid one or more negative outcomes? (yes or no)

4. Insufficient internal control mechanism? (yes or no)

5. Insufficient external control mechanism? (yes or no)

Note: The order of the first three factors may vary from person to person.

If five of the answers to the model "Cognitive Factors Affecting Whether a Person Commits Espionage" are yes then there is the possibility of espionage occurring. At the same time if one or more of the answers are no then it is likely that the individual at risk will not perpetrate espionage. Mr. Timm describes insufficient internal controls and external controls as follows.

> *An insufficient internal control mechanism to prevent the act.* The person does not have sufficient fear that his or her conscience would bother him or her; the person feels too little anticipatory shame or guilt. When envisioning the act, the person must see it as falling within the limits of his or her self image, or the act will not be done.
>
> The nature and strength of the individual's moral beliefs are important in determining the outcome. At least one of the following conditions is needed:

- *Disbelief that the act is morally wrong.* A foreign spy or undercover officer who is loyal to his or her true country or a person who feels a greater loyalty to certain people, groups or religious or philosophical beliefs would not believe the act of espionage to be wrong. The act's perceived reprehensibility is generally affected by the degree of selfishness involved, the act's potential for harming others on one's side, the person's intent, and the extent to which the person was coerced.

The person may be faced with competing role demands, as in the case of a mother whose child is held hostage by a hostile intelligence service that demands classified information. The determinant is the relative strength of the role that condones the act compared to the strength of the role that opposes it.

- *Rationalization of the act a priori.* People often rationalize with such comments as "This is a one-time violation just to get me through this rough period, and I will never do it again," "They have it coming," "It's for their own good," "Its for the good of humanity," "It really isn't anything the other side doesn't have," and "If I don't do it, somebody else will."

- *Belief that person is "special."* The person believes that special circumstances or personal attributes entitle him or her to disregard the applicable laws, policies, and doctrines.

- *Impaired mental reasoning.* The person is insane, is addicted to or influenced by drugs or alcohol, or has a low level of cognitive ability.

- *Undersocialization.* The person is a psychopath or sociopath.

> *An insufficient external control mechanism to prevent the act.* At least one of the following situations must be present:

- The individual perceives his or her locus of control to be external (that is, the person does not feel personally responsible for the consequences of his or her acts).

- The person does not consider the risks associated with committing the act and with being caught (that is, the person responds impulsively or immaturely).

- The person believes he or she has little status to lose. Either the person has little current status and does not envision that proceeding down the legitimate occupational paths open to him or her will satisfy his or her goals ever or quickly enough, or the person feels his or her life is sufficiently messed up or has sufficient potential to unravel that the person does not care whether he or she is punished.

  Also, the individual is not concerned about the impact the offense would have on others. Those with whom the person primarily identifies would not view the offense negatively, and the person has insufficient emotional ties to those who might be harmed by the act, such as family, friends, or colleagues.

- The person strongly believes that he or she will not be caught.
- The person strongly believes that he or she will not suffer any significant negative consequences even if caught (that is, the person does not feel sanctions will be imposed or does not fear them).

Mr. Timm also writes:

> Another personnel approach to thwarting espionage is to prevent people who may be predisposed to satisfy the model's conditions from being granted access to sensitive information. While many of the preaccess issues are currently used as criteria for adjudicating government security clearances, many others are not directly considered.
>
> Most of the issues that are not considered bear at least as much on the applicant's suitability to hold a given position as they do on security issues. Consequently, not only would their incorporation make acts of espionage less likely, but the resulting work force would be more productive and freer of interpersonal conflict.
>
> Expanding the criteria to include these issues would, however, necessitate developing objective procedures to assess the factors properly.

In regard to these statements, see Characteristics to Look for Before Granting Access to Sensitive Material (Figure 8-2).

Mr. Timm also writes that, "An additional measure is continuing evaluation. People and their circumstances change over time, sometimes for the worse."

It is also suggested by Mr. Timm that

> Continuing evaluations should look for any changes or problems in the screen criteria. In addition, evaluators should monitor behaviors that may reflect whether an employee has already engaged in espionage. The following categories are among those that should be considered:
>
> - *Behavior suggesting discontent with one's present situation.* Examples include poor job performance, feeling a need to hide job performance and the activities engaged in both during and after work,

Figure 8-2 Characteristics to Look for Before Granting Access to Sensitive Material. (From Howard W. Timm, "Who Will Spy," *Security Management*, July 1991, American Society for Industrial Security, 1655 North Fort Myer Drive, Suite 1200, Arlington, VA 22209. *Reprinted with permission.*

Before granting a person access to sensitive material, evaluators should examine whether the individual

- Has a good work record.
- Is able to get along well with colleagues and superiors.
- Has a tendency to discuss important issues and problems with superiors.
- Is not prone to grudges, revenge, or conflict.
- Has no alcohol or drug addiction.
- Has no close personal identification with widespread injustice and those who advocate illegal acts to remedy that perceived injustice.
- Is not a problem gambler or risk taker.
- Is not susceptible to blackmail.
- Is not susceptible to threats to relatives or friends in hostile countries.
- Has a tendency to associate with people in the same economic situation.
- Has good relations with family members.
- Is not a loner, has and values good, close, long-term friendships.
- Is financially responsible.
- Has few or no friends or family members who are hostile to U.S. policy or who are allied with hostile or competing countries.
- Has friends and family who would view espionage in extremely negative and unforgiving terms.
- Is happy with his or her present situation.
- Is considerate of others.
- Is optimistic.
- Views espionage against one's company or country as morally wrong.
- Has a conscience that acts up when he or she does something wrong.
- Believes he or she makes a valuable contribution to the organization.

- Tends to reject sleazy rationalizations for committing improper acts.
- Is not prone to emotional problems or insanity.
- Is not prone to acts of betrayal or walking away from commitments.
- Takes the responsibility for the consequences of his or her acts.
- Is not compulsive or immature.
- Is almost always satisfied with his or her current situation.
- Is comfortable with his or her status and career outlook.
- Enjoys work and the other activities in which he or she engages.
- Believes that if he or she committed a crime, he or she would eventually be caught and punished.

(Continued)

not finding work challenging or exciting, increased absenteeism, feeling one's supervisor does not care what one does or is out to get one, increased preoccupation with personal problems, pessimism, the feeling that one has to turn to strangers, going to bars to escape, feeling trapped, having unfavorable views about the organization or government, and feeling that the organization no longer appreciates one's potential to contribute meaningfully.

- *Behavior related to outcomes of espionage.* Examples include changes in financial condition, the purchase of luxury items inconsistent with one's income, association with people who demand or expect high-ticket items, and associations and romantic involvements with people hostile to U.S. policy.
- *Behavior suggesting an inability to resolve the guilt and fear stemming from the act of betrayal.* Examples include excessive drinking, use of drugs, excessive risk taking, the desire to be caught, suicide attempts, and other signs of emotional stress.
- *Behavior related to changing one's self-image to that of a person who commits espionage against the United States.* Examples include taking pride in one's espionage achievements, skills, and knowledge; acquiring espionage skills that serve to increase one's haul or decrease risk through planning, preparation, and careful target selection; acquiring additional contacts with the hostile or competing country; developing skills in dealing with security personnel; monetary, physical, or emotional dependence associated with committing acts of espionage; choosing work and assignments that facilitate espionage; enjoying life in the fast lane; devaluing commitment to honor, country, and legitimate work; justifying acts of espionage; becoming friendly with han-

dlers; poor or superficial relations with family, friends, colleagues, and superiors; and choosing reading material and films that provide technical information about espionage or support one's role.

Summary

1. Suspected espionage against the government should be reported to company security personnel and the Federal Bureau of Investigation.

2. Suspected instances of industrial espionage must be handled by trained professionals (private investigators).

3. Extreme care must be taken to document as much information as possible regarding the particular instance. This should include witnesses names, addresses, telephone numbers, and names and telephone numbers of relatives.

4. Once an investigation is under way, reveal its existence and details only to those individuals that need to know. The fewer people that know, the better the results of the investigation.

5. Avoid communications or confrontations with suspected employees, agents perpetrating the industrial espionage, or suspected clients of the agents.

6. Dismissal of employees should only occur when facts substantiate their knowing participation in perpetrating the industrial espionage.

7. Extreme care must be taken to ensure that employee rights are not disregarded.

8. Counterindustrial espionage may be used when industrial espionage is discovered as a means to gain time for investigation purposes.

9. Industrial espionage must be dealt with by professionals. Companies in the private investigation business should be contacted when it is suspected.

10. Audits and covert audits of computer systems or networks should be contemplated if industrial espionage is suspected or discovered. Audits may be handled by a computer consulting firm that specializes in these types of audits.

11. In suspected cases of espionage it is everyone's responsibility to notify appropriate security representatives.

References

1. Timm, Howard W. Ph.D. "Who Will Spy," *Security Management*, July 1991, pp.8–12, American Society for Industrial Security, 1655 North Fort Myer Drive, Suite 1200, Arlington, VA 22209. *Reprinted with permission.*

2. Kelly, Rob, "Do You Know Where Your Laptop Is?", *InformationWeek*, vol. 7, no. 2, 1992, pp. 28–30, CMP Publications, Inc., 600 Community Drive, Manhasset, NY 11030. *Reprinted with permission.*

PART 2
Fraud Prevention Strategies

9
Security

Introduction

Developing and implementing effective security policies and procedures is absolutely essential. This represents a significant challenge to management responsible for laptops, personal computers, minicomputers, mainframe computers, and networks. The security procedures presented in this chapter should be used as a baseline to developing and implementing security for most computing environments. Common sense in implementing security coupled with the full use of the available technology will yield the best results.

Security Policy and Procedures

Thomas Peltier is the information security advisor for General Motors Corporation. He directs the implementation of corporate information security policies, procedures, and the ongoing security awareness program. In an article titled "Policy Statement: The Cornerstone to All Procedures" published in the *Computer Security Journal,* Mr. Peltier writes[1]:

> Most computer security policies and procedures are based on the realization that the organization is completely integrated into the various computer systems.
>
> Management is beginning to understand that it is their responsibility to ensure that a system of internal controls has been established and maintained. This system provides reasonable assurances that the books and records reflect the transactions of the organization and that its established policies and procedures are carefully

followed. Failure in any of these areas can be viewed as a breech of senior management's fiduciary responsibility.

Developing a Policy

Developing a policy that fits your particular environment is essential. Both management and the employees affected must feel they have ownership in the policy. Additionally, policy should be reviewed by the human resources department and legal counsel. The policy must be supported throughout the company by its employees. Mr. Peltier writes:

> Because the top-down method is usually supported by management, it has a better chance of success, but many times it lacks reality. When top management decrees what the policy is to be, it often is too global or too restricted by their knowledge that they are ultimately responsible for the assets for the organization. The grass roots effort involves all the employees but often gets bogged down by input from people affected by the policy that contains each area's vested interests.
>
>   Your Goal is a policy that combines the best of both methods: sort of a `Top-roots' method. After you research your policy statement, have it reviewed by the people in the field and then get Top-management support. This method will provide you with the best possible policy and the highest level of support. For this policy to be effective, you will need both![2]

Security Policy

A security policy should detail policy and procedures for employees. The policy should describe specific behavior that is not considered acceptable. The policy may embrace more than just the computer system. Other sensitive areas of a business that should be not be revealed also may be addressed in the same policy.

Mr. Peltier suggests that the written policy should clear up confusion, not generate it. The policy must clearly state the objectives and answer the following questions:

- What is to be protected? State the obvious. Decide for your employees (and those that will review and audit your organization's controls) just what is important and what must be controlled. Start with a strong sentence describing as completely as possible just what this policy has been written to protect.

- Who is responsible? Include all levels of responsibility: who is responsible for abiding by the policy and who is responsible for ensuring compliance.

- When does the policy take effect? There are at least two dates to consider. The first date is for existing employees and the second date is for employees who join the organization after the policy has been adopted.

- Where within the organization does the policy reach? Is it only for a specific group of employees at company-provided facilities, or does it reach beyond the physical constraints of the building? Does the policy affect the employees when they travel or when the visit another country?

- Is policy enforcement different at organization headquarters than it is in remote locations? Is the enforcement different in different areas? Do the accountants have a different set of controls than the research engineers? Or is the policy in effect everywhere?

- Why has the policy been developed? This question leads into the sales aspect of your job. You must clearly explain why the controls should be established.

- How will the employees be monitored? How will the policy be implemented? Will there be a gradual phase in or will it be effective on the publication date? How will the organization ensure that all employees receive adequate training, or even if all employees have been made aware of the policy's existence?

When writing the policy, eliminate all unnecessary technical jargon. Each department within the organization has its own language. To be effective, your policy is going to have to be written in the business language of your organization.

Terms like IMS, CICS, TSO, RACF, ACF2, bits, bytes, baud rates, modems, and so forth are used so often by people in data processing that they assume everyone understands them. But for an employee in accounting, those terms may be meaningless.

To make sure you have succeeded in communicating to all employees, someone outside your work area should review your work. The policy development department is the likely candidate for critiquing your work; they will make certain that your policy is in the proper format and will identify technical jargon to eliminate.

A policy statement should not exceed one or two pages. The wording must be concise so the reader can have no doubt about objectives. The wording must be unambiguous so that no one can exempt himself or herself from the requirements.

Finally, know your readers. Knowing who will be reading your policy will have a direct effect on who it will apply to and how universal its acceptance will be. Perhaps you will need to modify the policy for different locations of the organization.

In a multinational organization, the policy statement will have to be modified for various foreign locations to meet local requirements. Try to be included in the review panel for any of these activities. Additionally, if your organization is in the defense business, then there are specific Department of Defense regulations that must be followed.

Written Policy Checklist

While the format of the policy will depend on your organization's publication style, specific items should be included, or at least considered, for each policy. The written policy normally includes the following items:

1. A declaration of what is to be protected or the purpose of the policy
2. To whom the policy applies
3. The parties responsible for enforcement
4. The ramifications of noncompliance
5. Which, if any, deviations are allowed
6. A description of the deviation
7. The audit trails available or required

In addition to the preceding items dealing with the contents of the policy, the employees should also be aware of which department has responsibility for updating the policy, how often it is to be reviewed and updated, and the date of the last revision.

Examples of Policy Statements

Review these corporate information and computer security policy statements using the written policy checklist to see how many of the points are incorporated in each policy.

Example 1.   Utility company. Computer systems are company assets and must be protected from accidental or unauthorized disclosure, modifications, or destruction. All employees and contractors have an obligation to protect these resources by adhering to good security practices. (Written policy checklist items 1 and 2, above)

Example 2.   Insurance company. The protection of assets such as employees, physical property, and information relating to the conduct of business is a basic management responsibility. Managers are responsible for identifying and protecting all assets within their assigned area of management control. They are responsible for ensuring that all employees understand their obligation to protect company assets. They are responsible for implementing security practices that are consistent with generally accepted practice and the value of the asset. Finally, managers are responsible for noting variance from established security practice and for initiating the indicated corrective action. (Checklist items 1, 2, and 3)

Example 3. Major U.S. bank. Information is a principal asset of the bank and must be protected to a degree appropriate to its vulnerability and its importance to the organization. Responsibility for information security rests with all employees on an ongoing basis. (Checklist items 1 and 2)

Example 4. Washington, D.C.–based bank. Information is a bank asset. Its access, use, or processing, whether on company-provided processing devices or noncompany-provided devices, at any site, is under the authority of all applicable regulations and corporate policies and standards. Steps shall be taken to protect information from unauthorized modification, destruction, or disclosure, whether accidental or intentional. It is the standard of the bank to limit access to information on a need-to-know basis to the smallest subset of authorized users. (Checklist item 1)

Example 5. California-based bank. Information is a bank asset and, as such, steps shall be taken to protect it from unauthorized modification, destruction, or disclosure whether accidental or intentional. The cost of such protection should be commensurate with the value of the information and the probability of the occurrence of a threat. (Checklist item 1)

Example 6. Manufacturing corporation. Other than as specifically authorized by the appropriate company section manager, use of computer assets is restricted to company business. When using computer assets, each employee is authorized to access only information that is required to do his or her job. Unauthorized access to any other information is strictly prohibited. (Checklist item 5 and maybe 1 and 2)

Example 7. Global manufacturing corporation. The protection of corporate assets such as physical property and information relating to the conduct of business is a basic management responsibility. Managers must identify and protect all assets within their assigned area of management control. They are responsible for ensuring that all employees understand their assigned area of management control. Managers are responsible for ensuring that all employees understand their obligation to protect company assets. They are responsible for implementing security practices that are consistent with those discussed in the corporate information security manual. Finally, managers are responsible for noting variances from established security procedures and for initiating the required corrective action. (Checklist items 1, 2, 3, 5, and 7)

Example.   Telecommunications company

Purpose.   The purpose of this policy is to help drive the company as a world-class leader in the internal use and management of information and data, to streamline the business processes and internal operations, and to enhance the company's competitive position in the marketplace. In this policy the terms "information" and "data" are based on the following definitions. Information is the representation of discrete facts.

Policy

- Information and data are corporate resources.
- Data will be safeguarded.
- Data will be shared based on company policies.
- Data will be managed as a corporate resource.
- Corporate data will be identified and defined.
- Databases will be developed based on business needs.
- Information will be utilized to enhance current offerings and pursue new business opportunities.

Goals.   Successful management of information and data is critical to the operation of the company. Through active planning, organization, and control of these corporate resources, we will

Manage information as a strategic asset to improve the profitability and competitive advantage of both our customers and the company

Implement databases that are consistent, reliable, and accessible to meet all corporate requirements

Maximize the business processes through excellent data management across all business units

Responsibilities.   Every manager is responsible for implementing and ensuring compliance with the company information policy and initiating corrective action if needed. In implementing this policy, each business unit head is responsible for

Communicating this policy to employees

Establishing specific goals, objectives, and action plans to implement the information policy and monitor progress in implementing the policy

Developing plans that drive information system and database development to satisfy both customers and corporate information needs

Actively supporting strong data management through data stewardship

Providing education and training in data management principles to employees

The policy has been signed by the chairman of the board. (Checklist items 1, 2, 3, and 7)[3]

Mr. Peltier states:

> Every data processing installation must have security procedures. These requirements can be mandated through existing federal, state or local laws, regulations, or by contract. Senior management is responsible for ensuring that policies and procedures are published and current. Security procedures should be examined to ensure that they add to the organization's needs and do not inhibit business objectives. The written policy should clear up confusion, not generate it. The wording should be unambiguous and free from unnecessary technical jargon.[4]

Mr. Peltier has recently completed a book entitled *Policies & Procedures for Data Security*. It has 168 pages in a three-ring binder. It is illustrated with tables and charts and is priced at $97 in the United States.

This book may be ordered by contacting The Computer Security Institute, Miller Freeman Inc., P.O. Box 7339, San Francisco, California 94120. Telephone: (408) 848-5926; FAX (408) 848-5784.

A security policy will only be taken seriously if it is enforced. Most companies do not prosecute employees involved in perpetrating a crime. Companies do not want publicity about computer crimes of which they are a victim. This doesn't solve the problem. An individual discharged for criminal conduct will merely repeat this type of behavior at the next job.

Companies should have clear guidelines in enforcing a security policy and prosecuting employees that have committed a criminal act. However, caution must be exercised to ensure that a suspected employee's rights are not violated. If an employee's rights are violated in the pursuit of gathering evidence, the company may be legally liable.

Companies should make employees aware of the security policy by discussing the policy at regularly held meetings. Employee awareness of the security policy is essential to its success. Everyone must understand their responsibility is not just limited to understanding the policy. By getting employees to support a security policy, they not only protect the interests of the company but they also protect their own interests. What happens if a competitor obtains information that reduces the profitability of your company, thereby creating a necessity for a reduction of forces? What happens if the information is related to the defense posture of this country?

Employees who support the security policy should be openly praised and recognized. Everyone should be encouraged to support the security policy and to recommend procedures that will improve security of the computer system.

Security Plan

It is the responsibility of management to provide a comprehensive security plan. The security plan must address the appropriate computer environment. Some guidelines are presented here that encompass laptops, notebook computers, personal computers, minicomputers, and mainframe computers. Any security plan must be based on common sense and the ability of management to make the most of existing technology to protect its computer systems and networks.

Laptops and Notebook Security

Laptops are currently used by the top executives of many corporations around the world. Laptops can be used by executives while they are traveling to download data from a main computer at their company's headquarters. Most laptops come with an internal modem that allows them access to sensitive data anywhere there is a telephone. Thieves who steal laptops or notebooks can use the stored telephone number and in some cases the password to access data at a company's corporate headquarters. The potential for loss by a victimized company is staggering. Not only can sensitive data be divulged to a competitor, but viruses and logic bombs may also be uploaded to a company's mainframe computer.

I particularly like the new Epson laptop that has a removable hard drive. This could easily be locked in a safe or a safety deposit box at a hotel. However, data encryption of data on the hard drive is still recommended. Diskettes used with the laptop or notebook should also be encrypted.

Recently, *InformationWeek* published a story titled "Do You Know Where Your Laptop Is?" by Rob Kelly. Mr. Kelly writes:

It was an expensive round of window shopping. On Dec. 17, 1990, a British Wing Commander parked his car in downtown London to browse through an automobile showroom. A Wing Commander in Great Britain's Royal Air Force, he was enjoying a few moments away from the mounting pressures leading up to the Gulf War, which would begin less than a month later.

But the Wing Commander made a huge mistake: He left his Laptop computer in his car. And although he was gone a mere five minutes, by the time he returned, the laptop had been stolen—as had U.S. General Norman Schwarzkopf's plans, stored in the computer's disk drive, for the upcoming strike against Iraq.

The Wing Commander paid dearly for his carelessness. Soon after the red-faced Wing Commander reported the incident, he was court-martialed, demoted, and slapped with a substantial fine. The computer was anonymously returned a week later—with disk drive intact.

The British Wing Commander may feel alone in his dilemma and rue the wrong turn his life has taken, but such episodes are any thing but isolated. Though electronic security sources say it's too soon to keep score yet on the exact number of laptop thefts, anecdotally, at least, it appears a computer crime wave is underway. According to electronic data experts, during the past eighteen months, as laptop purchases have soared, theft has taken off also.[5]

One might think these are all isolated incidents and that it can't happen to me. Laptop theft has specific targets, Mr. Kelly writes:

For instance at the Computer Security Institute (CSI), an organization that ironically comprises corporate security experts, a half-dozen members have already reported their laptops stolen, says Phil Chapnick, director of the San Francisco based group. And there are probably more that aren't speaking about it, he adds: "victims prefer to maintain a low profile." So do the perpetrators, obviously. But a picture of who some of them are is beginning to emerge, says John Schey, a security consultant for the federal government. He says a roving band of "computer hit men" from New York, Los Angeles, and San Francisco has been uncovered; members are being paid upward of $10,000 to steal portable computers and strategic data stored on those machines from executives at Fortune 1000 companies. Federal agents, Schey adds, are conducting a "very, very dynamic and highly energized investigation to apprehend the group." U.S. law enforcement authorities refuse to comment on the issue.[6]

Many companies are now reassessing their position on laptop security in lieu of these recent events. Mr. Kelly also writes that

By some estimates building in protection measures raises the price of a laptop by at most 20%. Beaver Computer Corp. in San Jose, Calif., for example, has a product to encrypt the data on a laptop's hard drive and floppy disks. With this, the information can't be accessed without an "electronic key" or password. BCC has installed this capability on its own laptop, the SL007, which seems to have passed muster with some very discriminating customers; sources close to the company say a major drug cartel in Colombia wants some of those machines to protect drug trafficking data.[7]

Laptops and notebook computers are great tools for productivity; I once wrote the business plan for a new technologies company on a laptop. I accomplished most of the work while traveling and staying at a hotel in Atlanta. A laptop with WordPerfect makes a great combination and allows you to work almost anywhere. Care must be taken to protect your work and sensitive data belonging to the company you work for.

The greatest risk when using laptops is communications to a mini or mainframe computer at a company's headquarters. Mr. Kelly writes:

> Security Dynamics Technologies Inc. in Cambridge, Mass., offers the credit card-sized SecurID which can be attached to most laptops. SecurID consists of a $60 device that is connected to the laptop, and additional hardware (cost $3,000 to $13,000) installed on the host. SecurID continuously changes the login used to dial into the host; by the time a hacker gets around to using a stolen log-on, for instance, it will be obsolete.[8]

Figure 9-1 Laptop and notebook computer guidelines.

1. When traveling do not check the laptop with your luggage, carry it with you.

2. If staying at a hotel and you have planned activities that require the laptop to be left behind, check the laptop at the desk. Do not leave the laptop in your hotel room.

3. Encrypt data on the hard drive and floppy diskettes.

4. Do not store your logon and password for the companies network or mainframe computer on the laptop or notebook.

5. The laptop should be kept in a locked drawer when not being used at the office.

6. While you have the laptop assigned to you by the company you work for, do not let anyone else use it.

7. If the laptop or notebook is reassigned to another employee of the company for which you work, delete any data which you have entered, unless instructed otherwise by your supervisor or management.

This may be an excellent strategy for companies that have dozens of laptops communicating with a host (mini or mainframe computer).

If you're a laptop or notebook computer user, Figure 9-1 contains some guidelines that may save you the embarrassment of informing your employers of the loss of a laptop. Included are methods for protecting sensitive data on the hard drive and floppy diskettes.

Personal Computer Security Guidelines

A security plan for a small business that uses a single personal computer can be as simple as the following guidelines. I recommend that the following plan be used for a small business with one or more personal computers.

1. Lock the central processing unit (CPU) when not in use or if a lock is unavailable install a menu software package that requires a password.

2. Control diskettes and other removable magnetic media. Anything that goes out the door of a business must be accounted for.

3. Make full and frequent backups of the directories and files on the personal computer. Store one copy off site, possibly at the home of the owner of the business. Secure diskettes and other magnetic media when not being used.

4. If a modem is used in the personal computer, ensure that the telephone number is divulged on a need-to-know basis. The telephone number should be routinely changed if an employee is discharged and had knowledge of the number.

5. If passwords are used with software on the system, change them routinely. When an employee leaves who had a log-in and password, remove the log-in and password immediately. Change passwords of other users immediately.

6. Obtain software that scans for viruses on the system every time the system is booted up. This kind of software can be obtained quite easily.

7. Buy a paper shredder and dispose of confidential printed materials only after shredding them.

Security is very simple at the personal computer level. At the mini and mainframe computer level security is more complex. The security plan here should be developed in accordance with the hardware, operating system, and software options available for the computer system being maintained. The following guidelines should be the basis for security of both mini- and mainframe computers.

Systems Controls

Systems controls are essential ingredients to maintaining security on mini and mainframe computers. The hardware vendor of either the mini or mainframe will have off-the-shelf software to enable the system administrator to monitor users. Some software may be available through various user groups at no charge.

Lisa Manzolillo and Richard Cardinalli state:

> Internal Monitoring programs are the most effective way to control unauthorized system intrusion. Such programs can assist management in controlling computer crime and provide assistance in monitoring and evaluating personnel activities. This is usually the weakest part of information system security. Most computer frauds could have been prevented if more stringent controls are implemented.[9]

Security for most computer systems can be augmented by acquiring additional software designed to monitor users. A variety of Peek and Poke software, as it is called, can allow an administrator to observe every keystroke made at a video display terminal interactively. Maintaining audit trails and transaction files remains the primary way of monitoring users. The security plan for mini- and mainframe computers, as shown in Figure 9-2, may be administered by the manager or system administrator that supports that particular computer system. In the case of mini or mainframe computers, the plan should be thoroughly documented and approved by higher levels of management.

Summary

1. Develop and implement a security policy.

2. Develop a security policy that defines in a contractual format what is expected of all employees.

3. Make awareness of the security policy as important as the company's profitability.

4. Enforce the security policy without exception.

5. Provide positive reinforcement for employees that support the security policy.

6. Develop and implement a security plan that best suits the computer system.

7. Thoroughly document the security plan and keep the information that it provides current.

Figure 9-2 Mini- and mainframe computer security guidelines.

1. Provide physical security of the computer system.
2. Maintain password security of the users and groups to which they belong.
3. Provide accountability for all magnetic media used.
4. Maintain backups of the database on site and off site.
5. Ensure that both hardware and software supporting communications are as secure as possible.
6. Shred documents when they are no longer needed.
7. Acquire software to monitor user activity that provides audit trails and user logs.
8. Do not allow users to load software from personal computers (including laptops and notebook computers) to the mini or mainframe computer.
9. Screen all software loaded on to the mini or mainframe computer for viruses and logic bombs.
10. Screen data transmissions to the mini or mainframe computer for viruses and logic bombs.

References

1. Thomas Peltier, "Policy Statement: The Cornerstone to All Procedures," *Computer Security Journal,* vol. 7, no. 2, 1991, p. 1, Computer Security Institute, 600 Harrison Street, San Francisco, CA 94107. *Reprinted by permission.*
2. Thomas Peltier, op. cit, p. 6.
3. Thomas Peltier, op. cit, pp. 8–12.
4. Thomas Peltier, op. cit, p. 13.
5. Rob Kelly, "Do You Know Where Your Laptop Is?," *InformationWeek,* 1992, p. 28, CMP Publications, Inc., 600 Community Drive, Manhasset, NY 11030. *Reprinted by permission.*
6. Rob Kelly, op. cit, p. 28.
7. Rob Kelly, op. cit, p. 30.
8. Rob Kelly, loc. cit.
9. Lisa Manzolillo and Richard Cardinalli, "Ethics and Computer Crime—a Guide For Managers," *Computer Security Journal,* vol. 7, no. 2, 1991, p. 9. (*Reprinted with permission from Computer Security Institute, 600 Harrison Street, San Francisco, CA 94107.*)

10
Audits

Introduction

Many small businesses start with a personal computer to manage finances and payrolls. It may be just one personal computer without a modem, running Quicken and MS/DOS. Conversely, a business may use a mini or mainframe computer and be connected to an international data network. In any case, the owner of a business or the manager of a computer system has a fiduciary responsibility to maintain the data on that system accurately. If data on the computer system does not accurately reflect all business transactions, a company may be in violation of the law. Audits of computer systems are primarily intended to verify that data pertaining to a business is being accurately and efficiently maintained on the computer system.

Personal Computers

On a yearly basis retain the services of a consulting firm or consultant to audit software systems supported by a personal computer. If more than one personal computer is used by a small business, audits conducted twice a year may be advisable. Solicit information on possible hardware and software upgrades to the system that may be beneficial to the business or the performance of the system. Most importantly, solicit recommendations on security for the system.

While laptops and notebook computers may not be the subject of an audit specifically, any company's security plan must include these types of computers. Therefore companies that use these devices should expect auditors to inquire on what procedures are in place for safeguarding the data. In addition to questions on procedures designed to safeguard data, procedures on safeguarding communications via modem to a mini- or mainframe computer at the company's headquarters should also be the subject of the audit.

Mini- and Mainframe Computers

Both the minicomputer environment and the mainframe computer environment are complex environments. These environments are similar in that they have groups of people maintaining them on a day-to-day basis. However, it is the system administrator that is usually responsible for security, operations, performance, and documentation.

Security on the system should be designed to let the users perform their required daily tasks and at the same time ensure that the operating system, file system, and program directories used to support the day-to-day operations are not corrupted. Integrity of the data on the system is also crucial and should be closely monitored by the system administrator.

Various operating systems grant users read, write, modify, and delete privileges in different ways. It is the system administrator's responsibility to decide the assignment of these privileges to users on the system. Privileges are usually set up when a user log-in and password are created by the system administrator. Group privileges also may be created and assigned for a user that control the read, write, modify, and delete privileges within a specific group. On some systems, group managers may perform this same task of assigning group privileges. All of this is intended to control the user down to the lowest level of detail and yet not prevent the user from performing required tasks.

The responsibilities of any system administrator are based on the hardware, operating system, and other software installed and may vary from site to site. The system administrator is in a position of trust. An entire businesses's performance may hinge on the performance of its computer environment and it is the System Administrator who controls that environment.

System administrators may not always be data processing professionals or have degrees in computer science. Minimally they may know little more than how to program and understand the operating system. Some system administrators are certified to support their particular hardware and operating system environments.

Any individual that performs system administrator duties is in a position to make the system proprietary to themselves. Even individuals that only manage subsystems on a computer can make the system proprietary to themselves. This is sometimes thought of as a way of creating job security. It is imperative to prevent attempts by individuals to make systems proprietary. The easiest way to prevent this is to perform audits. Under some circumstances, audits that are unannounced also may prove beneficial.

It is essential for departments that maintain on site computer systems to be audited at regular intervals. This is an activity that should be given the highest priority by any manager responsible for maintaining a computer system. The audit of the system should not be approved or influenced by the manager responsible for maintaining the computer system.

The criteria for every audit should be customized to fit the hardware, operating system, communications, and other software on the system. Approval for audit criteria should occur at least one level above the manager responsible for the computer system to be audited.

The audit is furnished to higher levels of management to ensure that they are aware of the status of security, operations, performance, and documentation. It is essential that the entity performing the audit be free from influence and by that deliver an impartial report.

While an audit is being conducted, the director, manager and system administrator for the computer system must be available to answer questions on both hardware and software. The entire staff that supports a computer system will be interviewed and observed performing procedures for which they are responsible. The general areas covered by an audit are shown in Figure 10-1.

Figure 10-1 Audit criteria.

I. Security
   A. User log-in and password
   B. Group privileges
   C. Directory and file privileges
   D. Communications
      1. Local
      2. Remote (networks)
   E. Security or monitoring software
   F. System logs
   G. Audit trails
   H. Security policy
   I. Security plan
   J. Security awareness
   K. Shredding of unwanted printed materials

(Continued)

II. Operations
    A. Scheduled activities
        1. Daily
        2. Weekly
        3. Monthly
        4. Quarterly
        5. Yearly
    B. Catastrophe preparedness
    C. Archive of file systems
        1. Test
    D. Restoration of file systems
        1. Test
    E. File system maintenance
    F. Storage of magnetic media
    G. Scheduled maintenance of hardware
    H. Development partition or directory
    I. Test partition or directory
    J. Testing procedures
    K. Mirrored partitions
    L. Mirrored disks

III. Performance
    A. Benchmark testing
    B. Response times
    C. System configuration
        1. Software
        2. Hardware
    D. Memory utilization
    E. Storage utilization
    F. Performance tools
    G. Network communications

IV. Documentation
    A. Hardware
    B. Operating system
    C. Third-party software
    D. Developed software
        1. System
        2. Programmer
        3. User
        4. File definitions
        5. Flow charts
        6. Tables
    E. Online storage
    F. Offline storage
    G. Availability
    H. Updates

Audit Strategy and Benefit

The audit criteria is analyzed by asking the question, Who? What? When? and How? thereby developing all pertinent details to a task or procedure. Why a task or activity is performed is also scrutinized to see if it should continue to be performed or modified.

Once the criteria for an audit have been established, the audit begins. The lowest levels of detail are reviewed in an audit. Every file, program, and table on the storage devices or other media that is part of online storage should be accounted for as to purpose and use.

Audits also can be used as a reference or baseline when the audit is performed again. Information obtained in an initial audit is reviewed against the current audit to detect areas of increased usage and performance problems. This data can be used to help plan for future hardware and software upgrades to the system.

The idea behind the audit is that you gain, maintain and improve control of the computer system on which you depend. Individuals that maintain the computer systems hardware and software should know their work is subject to review from an outside consulting firm. These regularly scheduled audits can improve the quality and performance of a computer system.

I have seen companies use internal auditors to review systems and have seen dismal results from those same audits. Part of the reason for poor-quality audits is that the auditors did not possess sufficient skills or experience. The auditors were influenced by company politics on some occasions and this lead to audits that consisted of glossy compliments. However, on large computer systems there may be real benefit in comparing an internal audit to an external audit performed by a consulting firm.

It is management's prerogative to perform audits that are announced or unannounced. However, regularly scheduled audits are recommended. Computer systems that are not exposed to the process will invariably decline in performance and thereby increase costs to maintain the computer system. On occasion, I have seen the entire life span of the best computer systems shortened dramatically.

I recommend that bonuses and pay increases should be directly linked to passing audits. This kind of incentive will prolong the life span of both hardware and software that combined make an efficient computer system.

The cost of an audit can vary. It is dependent on the criteria approved for audit and the level of cooperation from the group supporting the computer system to be audited. The amount of money it can save in terms of dollars may be hard to define. The usual duration is proportional to the size and type of systems involved.

Failed Audits

Audits should be considered failed if any portion of the criteria reviewed is unsatisfactory. The consulting firm reports information on criteria it discovers is unsatisfactory to the appropriate manager at the company audited. The initial report should be passed to management with clear-cut recommendations to resolve areas of the criteria that are unsatisfactory.

Failure of an audit does not constitute grounds for dismissal of a director, manager, or system administrator. However, it can point to areas that require improvement in the day-to-day management of a computer system.

Corrective Action

In the case where security needs to be changed or modified for a user or file system, no delay should be tolerated. Where operations, performance, or documentation is in question, a delay of sufficient duration for analysis may be required before a solution can be put forth. For each instance, a specific amount of time should be established for completion of corrective actions.

When the time allotted is up, the corrective action must be verified and tested again and again if necessary. When the audit is performed again at the next regularly scheduled time, these areas of previous problems should be scrutinized closely.

Covert Audits

Covert audits are initiated when management has suspicions they want confirmed or denied without disturbing normal production and arousing suspected individuals. On more than one occasion, I have been retained to perform a covert audit. Covert audits are particularly useful in situations where higher levels of management are concerned about the computer systems they depend on and have reason to suspect something is wrong. Covert audits should be considered when data gathered from normal audits are unduly influenced by management at the department level.

Covert audits can also be useful when a company is preparing to cease a relationship with a vendor or one of its own employees. In this situation, the audit is performed by observing operations being performed and determining their functionality. The covert audit should be considered when misuse of a computer is suspected and management responsible seems unable to respond.

Signals for a covert audit are presented below. If one of the seven conditions presented occurs, then a covert audit is recommended. However, it must be understood that if one of these seven conditions or signals occurs, then someone in charge of the computer system or network is not doing his or her job.

Covert audits are a means of substantiating suspected instances of wrong doing by employees without disrupting business. The best results of a covert audit are obtained when the presence of the auditor or consultant performing the covert audit is undetected. The fewer individuals who know about the covert audit or of the consultant's presence the better. The consultant should provide information based on facts. However, knowing the mood of the employees or their over-all morale may be helpful to management. The consultant should be able to distinguish between the subtleties of feelings and facts. For more details on selecting a consulting firm to perform this type of audit, refer to Chapter 12.

Signals for a Covert Audit

1. Misrepresentation (by management or vendor)

2. Sabotage

3. Data omission

4. Theft of confidential information

5. Unauthorized use of computer or network resources

6. Undocumented changes to a computer system or network made by an individual or vendor

7. Espionage

The key to preventing computer fraud is knowing who is going to do it. Access is really the first determining factor in every case I have ever come across. Certainly the motivation for computer fraud can be divided between two categories. The first is greed, and the second is malicious intent.

In Figure 10-2, I list, in order of frequency, the most common to the least common perpetrators of computer fraud. This data is presented on cases I have personally encountered and is not based on any national statistics. I am extremely pessimistic about statistics of any kind because the bulk of computer fraud goes unreported. The professional categories listed all share one thing in common—access. Access by these professional categories to the computer system and the network to which it is attached must be scrutinized closely during an audit.

All of the professional categories listed in Figure 10-2 are also in positions of trust to varying degrees. The access and trust placed with

Figure 10-2 Those most likely to commit computer fraud. (The categories in this figure are presented in order of incidence, from the highest to the lowest.)

Vendors

Users

Programmers

Systems programmers

MIS managers

Analysts

Computer operators

Executives

Data entry clerks

Clerical staff

Consultants

an MIS manager is significantly greater than that of a user of a computer system. The amount of damage that can occur, therefore, is proportional to the amount of access and trust a company may have in an employee or vendor.

Computer crimes represent a potentially embarrassing situation to the victims. Many companies would rather dismiss an employee for computer fraud than prosecute the individual.

Covert audits are ideally conducted by one or two personnel with the freedom to cut through red tape if necessary. The identities of persons conducting this type of audit should be disclosed on a need-to-know basis. Only the manager who authorizes the audit should know who is performing the audit and what they are looking for.

In this situation, preferential treatment from management can work against the individuals conducting this type of audit. Actual training of an individual conducting a covert audit on low-level operational tasks and activities can provide valuable insight.

No one would question why the individual was taking detailed notes under those circumstances. Questions from the individual would be expected from everyone supporting the computer system or network. Gathering of some printed materials would also be expected.

Information collected during this type of audit would primarily be on a particular problem area. A full audit cannot be conducted under these circumstances. The information compiled has to be based on fact. Notes, observations, and printed output are all that are gathered under these circumstances.

Covert audits can provide information on potential risk situations where security procedures have broken down. In cases where industrial espionage has occurred, this may be a means of identifying employees that represent a potential risk to the internal security of a company.

A formal report to the manager initiating the covert audit would conclude the activity. Any actions taken after the report is viewed by management are at their discretion. The report should be held in strict confidence by the entity or individual conducting this type of audit. The individual that conducted the audit should be available to testify or be deposed if necessary.

A covert audit can bypass several layers of management in some companies and provide unbiased information. The benefit gained from an audit of this type is that you may be able to head off potential problems before they get out of control.

In Chapter 6, Case 12, the government contractor involved could not account for $25 million. Regular audits and covert audits might have controlled the losses in that case.

Summary

Audits conducted on an announced or unannounced basis can prevent computer fraud of most types. Audits can certainly be used by higher levels of management to ascertain if their computer systems or networks are being managed efficiently. Certainly the possibility always exists of discovering, during an audit, activity that consists of mismanagement or computer fraud.

Mismanagement of computer systems and networks creates the environment for unscrupulous individuals to perpetrate computer fraud. Audits can be the early warning system for management and can ensure that proper management is maintained. Covert audits are particularly useful in situations where higher levels of management are concerned about the computer systems they depend on and have reason to suspect something is wrong. Covert audits should be considered when data gathered from normal audits are unduly influenced by management at the department level.

Audits

Personal Computers (Small-Business Environment)

1. Retain the services of a consultant to audit the personal computer and the software systems it supports on a yearly basis.

2. Frequency of audits should be scheduled proportionately to the number of computer systems a small business maintains.

Mini- and Mainframe Computers (Medium to Large Business Environment)

3. Retain the services of a consulting firm to perform audits on mini or mainframe computers. This activity should occur on a semiannual basis.

4. Unannounced audits for computer systems that are not operating to optimum performance levels or experiencing security problems are recommended.

5. Audits should be performed by experienced outside consulting firms.

6. Audits should be approved and initiated at one level above the management responsible for maintaining the computer system being audited.

7. Bonuses and pay increases for personnel supporting a computer system should be based on passing audits successfully.

Failed Audits

8. Audits should be considered failed when any portion of the criteria for the audit fails to meet expectations of the company's management that approved the criteria.

9. Recommendations presented by the entity performing the audit to correct deficient areas of the criteria should be implemented within a reasonable period of time.

10. Areas of audit criteria reported as deficient or failed previously should be checked and tested until they are deemed acceptable by management.

Covert Audits

11. Covert audits should be performed with extreme caution by individuals that are competent enough not to violate the rights of someone who is suspected of wrongdoing.

12. Covert audits are strongly recommended when any of the following activities are suspected:

   - Misrepresentation (by management or vendor)
   - Sabotage

- Data omission
- Theft of confidential information
- Unauthorized use of computer or network resources
- Undocumented changes to a computer system or network made by an individual or vendor
- Espionage

13. Covert audits are a means of discovery. Information pertaining to them must be kept confidential.

14. Fact and not suspicion must be the deciding issue in determining wrongdoing by anyone.

11

Communications, Networks, and Telecommunications

Introduction

Communications and networks enable all computer users to take advantage of their organization's computing capabilities by exchanging information and sharing resources. Small computing systems (personal computers) can access the resources of larger systems, while larger systems can offload applications best handled by personal computers. Networks encourage the flow of information throughout a business and increase productivity. Any computer system can become a shared resource by connecting it to a network. Sharing of small computing resources like personal computers or workstations on a *local area network* (LAN) allows sharing of information in a building or cluster of buildings.

Communications

Most people understand what a modem is and I am not going to explain how they work. Modems open a door to communications utilizing a personal computer or a dumb terminal that can be almost unlimited in scope. A modem also can be a liability because not only can you use it to communicate with other systems, but other entities can also use the modem to communicate with you and with systems it is directly connected to. This makes communication a two-way street and enables both dialing out and dialing in to computer systems.

While I was working at a government contractor's site, modem communications were permitted so that designated users of the system were able to access the system from home. In the event of some urgent problem, this allowed myself and the others I worked with to respond without making a long drive to the site and made our response to system problems more timely.

Some manufacturers of computer equipment like Digital Equipment Corporation (DEC) support their users' computer systems by dialing in on a modem specifically designated for use by their technical staff to perform diagnostics remotely. These modems are specifically optioned and set for use by these technical representatives. This represents a defense against individuals who may attempt to communicate with the computer system but are not authorized to do so.

Other computer manufacturers also provide support by dialing in to a modem connected to a computer system for diagnostics that has options and settings allowing almost anyone to access the system. While there may be a specific log-in and password for this purpose, the risk is that the password and log-in may fall into the wrong hands. I recommend changing the password frequently on modems that specifically support remote diagnostics.

Case 17

A manufacturer of data storage devices located in the Midwest suffered the loss of a database. The loss of the database was directly attributable to a user logged in on a modem. The cost to restore this particular database was over $100,000. Even if the database is backed up, the data entered since the last backup of the database has to be reentered.

The manufacturer had encountered a downturn in its business and had been in the process of reorganization. Reduction of forces had been going on for some months. This was an effort of this company's management to streamline its business and remain profitable.

The theft of the database was a malicious act to say the least. The individual who perpetrated this destructive act was never caught. The loss of this database was public knowledge at the time it occurred and was published in the local newspapers.

Analysis

This was a preventable situation which dial-back modems would have discouraged and possibly prevented. This type of modem works in the following way. First it is contacted by the calling modem and then its telephone number is recorded. The receiving modem then checks to see if the calling modem's telephone number is in its table. If the calling modem is not in the receiving modem's table, then no communications are established. Many vendors of communications hardware offer variations of this procedure.

This kind of malicious act was probably perpetrated by a disgruntled employee. Clearly this was an attempt to tweak the noses of management of this company and possibly demonstrate the inefficiency of management responsible for maintaining the database.

For some months this company had been laying off employees. Passwords should be changed when employees are first notified of a layoff. No delay can be allowed under these circumstances in changing passwords. Frequently changing passwords or log-ins that are used for remote access can be crucial in maintaining security of computer systems, networks, and databases.

Networks

Networks are plentiful. These days when consumers buy a personal computer, they also may receive complementary software for CompuServe or Prodigy. CompuServe and Prodigy provide a wide variety of network services to the public.

Network administrators are similar to system administrators in their responsibilities. System administrators contact network administrators when setting up communications and establishing the details of passing data back and forth. The network administrator is responsible for creating network log-ins, passwords, and providing the criteria for transmitting data.

The development and implementation of a Network Security Policy is essential. Some formulation of security for users and groups is built in to software supporting LANs. Novell NetWare provides comprehensive security for the LAN environment. It is entirely possible that a gateway to a larger network could reside on a LAN, giving users access to an even larger Internet or wide area network (WAN). User awareness of a network security policy must be a priority for the network administrator.

Novell NetWare is a very popular and successful system for supporting LANs. Novell supports multiple protocols and utilizes servers. This system supports servers that use standard structured query language (SQL). Security offered with this product is exceptional. There are other LAN products on the market, but Novell is the dominant one. The Novell LAN is administered by a network administrator. The security and topology should be reviewed during an audit.

Networks are made up of bridges, routers, brouters (a combination bridge and router), gateways, and hosts (mainframe computers). All of these pieces of equipment have unique network addresses. Some networks are engineered to provide redundant pathways for data transmission. Packets of data with unique network addresses are routed from the various components until it reaches its final destination.

Network administrators must enforce log-in and password security. Sharing of log-ins and passwords must be discouraged in the strongest possible way. Changing log-ins and passwords of terminated employees has to be performed as soon as their changed status is known.

User logs and audit trails must be maintained on users. Frequent examination of logs and audit trails are recommended. Users that are working beyond their normal work areas should be scrutinized. Network administrators should establish a rapport with users and make inquiries regarding their work patterns. Network administrators should strive to improve the network environment so that users get quality services and at the same time a secure network environment.

Schlumberger, a French company, has a network called SINET (Schlumberger International Network) that is a transmission control protocol/internet protocol (TCP/IP) network. This is a state of the art network and Schlumberger continues to improve it. I myself have used SINET to send and receive mail from Europe. It is a worldwide network and can be easily accessed.

The Department of Defense sponsors its own TCP/IP network called the Defense Research Projects Agency (DARPA) network. The Department of Defense relies on multiple networks to transmit and receive data all over the world. For obvious reasons, I am not going to discuss them in detail.

Data encryption is used by both defense networks and commercial networks. In the commercial sector financial institutions use data encryption. This method of protecting data being transmitted eliminates all but the very sophisticated who would gain access illegitimately.

Viruses and Worms

Viruses proliferate because users share software among themselves. Viruses are primarily transmitted by sharing diskettes and by downloading software using a modem. A *virus* is a program deliberately written by someone and intended to inflict indiscriminate damage to software and databases. Viruses are not created by accident—they merely perform their designed function. Viruses are started by someone placing them in a bulletin board or software that is to be distributed.

On March 6, 1992, the 517th anniversary of Michelangelo's birth, a virus bearing the artist's name created what almost amounted to a media event. This virus was on personal computer systems, waiting for March 6 before executing its function. Everyone was concerned about the impending damage that was to occur. Some damage was inflicted by this virus. However, because so many people are scanning software and practicing safe computing, the impact of the virus was short-lived. Sometimes the virus is detected and successfully removed without damaging software or data.

Peter Stephenson has been an independent network consultant for 11 years. He specializes in enterprise network design, analysis, and information security in the LAN environment. He is the author of seven books on personal computing and is a regular columnist for *LAN Magazine.*

Mr. Stephenson presented an article titled "Implementing the Secure PC LAN—Guidelines for Information Security" in the *Computer Security Journal.* In this article Mr. Stephenson states:

> Worms and trojan horses are included under the category of virus attacks. A virus is a program fragment that attaches itself to an executable program or resides in workstation memory. It requires another program to execute. Viruses replicate every time the executable program to which they are attached executes. By the time their payload is scheduled to go off, the probability of damage is high since the virus has infected a large number of programs.
>
> A worm, on the other hand, is a self-contained, self-executing program that not only replicates itself but it also does ongoing damage. The usual damage done by a worm is the theft of resources. Worms will use up disk space or CPU resources, slowing the computer system down to a crawl. An insidious type of worm may move about the LAN collecting user names and passwords and depositing them in a clandestine file for later use by an intruder.
>
> A trojan horse is a program that carries a virus or worm into a system. The trojan horse is an innocent looking application or game that releases its cargo when executed. If it is carrying a virus, it starts the process of attaching and replicating. If it carries a worm, the worm executes and begins its damage agenda. Trojan horses are usually games, utilities, or hacked programs that are tempting to users.
>
> Here again, the personal computer LAN environment differs significantly from the mainframe world. Programs intended for use on mainframes are large, sophisticated, and expensive. They are almost always installed on the computer in an orderly manner by experts who not only know the program but know where it came from.
>
> Personal computer LAN programs, in contrast, are small, simple to use and install, and inexpensive and often are installed by the users themselves who may have no idea where the program came from. Often, the programs are downloaded from bulletin boards or shared by coworkers. Personal computer LAN administrators can protect against virus infections by treating the LAN and new programs in the same way that mainframe administrators do. Don't allow users to add programs. Screen every new piece of software

for viruses before installing. Never share software. It's illegal and it's dangerous.[1]

Some viruses specifically attack the file allocation table (FAT) located on the hard drive of a personal computer. The table tells the operating system where each file physically exists. Once a virus has corrupted the FAT, the computer may not know what the used and unused portions of the disk are, allowing files to be written over. This ultimately renders the hard drive useless. Both the $5\frac{1}{4}$- and the $3\frac{1}{2}$-inch diskettes also have FATs.

Some viruses reside in the boot sector and are loaded into memory when a personal computer is booted. Floppy drives that are then used receive the virus from active memory.

Other hardware beside the hard drive may be at risk from viruses. It is possible for a virus to reset the scan rate of a monitor. Resetting the scan rate may actually destroy the monitor over a period of time if not discovered. This particular virus unfortunately will only affect the higher-priced video graphics array (VGA) and color graphics adaptor (CGA) monitors that use software to set the scan rate of the monitor.

Most viruses attach themselves to an executable file. When the file or program executes so does the virus. Typically these files are files that have filename.COM, filename.EXE, or filename.SYS extensions. Every time the file that contains the virus is executed, the virus proliferates throughout the diskette or hard drive.

Where Do Viruses Come From?

Bulletin boards are proliferating across the country. Currently there are over 4000 publicly accessible bulletin boards in the United States alone. Almost 10 million households in this country have modem-equipped personal computers. Bulletin boards support user groups, general information, matchmaking, and games. Software downloaded from bulletin boards should be scanned for viruses as a matter of routine.

Bulletin boards are a common distribution point for viruses. However, it is the sharing of diskettes and personal computing devices that dynamically spreads a virus. Using write protect tabs on diskettes will prevent the spread of a virus to a diskette. This also means that the diskette can only be read and not written on.

Who Creates Viruses?

Computer viruses are deliberately written by individuals with varying degrees of proficiency. Some viruses are written as malicious pranks.

However, it has been asserted that some viruses are written by professional programmers as an attempt to discourage illegal copying of software.

Additionally it has been asserted by some that software companies have deliberately written software to seek out and corrupt competing software products, thereby diminishing the reliability of competing software and enhancing the reliability of their own.

However, my personal view is that some viruses like Michelangelo were created by one or two individuals as a malicious prank. These individuals' level of expertise indicates that they probably make their living by programming or designing software.

Tom Sheldon, the author of *NOVELL NetWare 386: the Complete Reference*, writes:

> One of the responsibilities of a network manager is to provide adequate security for the system and its data. While NetWare itself provides a number of security features, you should take additional steps to ensure that the installation is protected from accidents, natural catastrophes, and intentional harm. Computer viruses are most dreaded of all. They are constantly being written or improved by programmers whose only intention is to test their skill at cracking a security system and watching the results. And the results may be global, as was a recent virus in the telephone system.[2]

Scanners

Scanners are an effective preventive measure against viruses—I use them myself. The best way to keep your system from getting infected is to play safe. Don't exchange disks and programs with sources you don't know. Scan all new disks with virus protection software before using.

Users of personal computers must be prohibited from uploading data and programs to networks, minicomputers, and mainframe computers. The uploading of data and programs to networks, minicomputers, and mainframe computers should only be facilitated by the appropriate network or system administrator.

There are several scanners on the software market. One scanner that is particularly comprehensive in its approach is available from Central Point Software. I have used this product at client sites and I am impressed with its approach. The documentation provided with it is well presented and easy to use. The DOS version of the Antivirus software for DOS detects known and unknown viruses. It also provides for the removal of viruses from infected files. Additionally the software can immunize files against infection. The Antivirus software can be memory resident and be executed from within an autoexec.bat file.

The Antivirus software also offers support of LANs. The continuous antivirus protection (CAP) service offered by Central Point Software is an excellent strategy. This service allows the user of the software to keep up with recently discovered viruses for a nominal charge. Significantly, Central Point Backup contains its own internal anti-virus protection. Frequent data backups will protect the user from data loss in the event of a virus.

In the final analysis, however, I must state categorically that scanners will not detect all viruses. They can be of help with viruses they know about, not the ones they don't.

Logic Bombs

Scanners will detect viruses they know. Scanners will not detect other types of insidious programs like logic bombs. A logic bomb, i.e., a program or subroutine triggered unknowingly by a user, which can delete any part of a computer system, created on a computer system would not be detected by a scanner. Depending on the programmer who creates the logic bomb and depending on this individual's level of expertise it could be extremely hard to detect. Personal computers, mini- and mainframe computers, and networks are all at risk from this type of program.

The network administrator's or system administrator's best defense against logic bombs is to maintain a record of every file in a directory and every directory within directories. The purpose and function of files in directories must be ascertained. I frequently use programs that do nothing more than write the name and size of files and directories to a file. By running the program that catalogs the files and directories and then making a simple comparison to previous output, you can quickly identify possible problems of this type.

Network History

I would like to cite a particular instance that occurred in 1990, 2 years before the end of the Cold War. A trained astronomer who worked on a network that was connected to another defense network observed and helped catch East German agents. These agents were attempting to communicate with the defense network so they could receive classified data.

An even more regrettable incident occurred in 1988. This incident was a prank but it was significant. An extremely bright young man introduced a virus into the ARPANET network (a network originally funded by the Advanced Projects Research Agency) thereby rendering it useless until the virus could be eliminated. This incident was treated as a criminal act and the individual was given a year in prison.

An individual gained access to the computer system of a bank in Los Angeles and managed to transfer millions of dollars to an account he controlled. This individual used the funds in his account to buy diamonds. It was the large purchase of diamonds that aroused the authorities' interest and eventually led to the individual's arrest. This incident received a lot of attention in the press at the time. The transactions performed by the individual in this situation went unnoticed by the bank.

The transaction itself would have been almost impossible to detect at the network level. However, the transaction could have been better monitored at the host or mainframe level. Transactional monitoring of users on some computer systems is an effective countermeasure.

Some defense networks in this country at one time used satellites as part of their networks. This country's intelligence agency, and those of other NATO member governments, discovered that communications using satellites were being monitored during the Cold War. Now most of those same networks are terrestrial-based. Terrestrial-based networks are in conduits below ground.

Network Audits

Some networks are administratively handled by one network manager with multiple regional network managers. The regional network managers are responsible for managing a specific region of the network. This would include user security and updating new addresses of bridges, routers, brouters, gateways, and hosts. This activity would be coordinated with the network manager. The network manager and regional managers maintain documentation on the networks they support. That documentation is first reviewed in preparing for an audit of a network. Networks are very vulnerable but can be audited.

Audits of networks are more sophisticated than those of computer systems residing on the network. The starting point is the LAN and the workstation or personal computer, then servers. Gateways on the LAN are then reviewed. Alternately the LAN might be connected to an Ethernet backbone network that has gateways to a metropolitan area network (MAN), Internet, or WAN networks. Next the network connected to the gateway is reviewed. Then computer systems or hosts residing on Internet or WAN networks are reviewed. Conversely an audit of a network could begin at the highest level (Internet or WAN) and work its way down to that portion of the network maintained by the entity requesting the audit.

The entire security and topology of the network should be reviewed and tested at regular intervals. Testing to see if established security procedures are effective and cannot be circumvented is essential. Audit criteria is dependent on the type of hardware and software used and the topology of the network. Approval for audit criteria should occur at least one level above the manager responsible for the network to be audited. Once the criteria for an audit has been established, the audit begins. The lowest levels of detail in the network can be reviewed in an audit.

The network audit is furnished to higher levels of management to ensure that they are aware of the status of security, operations, performance, and documentation. It is essential that the entity performing the audit be free from influence and thereby deliver an unbiased report.

While the network audit is being conducted, the network administrator must be available to answer questions on all aspects of the network. The staff that supports the network should be interviewed and observed performing procedures for which they are responsible. The general areas covered by a network audit are presented. The reader is encouraged to amend and redefine the material presented in Figure 11-1.

The network audit criteria presented here represents areas that might be audited on a LAN. The information is not intended to represent all the details or the lowest level of detail that would be reviewed in a network to be audited. The amount of criteria and the depth to which it is reviewed would vary depending on the installation. Additionally the amount of time and labor to perform an audit might be considerable. It might be prudent to select only a portion of the criteria, perhaps security and then later performance, operations, or documentation.

Network audits also can be used as a reference or baseline when the audit is performed again. Information obtained in an initial network audit is reviewed against the current audit to detect areas of increased usage and performance problems. This data can be used to help plan for future hardware and software upgrades to the network.

Network administrators can prevent the majority of data intrusion by adhering to good management. The following is a list of recommendations that can be used as an overall strategy for a network.

Figure 11-1 Network Audit Criteria

LAN—Network Administrator ————————————

I. Topology
  A. Hardware
    1. Servers, routers, bridges, gateways, etc.
      (a) Address
      (b) Manufacturer
      (c) Description
      (d) Warranty
      (e) Capacity
      (f) Protocols
      (g) Routing
      (h) Interface cards
      (i) Cabling
      (j) Transmission speed
      (k) Physical location
    2. Workstations
      (a) Address
      (b) Manufacturer
      (c) Software configuration
      (d) Hardware configuration
      (e) Protocols
      (f) Interface card
      (g) Cabling
      (h) Transmission speed
      (i) Physical location
    3. Printers
      (a) Local
      (b) Remote
      (c) Physical location
      (d) Description
      (e) Print server

II. Security
  A. Network administration
    1. Alternate administrator
    2. Workgroup managers
    3. User account manager
    4. Other network administrators
  B. Management software
    1. Monitoring
      (a) User logs

    (b) Audit trails

    (c) Intruder detection

   2. Management triggers

   3. Management managers

  C. User

   1. Access rights

    (a) Directory

    (b) File

   2. Group rights

    (a) Directory

    (b) File

   3. Applications used

  D. Physical security of equipment

III. Performance

  A. Diagnostic testing

   1. Cable tracers

   2. Continuity testers

   3. Diagnostic software

   4. Time domain reflectometers

   5. Diagnostic software

   6. Protocol analyzers

  B. Packets

   1. Send or receive

    (a) Too big to count

    (b) Too small to count

    (c) Miscellaneous errors

    (d) Retry count

    (e) Checksum errors

    (f) Receive mismatch count

    (g) Total packets

  C. Buffers

   1. Dirty cache buffers

   2. Packet receive buffers

   3. Directory cache buffers

   4. Original cache buffers

   5. Total cache buffers

  D. Utilization

   1. Processor busy time

  E. File server uptime

   1. Time the server has been running

  F. Memory usage

(Continued)

IV. Operations
  A. Scheduled activities
    1. Daily
    2. Weekly
    3. Monthly
  B. Catastrophe preparedness
  C. Archive of file systems
    1. Test
  D. Restoration of file systems
    1. Test
  E. File system maintenance
  F. Storage of magnetic media
  G. Scheduled maintenance of hardware
  H. Test partition or directory
  I. Testing procedures
  J. Mirrored partitions
  K. Mirrored disks

V. Documentation
  A. Hardware
    1. Warranty
    2. Serial number
    3. Maintenance
    4. Spares
  B. Operating system
  C. Third-party software
  D. Developed software
  E. System outages
  F. Drawings of the network
  G. Offline storage
  H. Availability
  I. Updates

Quick Network Checklist

In researching material for this book, I reviewed two guidelines that I think every network administrator should implement. The first guideline presented is from Tom Sheldon's book entitled *NOVELL NetWare 386: The Complete Reference.*[3] The second guideline is from the article written by Peter Stephenson entitled "Implementing the Secure PC

LAN—Guidelines for Information Security."[4] These two guidelines when used together present a comprehensive checklist and represent years of experience and insight into managing for a secure network. In addition to these guidelines, I add two more recommendations for managing a secure network. Mr. Sheldon writes:

- Minimize the number of users who have supervisor privileges. In reality there should be only one supervisor who has complete access to a file server. All other users should be classified as managers with restricted rights, especially to the SYS:SYSTEM directory.
- Flag all executable application files with the Read Only attribute, and do not give other users the rights to change the attributes.
- Secure all backups.
- Lock the file server console at all times.
- Use diskless workstations in remote or unsupervised areas to ensure data is not downloaded from the server to a disk and carried out of the building.
- Train users to log out of their workstations properly so unauthorized users cannot walk up and begin using their stations.
- Use physical locking devices to prevent theft of equipment. Even though a server system may be locked down, you still need to ensure that its internal hard drives are not removed. The data on those drives is the most important part of the network.
- Centralize servers and other network equipment into a single management area, and then lock the area. Use access devices such as fingerprint readers or magnetic cards to gain access to the area.
- Secure the cable system from unauthorized taps. This can be done with management software that monitors all nodes on the network. Fiber optic cable can also be used.[5]

Peter Stephenson writes:

Administrators can prevent as much as 80% of all LAN data loss simply by practicing good LAN management and common sense. Some things that administrators can do to help things along are:

- Have a written security plan and apply its policies and practices diligently. Make sure your users have read it and understand it.
- Configure your servers and volumes properly for maximum compartmentalization of users. Rely on a need to know as a guideline for access to data and applications.
- Practice safe computing. Screen all new software before installing it. Don't permit software sharing.
- Encrypt sensitive data on the network drives.
- Ensure that passwords and user lists are encrypted.

- Limit outside access through modems and internetworks as much as possible. Insist upon reauthentication when a user enters your system from another network or system. Close backdoors.
- Enforce the use of strong passwords, prohibit password sharing and lock users out of the network after three log-in failures until you know what the problem is.
- Apply good audit trails and user logs and scan them regularly for divergences from normal patterns. Roam your LAN frequently and become familiar with it and its users and their patterns.
- Above all, realize that you must secure LANs from the workstation in, towards the file server and always assume that your best access control efforts will, some day, fail. Plan accordingly.[6]

In addition to these guidelines, I would like to add these two recommendations.

- Force periodic password changes and require the password to be unique. A combination of numeric and alpha characters is recommended.
- Use and maintain dial-back modems that verify the telephone number of the calling or sending modem.

Peter Stephenson states:

> Providing good information security in the PC LAN environment is a far more significant challenge than on virtually any other type of system. The obvious reason for the high potential for damage from well meaning, legitimate users with poor training or compartmentalization stems from the nature of PCs themselves.
>
> As a network administrator, your job is to raise the awareness of your users in the area of security, configure your network properly and be vigilant for malicious intrusion. There are many tools on the market to help you with these tasks, but your best tools are your own common sense and experience. LAN security may be tough. LANs may inherently be more vulnerable than other platforms. Users may be more sophisticated, relatively speaking, on PC LANs than on mainframes. But, as an administrator, you can still have the upper hand.
>
> The very weakness that intruders exploit and untrained users fall prey to are more easily managed on PCs than on any other platform. Know your system and know your users. If you keep your eyes open and your audit trail running, you'll stop almost all trouble on your LAN before it gets started.[7]

LANs are the first layer in a many-layered communications environment available today (Figure 11-2). From the LAN via a gateway users

```
┌──────────────────────────────────────────────────────────┐
│ Low Level                                                  │
│                                                            │
│ ─────────────────────── Local Area Networks ───────────── │
│ ─────────────────── Metropolitan Area Networks ────────── │
│ ───────────────────── Wide Area Networks ──────────────── │
│ ──TYMNET ───────────── TELENET ────────INTERNET ──────     │
│ High Level                                                 │
│                                                            │
└──────────────────────────────────────────────────────────┘
```

Figure 11-2   Network layers.

have a limitless horizon of networks with which to communicate. It is essential that this layer be secure as possible.

By using a gateway or modem, a user can access LANs, MANs, and WANs with little effort. It is essential that LAN security be as tight as possible. LANs are the first network layer a user may communicate with in some environments.

Telecommunications Networks

Telecommunication networks support voice and data communications. The networks are owned by American Telephone and Telegraph (AT&T), MCI, GTE, Sprint, PACTEL, and many other major corporations in this country. These companies provide competitive services to their customers. All these companies suffer theft of resources. These companies have fraud control units that are dedicated to eliminating theft of resources.

I am going to provide two case histories that illustrate the magnitude of the problems faced by telecommunication carriers in this country. The first case involves a telecommunications company, and the second case involves a network component manufacturing company.

Case 18

In September 1986, I was hired as senior systems analyst for a major telecommunications company. While working for the telecom company, I became involved in presenting a solution to busted authorization codes on their network. These authorization codes allow users of the network to place calls using an authorization code imprinted on a plastic card.

I had conversations with the manager directly responsible for the problem. He informed me that the telecom company was losing a million dollars per month from busted authorization codes. A significant amount of the calls made with busted authorization codes were used to call Colombia in South America. Obviously drug traffickers not wanting to have calls placed to that country on their own telephone bills used this method to conduct business.

Another engineer and I immediately began analysis of busted authorization codes. We conferred with other engineers and software programmers to come up with a cost-effective solution that would enable automatic determination of when authorization codes were compromised or busted. Most of the software and hardware was already in place. Very little actual research and development would be necessary. Within about 30 days of starting the assignment I forwarded a proposal.

The proposal requested about 8000 hours to install and test a system. The system would

- Generate reports on suspected busted codes on a near real-time basis

- Perform automatic notification of suspected busted codes to Pacific Division Investigations.

- Perform deactivation of busted authorization codes using a program already developed and working

- Update appropriate databases automatically.

While I was waiting to get approval to proceed with this project, the telecom company decided to lay off about 25,000 personnel nationally. The facility I worked at was affected. Almost everyone there that I worked with was laid off, including myself. The severance package was good and I got the whole month of December off which I didn't mind. I kept the proposal to management on controlling the busted authorization codes.

In 1992, I was contacted by the telecom company, which was starting a big fraud control project. I was interviewed as a candidate to head this project. I managed to find the 6-year-old proposal and go over it before the interview. In the telephone interview I had with the telecom company, busted authorization codes were the topic of conversation. The telecom company had now decided to develop a fraud control workstation that would detect and deactivate busted authorization codes.

The real significance of busted authorization codes for the telecom company is that 6 years had elapsed since I had performed an analysis of the problem. At that time the company was incurring losses of $1 million per month from theft of resources. Surely that figure had risen since then. If the cost per year was $12 million, then the total figure for losses over 6 years would be $72 million.

Analysis

The telecommunications company's problem with busted authorization codes has received media attention. The television show "Fight Back" with David Horowitz had an episode that actually showed him obtaining a code and using the authorization code to place a call.

There are two distinct categories of explanation of how authorization codes are obtained by so many individuals. First, a customer of the telecom company purposely divulges an authorization code to someone else. The code then gets passed around among friends and associates, eventually finding its way into the possession of someone who really abuses the authorization code for his or her own purposes. Second, the telecom company's own employees divulge the authorization codes to individuals who again abuse the code for their own purposes whatever they may be. Security of authorization codes and the telecom company's employees who have access to authorization codes should be under constant review.

I have an authorization code I use every day, and I have memorized the number. The card on which the code is printed never comes out of my wallet.

Case 19

This case is a little different from Case 18 and I am using the former case as background for this one. A manufacturer of network components with plants and facilities throughout the country used a voice and data network to perform its day-to-day business. The network was comprised of lines leased from AT&T.

The network had been in place for a few months when the AT&T fraud control unit contacted the director of management information services (MIS). AT&T fraud control representatives notified the director of MIS that his network was being used by drug traffickers. The network was being used in the evening hours to conduct drug transactions. Calls through the network were placed only to Puerto Rico, and from there the calls were being forwarded to Colombia.

Analysis

In discussing the situation with the director of MIS for the company involved, he stated that he did not feel that this meant an employee had assisted the drug traffickers. However, I saw that the drug traffickers must have been made aware of the network's existence and how it could be used by them.

This was not a public network—it was designed to support voice and data communications for a manufacturing company. It is my opinion that an employee may have compromised the network or an employee of a vendor who had assisted in its installation had compromised the network.

This kind of network is ideally suited to drug traffickers. It represents a low-profile way to communicate to drug contacts in Colombia. Obviously AT&T fraud control officials knew what was going on. Analysis of the manufacturer's network revealed that there was increased activity in the off-business hours. The director of MIS seemed to feel that there was nothing he could do about the drug traffickers and that none of his people would compromise his network.

My recommendation in this particular instance would be to increase security on the network so that drug traffickers could not use it. Authorization to use the network internally should be reviewed. People authorized to use the network should be constantly reminded to keep details regarding access confidential.

I was particularly struck with the complacency of the director of MIS. Theft of resources did not seem to be important to him. Announced and unannounced audits of computer systems and networks under these circumstances would be advisable. A covert audit of personnel directly involved in maintaining and managing network communications would also be recommended in this situation.

Because employees of the manufacturer might be directly involved in supporting voice and data communications for drug traffickers, and because of the potential liability to the manufacturing company, a private investigation service company should have been retained. Such a firm could identify employees at risk and advise the manufacturing company accordingly.

Transactions of the drug traffickers in this case could easily be hidden in files that had similar names to filename conventions used by the manufacturing company. These same files might have had file extensions that ended in filename.txt, filename.dat, or filename.exe. This situation underscores the importance of being able to identify every file on a network, computer, or server.

Once a network administrator is alerted to this kind of situation, it should take little effort to identify files that do not belong on the network. Conversely a company in this situation might assist the appropriate law enforcement agency in apprehending drug traffickers and unwanted intruders on the network.

Summary:

1. Safeguarding access to public and private voice and data networks is everyone's business. The public and business community must work together.

2. Unauthorized access to public and private networks must be dealt with immediately upon discovery. Management and telephone company fraud control representatives as well as law enforcement officials must be notified promptly.

3. Private networks may discover unauthorized use by sampling traffic levels around the clock. Unusually high levels of access at off-business hours are suspect.

References

1. Peter Stephenson, "Implementing the Secure PC LAN—Guidelines for Information Security," *Computer Security Journal*, vol. 7, No. 2, 1991. (*Reprinted with permission, Computer Security Institute, 600 Harrison Street, San Francisco, CA 94107.*)

2. Tom Sheldon, *NOVELL NetWare 386: The Complete Reference*, Osborne McGraw-Hill, Berkeley, 1990. (*Reprinted with permission.*)

3. Tom Sheldon, op. cit.

4. Peter Stephenson, op. cit.

5. Tom Sheldon, op. cit.

6. Peter Stephenson, op. cit.

7. Peter Stephenson, op. cit.

PART 3
Consulting Firms, Checklists, Questionnaires, and Audit Criteria

12
Consulting Firms

Introduction

The consulting firms in this country are too numerous to count. Finding the right one for you or your company can mean the difference between success and failure. All the big accounting firms like Price Waterhouse, Ernst Young, Coopers & Lybrand, and Deloit Touche offer excellent services. Smaller consulting firms also offer quality services.

Consulting firms consult on a wide variety of computer systems, data communications, and telecommunications issues for the business community. These firms provide recommendations and solutions to various problems a business can encounter. Ideally the reason to hire a consulting firm is to get their analytical solution of a particular business issue. It is the responsibility of the consulting firm and its consultants to provide ethical and unbiased solutions to their clients. Many consulting firms also provide the human resources for projects undertaken by a business that it wouldn't normally have on staff. Under these circumstances, it is the professional expertise and the temporary labor that they can provide on short notice which makes consulting firms attractive. Professional categories available from consulting firms are listed in Figure 12-1.

I recommend retaining consulting firms and/or consultants for two distinct purposes. The first is to perform audits and covert audits of either computer systems or networks to which they are attached. The second is to perform vendor and product evaluation. Vendor and product evaluation performed by a consulting firm can ensure that you're getting quality goods and services from a vendor.

Data entry operator

Word processing operator

Technical writer

Computer operator

Programmers and programmer analyst

Support analyst

Analyst/project manager

Software engineer

Data communications engineer

Telecommunications engineer

Auditor (computer systems and networks)

Management consultant

Figure 12-1 Professional categories available from consulting firms.

Caution should be exercised when selecting a consulting firm. Determine the consulting firm's area of expertise since most consulting firms specialize. Some consulting firms do little more than provide labor to complete software development projects. Others provide comprehensive across-the-board solutions according to the needs of a client. This can best be determined by talking to the consulting firm and its clients. Obtain a copy of the firm's client list and call some clients to ascertain their level of satisfaction with the services provided by the consulting firm. Review professional resumes of consultants that will be provided by the consulting firm. It may be especially advantageous to talk to clients that received the same type of services your company is interested in obtaining.

It is essential in the process of retaining a consulting firm that their client list be disclosed. This ensures that the consulting firm is not in a conflict of interest situation. The consulting firm may require that a nondisclosure agreement be signed before they release a client list. Consulting firms that are unwilling to provide client information should not be considered. Nondisclosure should be construed as an indication that the consulting firm has a poor track record with clients.

Consulting firms that are just getting started and have few clients should be evaluated on the experience of their personnel. They may have extremely competent personnel ready to perform quality work. This can be determined by reviewing the professional resumes of their staff. Most consulting firms provide professional resumes of their staff to clients. Small consulting firms may be just as well qualified to perform audits or product evaluation as the larger and more well-known consulting firms. These firms may be able to respond in a timely manner to a preliminary request. Additionally these smaller companies may present a lower estimate to perform the work. Neither a timely response nor a lower estimate should be the deciding factor. Whether you need an audit, product evaluation, or system analysis, you want the best qualified consulting firm to perform the analysis.

Audits

The audit criteria must fit the particular computer system or network topology. Ask the consulting firm's representative how they perform audits and have them give you an estimate. Have the consulting firm provide you with copies of previously conducted audits.

A consulting firm may have to perform a quick survey of a computer system or network being considered for an audit. This will ensure that their estimate to perform the work is accurate. The consulting firm's proposal to perform the work should include criteria for the audit. The time required to perform the audit and expected completion date should also be stated in their proposal.

Once the criteria for the audit is approved you may compare it to the sample audit criteria in Chapter 16 and sample network audit criteria Chapter 17. Approval of the criteria for either a computer system or network should occur at least one level above the manager responsible for the system being audited.

At least two consulting firms should be solicited to present proposals for performing an audit. Selection should be based on competency, experience, and price to perform the work. The audit can provide a means of discovery. Situations that management should be made aware of and might not otherwise know may surface. The real benefit of using a consulting firm is that you should expect an unbiased and thorough audit. Whether it is an audit of a computer system or a network, you should expect a professional response with recommendations to improve security, performance, operations, and documentation.

In the last two decades, computers have been used to perpetrate fraud by substantiating claims of companies that misrepresented their actual financial position. In other words, the computer generated reports that deliberately misstated the facts. Information was deliberately altered by the perpetrators of the fraud. Auditors not only have to substantiate that the computer system is working correctly, but they must also ensure that the data that resides on the database is based on fact.

Therefore the consulting firm selected to perform an audit should provide aggressive auditors who are not afraid of asking questions. Consulting firms that fail to conduct an audit aggressively and ethically fail in their fiduciary responsibilities. Certainly any consulting firm that knowingly substantiates data reported by a company regarding its financial position are accessories to fraud.

Avoid long-term contracts with consulting firms that provide audits. A consulting firm should be used for a computer system or network audit once or twice and then replaced by another consulting firm. This prevents complacency on the part of the consulting firm and their auditors. The auditors will realize that they have no favor to garner from employees of the company they are auditing. Ideally the attitude of the auditor or consultant conducting an audit should be one of aggressively substantiating the lowest level of detail regarding either the computer system or network.

Covert Audits

Covert audits are initiated when management has suspicions they want confirmed or denied without disturbing normal production and arousing suspected individuals. Covert audits are particularly useful in situations where higher levels of management are concerned about the computer systems they depend on and have reason to suspect something is amiss or wrong.

Covert audits also can be useful when a company is preparing to cease a relationship with a vendor or one of its own employees. In this situation, the audit is performed by observing operations being performed and determining their functionality.

The covert audit should be conducted by a consulting firm or consultant that has experience. The consultant that actually performs the work has to be able to comprehend the legal boundaries involved. In addition to this, the consultant must be able to document and substantiate criminal acts while not arousing the suspicions of the individuals involved. The consultant performing the audit may work with a private investigation services company and/or law enforcement agency depending on the circumstances.

The best results of a covert audit are obtained when the presence of the auditor or consultant performing the covert audit is undetected. The fewer people who know about the covert audit or of the consultant's presence the better. The consultant should provide information based on facts. However, certainly knowing the mood of the employees or their overall morale may be helpful. The consultant should be able to distinguish between feelings and facts.

Product Evaluation

Many companies may not have the technical expertise on staff to perform product evaluation of software or hardware. In this situation the best course of action is to retain a consulting firm to perform the product evaluation. Product evaluation is time-consuming and labor-intensive. A consulting firm should be retained only on significant purchases. Elements of the product evaluation are listed on the vendor customer evaluation forms in Chapter 15. They must be used in conjunction with a customer listing from the vendor whose product is being evaluated.

Interviewing past clients of a consulting firm will reveal their level of satisfaction with services provided. This process can be conducted by telephone in as little as 15 minutes. Consulting firms that have had problems in providing goods or services are usually discovered in this process. Consulting firms that are unwilling to participate in this process should not be considered viable.

Consulting firms that have a business relationship of any type with a vendor being evaluated should not be used. The consulting firm cannot provide an unbiased and impartial product evaluation if a conflict of interest exists.

Reports

Whether it is an audit, covert audit, system analysis, or product evaluation the client of the consulting firm should expect to receive a written report which fully details their findings and recommendations. The level of detail may be even specified contractually before the work is commenced.

Information supporting recommendations should be provided. A research of pertinent periodicals may also yield valuable information. However, most articles in trade periodicals are sponsored by the vendor of the product. I have written several articles of this type. Sources of information that substantiate conclusions presented in a report should be provided. The report itself should be signed and attested to by a representative of the consulting firm.

Summary:

A consulting firm should be used when in-house expertise is not available to perform analysis of a system. Whatever the system is, the consulting firm should be selected on having the expertise to provide unbiased analysis and recommendations that will be of benefit to the recipient or client. Many consulting firms specialize in specific areas, telecommunications, data communications, software development and support, and security. Make sure the consulting firm you select is appropriate for the work to be performed.

1. Solicit proposals from two different consulting firms which can provide the same level of service.

2. Review the client list of perspective consulting firms, contact their clients, and ascertain their level of satisfaction with services provided.

3. Review the professional resumes of consultants provided by the consulting firm.

4. The selection of a consulting firm should be based on price, experience, quality, and availability to perform the work.

5. Retain the services of the consulting firm on a contractual basis.

6. Depending on the planned duration of the work to be performed, require weekly and monthly status reports.

7. Reports should indicate hours expended, what the hours were expended on, and how many hours are required to complete the assignment.

13
Quick Checklist

Introduction

The quick checklist is a list that can be reviewed quickly by readers at their discretion. The quick checklist is a composite of the summary information.

Misrepresentation

1. Check customer references of a potential vendor. Use the vendor customer evaluation questionnaires. See the samples for software and hardware in Chapter 15.

2. Visit other clients of a vendor and observe them using the vendor's product.

3. Retain the services of a reputable consulting firm or consultant to perform an analysis of the product to be purchased. Make sure that the consulting firm or consultant retained has no affiliation with the product and is unbiased.

4. Contractually withhold final payment for the product until it is successfully installed and accepted by you.

5. When acquiring software through a vendor, be sure that you have received the documentation, warranty information, serial number, activation key code, and registration card.

6. Receive hardware purchases directly from the manufacturer when ever possible. Be sure warranty information and registration cards for the equipment are included.

Contractual Agreements

1. Retain a consulting firm when making significant purchases of either hardware or software.

2. Retain legal counsel to review potential contracts if this service is not offered by the consulting firm.

3. Include all marketing literature from the vendor as exhibits in the contract.

4. The contract itself should detail as closely as possible the functional requirements of the system whether it is hardware or software.

5. Withhold 25 to 50 percent of the final payment from the vendor until the system has been accepted as successful.

6. State contractually that for unsuccessful implementations of hardware or software the vendor is subject to financial penalties.

7. Make provisions in the contract that require payments to vendors dependent on meeting a schedule of deliverable items.

8. If possible, develop your own contract; don't sign the vendor's contract.

9. Make sure all vendor guarantees and warranties are fully stated with their limitations in the contract.

10. All contracts should be made in triplicate, signed by authorized representatives, and notarized. Always retain the original copy.

Sabotage

1. Conduct business with software and hardware vendors pursuant to the provisions of a contract.

2. If conditions under which a vendor is performing work change, create a written addendum or add a change order to the contract.

3. If any vendor shows signs of attempting to perpetuate a relationship for financial gain, suspend the relationship. The business relationship may be resumed after an audit is performed that lays to rest any suspicion of this type of activity.

4. If a vendor is not performing up to reasonable expectations, it should be replaced. Never suppose its performance will improve with time.

5. In the event of a system failure determine the cause by looking at the system messages printed on the system console or the system printer. If the system has a mail module, check to see mail has been sent to the system administrator.

6. Have regular audits performed by an outside consulting firm or consultant.

Source Code

1. When acquiring software systems, establish the price for source code contractually.

2. If the price for source code is unreasonably high or if you do not anticipate changing the software, establish an escrow.

3. If changes in software are anticipated that may give competitors an advantage in the market you share, consider acquiring the source code and performing the changes internally. This type of work also might be performed by a third party or consulting firm.

Copyright

1. Apply for the copyright as soon as possible.

2. Details of the copyright submission should be kept confidential.

3. During the development of software, avoid allowing a single individual access to the entire system being developed.

4. Apply for a new copyright when significant changes are made to the system or a new version is to be released.

5. Affixation of the copyright notice to documentation and source code should occur as they are being created.

Data Omission

1. During the implementation of both hardware and software, audits conducted by an outside consulting firm, timed to coincide with the completion of activities and milestones, are essential.

2. Databases should be regularly checked to ensure that data is being entered correctly.

3. Management and supervisors responsible for data on any computer system should be aware of the Foreign Corrupt Practices Act and the Computer Security Act.

Fraud in Government

1. Suspicions or concerns of possible wrongdoing should be documented and presented verbally and in writing to your superiors first.

2. Do not discuss the circumstances regarding the incident with fellow employees.

3. If you suspect that the wrongdoing may be perpetrated by immediate supervisors or managers, go to the next highest level and the next above that if necessary. If you are a member of a union, notify the shop steward.

4. If you are an employee of local, state, or federal government and suspect criminal activity, report it to the proper law enforcement agency.

5. Maintain a copy of documentation in your possession along with any names, dates, and other information pertinent to the incident.

6. You have a legal and moral responsibility to report illegal or unlawful acts by government employees.

7. If you are not sure of the circumstances but feel something is wrong, consult with an attorney.

8. The federal government now offers rewards for whistle blowers. A percentage is paid based on the amount of money involved in the fraud or criminal act perpetrated.

Espionage

1. Suspected espionage against the government should be reported to company security personnel and the Federal Bureau of Investigation.

2. Suspected instances of industrial espionage must be handled by trained professionals (private investigators).

3. Extreme care must be taken to document as much information as possible regarding the particular instance of suspected espionage. This should include witnesses' names, addresses, and telephone numbers,and names and telephone numbers of relatives.

4. Once an investigation is under way, reveal its existence and details only to individuals that need to know. The fewer people that know, the better the results of the investigation.

5. Avoid communications or confrontations with suspected employees, agents perpetrating the industrial espionage, or suspected clients of the agents.

6. Dismissal of employees should only occur when facts substantiate their knowing participation in perpetrating the industrial espionage.

7. Extreme care must be taken to ensure that employee rights are not disregarded.

8. Counterindustrial espionage may be used when industrial espionage is discovered as a means to gain time for investigation purposes.

9. Industrial espionage must be dealt with by professionals. Companies in the private investigation business should be contacted when it is suspected.

10. Audits and covert audits of computer systems or networks should be contemplated if industrial espionage is suspected or discovered. Audits may be handled by a computer consulting firm that specializes in these types of audits.

11. In suspected cases of espionage it is everyone's responsibility to notify appropriate security representatives.

Security

1. Develop and implement a security policy.

2. Develop a security policy that defines in a contractual format what is expected of all employees.

3. Make awareness of the security policy as important as the company's profitability.

4. Enforce the security policy without exception.

5. Provide positive reinforcement for employees that support the security policy.

6. Develop and implement a security plan that best suits the computer system.

7. Thoroughly document the security plan and keep the information that it provides current.

Audits

Personal Computers (Small-Business Environment)

1. Retain the services of a consultant to audit the personal computer and the software systems it supports on a yearly basis.

2. Frequency of audits should be scheduled proportionately to the number of computer systems a small business maintains.

Mini- and Mainframe Computers (Medium- to Large-Business Environment)

3. Retain the services of a consulting firm to perform audits on mini- or mainframe computers. This activity should occur on a semiannual basis.

4. Unannounced audits for computer systems that are not operating to optimum performance levels or experiencing security problems are recommended.

5. Audits should be performed by experienced outside consulting firms.

6. Audits should be approved and initiated at one level above the management responsible for maintaining the computer system being audited.

7. Bonuses and pay increases for personnel supporting a computer system should be based on passing audits successfully.

Failed Audits

8. Audits should be considered failed when any portion of the criteria for the audit fails to meet expectations of the company's management that approved the criteria.

9. Recommendations presented by the entity performing the audit to correct deficient areas of the criteria should be implemented within a reasonable period of time.

10. Areas of audit criteria reported as deficient or failed previously should be checked and tested until they are deemed acceptable by management.

Covert Audits

11. Covert audits should be performed with extreme caution by individuals competent enough not to violate the rights of individuals suspected of wrongdoing.

12. Covert audits are strongly recommended when any of the following activities are suspected:

   - Misrepresentation (by management or vendor)
   - Sabotage
   - Data omission
   - Theft of confidential information
   - Unauthorized use of computer or network resources

- Undocumented changes made to a computer system or network by an individual or vendor
- Espionage

13. Covert audits are a means of discovery. Information pertaining to them must be kept confidential.

14. Fact, and not suspicion, must be the deciding issue in determining wrongdoing by anyone.

Consulting Firms

1. Solicit proposals from two different consulting firms which can provide the same level of service.

2. Review the client list of perspective consulting firms, contact their clients, and ascertain the level of satisfaction with services provided.

3. Review the resumes of consultants provided by the consulting firm.

4. The selection of a consulting firm should be based on price, experience, quality, and availability to perform the work.

5. Retain the services of the consulting firm on a contractual basis.

6. Depending on the planned duration of the work to be performed, require weekly and monthly status reports.

7. Reports should indicate hours expended, what the hours were expended on, and how many hours are required to complete the assignment.

14

Quick Network Checklist

Introduction

Maintaining security in the network environment is the primary objective of the network administrator. The Quick Network checklist is provided as a guideline or starting point to develop a secure network environment. The importance of the Checklist is such that its evolution and the list itself, previously presented in Chapter 11, bear repetition.

In researching material for this book, I reviewed two guidelines that I think every network administrator should implement. The first guideline presented is from Tom Sheldon's book titled *NOVELL NetWare 386: The Complete Reference*.[1] The second guideline is from the article written by Peter Stephenson titled "Implementing the Secure PC LAN—Guidelines for Information Security."[2] These two guidelines when used together present a comprehensive checklist and represent years of experience and insight into managing for a secure network.

Quick Network Checklist

In addition to these guidelines, I add two more additional recommendations for managing a secure network. Tom Sheldon writes:

- Minimize the number of users who have supervisor privileges. In reality there should be only one supervisor who has complete access to a file server. All other users should be classified as managers with restricted rights, especially to the SYS:SYSTEM directory.

- Flag all executable application files with the Read Only attribute, and do not give other users the rights to change the attributes.
- Secure all backups.
- Lock the file server console at all times.
- Use diskless workstations in remote or unsupervised areas to ensure data is not downloaded from the server to a disk and carried out of the building.
- Train users to log out of their workstations properly so unauthorized users cannot walk up and begin using their stations.
- Use physical locking devices to prevent theft of equipment. Even though a server system may be locked down, you still need to ensure that its internal hard drives are not removed. The data on those drives is the most important part of the network.
- Centralize servers and other network equipment into a single management area, and then lock the area. Use access devices such as fingerprint readers or magnetic cards to gain access to the area.
- Secure the cable system from unauthorized taps. This can be done with management software that monitors all nodes on the network. Fiber optic cable can also be used.[3]

Peter Stephenson writes:

Administrators can prevent as much as 80% of all LAN data loss simply by practicing good LAN management and common sense. Some things that administrators can do to help things along are:

- Have a written security plan and apply its policies and practices diligently. Make sure your users have read it and understand it.
- Configure your servers and volumes properly for maximum compartmentalization of users. Rely on a need to know as a guideline for access to data and applications.
- Practice safe computing. Screen all new software before installing it. Don't permit software sharing.
- Encrypt sensitive data on the network drives.
- Ensure that passwords and user lists are encrypted.
- Limit outside access through modems and internetworks as much as possible. Insist upon reauthentication when a user enters your system from another network or system. Close back-doors.
- Enforce the use of strong passwords, prohibit password sharing and lock users out of the network after three log-in failures until you know what the problem is.
- Apply good audit trails and user logs and scan them regularly for divergences from normal patterns. Roam your LAN frequently and become familiar with it and its users and their patterns.
- Above all, realize that you must secure LANs from the workstation in, towards the file server and always assume that your best access control efforts will, some day, fail. Plan accordingly.[4]

In addition to these guidelines, I would like to add the following three recommendations:

■ Force periodic password changes and require the password to be unique. A combination of numeric and alpha characters is recommended.

■ Use and maintain dial-back modems that verify the telephone number of the calling or sending modem.

References

1. Tom Sheldon, *NOVELL NetWare 386: The Complete Reference*, Osborne McGraw-Hill, Berkeley, 1990. (*Reprinted with permission*.)

2. Peter Stephenson, "Implementing the Secure PC LAN—Guidelines for Information Security," *Computer Security Journal*, vol. 7, no. 2, 1991. (*Reprinted with permission, Computer Security Institute, 600 Harrison Street, San Francisco, CA 94107.*)

3. Tom Sheldon, op. cit.

4. Peter Stephenson, op. cit.

15
Vendor Customer Evaluation Questionnaires

Introduction

Customer questionnaires can be especially useful in determining the worthiness of software, hardware, and the vendor. I used the Vendor Customer Evaluation Questionnaire (software) presented in this chapter at an aerospace company to determine the worthiness of a software product and its vendor. Customers can be surveyed in 15 minutes by telephone. Points can be equated to answers from customers of the vendor. When evaluating multiple vendors, this can be especially helpful. The two Vendor Customer Evaluation Questionnaires may not fit every situation but can be used for software and hardware evaluation. Either questionnaire can be used as a guide for developing your own.

Vendor Customer Evaluation Questionnaire (Software)

1. Site name _____

2. Site location _____

3. Site contact name _____

   Title _____

   Data processing experience in years _____

4. Site contact telephone number _____

5. Alternate site contact name _____

   Title _____

   Years of experience _____

6. Alternate site contact name _____

7. What modules of the vendor's software are installed? _____

8. When was each module installed (phased)? _____

9. Was vendor support of implementation satisfactory?

   Circle one   1   2   3   4   5

10. Was the delivery schedule maintained by the vendor?

    Y or N_____

11. Did the vendor provide on site support for the implementation?

    Y or N _____   Circle one   1   2   3   4   5

12. How many vendor personnel were required for the imple-
    mentation?_____

13. How many customer personnel were required for the imple-
    mentation?_____

14. Was the vendor implementation plan accurate?

    Circle one   1   2   3   4   5 _____

15. How long did the implementation take? _____

    _____

16. Are the installed modules performing satisfactorily?

    Circle one   1   2   3   4   5 _____

(Continued)

17. If not what are the reasons? _____

    Software? _____

    Hardware? _____

18. What are the personnel requirements to maintain the installed modules? _____

19. Are the costs to maintain acceptable to the customer? _____

    _____

20. Is the customer satisfied with vendor support in the areas of new releases and upgrades for the software?

    Y or N _____ Circle one   1   2   3   4   5_____

21. Is the documentation accurate? _____

    Y or N _____ Circle one   1   2   3   4   5_____

22. Is the documentation maintained concurrently with new releases and upgrades? _____

    Y or N _____ Circle one   1   2   3   4   5_____

23. Is the vendor responsive to support calls? _____

    Y or N _____ Circle one   1   2   3   4   5_____

24. Is the time for vendor support excessive? _____

    Y or N _____ Circle one   1   2   3   4   5_____

25. Is the customer satisfied with the vendor? _____

    Y or N _____ Circle one   1   2   3   4   5_____

26. Is the customer satisfied with the systems performance? ____

    Y or N _____ Circle one   1   2   3   4   5_____

27. Has the performance of this software diminished since its implementation? _____

    Y or N _____ Circle one   1   2   3   4   5_____

28. If performance has diminished, which module of the system was affected? _____

29. Why has this particular module diminished in performance?

    _____

30. What is the most undesirable aspect of the system? _____

_____

31. What is the most outstanding feature of the system? _____

_____

32. Would the customer recommend the software? _____

33. Was the training offered on the software adequate? _____

_____

34. Interviewer's perception of customer.

   Knowledge of the software product

   Circle one   1   2   3   4   5

   Knowledge of communications

   Circle one   1   2   3   4   5

   Degree of enthusiasm expressed

   Circle one   1   2   3   4   5

   Technical expertise

   Circle one   1   2   3   4   5

   Overall perception of the installation

Note: The Circle one   1   2   3   4   5 rating system
   is employed, where 5 is the highest score.

Vendor Customer Evaluation Questionnaire (Hardware)

1. Site name _____

2. Site location_____

3. Site contact name _____

    title _____

    data processing experience in years _____

4. Site contact telephone number_____

5. Alternate site contact name _____

    Title _____

    Years of experience _____

6. Alternate site contact name _____

7. What model of computer is installed? _____

8. What operating system is installed? _____

9. Was vendor installation satisfactory?

    Circle one   1   2   3   .4   5

10. Was the delivery schedule maintained by the vendor?

    Y or N_____

11. Did the vendor provide on-site support for the installation?

    Y or N _____ Circle one   1   2   3   4   5

12. How many vendor personnel were required for the installtion? _____

13. How many customer personnel were required for the installation? _____

14. Was the vendor installation plan accurate?_____

    Circle one   1   2   3   4   5

15. How long did the installation take? _____

16. Is the extended operating system working satisfactorily? ___

    Circle one   1   2   3   4   5

    _____

(Continued)

17. If not, what are the reasons?_____

    Software? _____

    Hardware?_____

18. What are the personnel requirements to maintain the
    installed system? _____

19. Are the costs to maintain acceptable to the customer? _____

    _____

20. Is the customer satisfied with vendor support in the areas of
    new releases and upgrades for the operating system. _____

    Y or N _____ Circle one   1   2   3   4   5 _____

21. Is the documentation accurate? _____

    Y or N _____ Circle one   1   2   3   4   5

22. Is the documentation maintained concurrently with new
    releases and upgrades? _____

    Y or N _____ Circle one   1   2   3   4   5 _____

23. Is the vendor responsive to support calls? _____

    Y or N _____ Circle one   1   2   3   4   5 _____

24. Is the time for vendor support excessive? _____

    Y or N _____ Circle one   1   2   3   4   5 _____

25. Is the customer satisfied with the vendor? _____

    Y or N _____ Circle one   1   2   3   4   5 _____

26. Is the customer satisfied with the systems performance? ___

    Y or N _____ Circle one   1   2   3   4   5 _____

27. Has the performance of this hardware diminished since its
    implementation? _____

    Y or N _____ Circle one   1   2   3   4   5 _____

28. If performance has diminished, what is the reason? _____

29. Did the vendor provide a field engineer to determine the
    cause of performance problems? _____

30. What is the most undesirable aspect of the hardware? _____

    _____

(*Continued*)

31. What is the most outstanding feature of the hardware? _____

_____

32. Would the customer recommend the hardware? _____

33. Was training on the operating system and hardware ad-
quate? _____

34. Interviewer's perception of customer:

Knowledge of the software product

Circle one   1   2   3   4   5

Knowledge of communications

Circle one   1   2   3   4   5

Degree of enthusiasm expressed

Circle one   1   2   3   4   5

Technical expertise

Circle one   1   2   3   4   5

Overall perception of the installation _____

_____

Note: The circle one   1   2   3   4   5   rating system
is employed, where 5 is the highest score.

16

Sample
Audit Criteria

Introduction

The criteria presented here are only a sample and should not be viewed as anything more than a guideline. This list of criteria is a top-down list. Some items could have been presented in a layered or exploded format.

I. Security
    A. User log-in and password
    B. Group privileges
    C. Directory and file privileges
    D. Communications
        1. Local
        2. Remote (networks)
    E. Security or monitoring software
    F. System logs
    G. Audit trails
    H. Security policy
    I. Security plan
    J. Security awareness
    K. Shredding of unwanted printed materials

II. Operations
    A. Scheduled activities
        1. Daily
        2. Weekly

   3. Monthly
   4. Quarterly
   5. Yearly

  B. Catastrophe preparedness
  C. Archive of file systems
   1. Test

  D. Restoration of file systems
   1. Test

  E. File system maintenance
  F. Storage of magnetic media
  G. Scheduled maintenance of hardware
  H. Development partition or directory
  I. Test partition or directory
  J. Testing procedures
  K. Mirrored partitions
  L. Mirrored disks

III. Performance

  A. Benchmark testing
  B. Response times
  C. System configuration
   1. Software
   2. Hardware

  D. Memory utilization
  E. Storage utilization
  F. Performance tools
  G. Network communications

IV. Documentation

  A. Hardware
  B. Operating system
  C. Third-party software
  D. Developed software
   1. System
   2. Programmer
   3. User
   4. File definitions
   5. Flow charts
   6. Tables

  E. Online storage
  F. Offline storage
  G. Availability
  H. Updates

17
Sample Network Audit Criteria

Introduction

The criteria presented here are only a sample and should not be viewed as anything more than a guideline. These criteria, like the sample audit criteria in Chapter 16, are a top-down list. Some items could have been presented in a layered or exploded format.

Network Audit Criteria

The following are for a LAN—administrator:

I. Topology
    A. Hardware
        1. Servers, routers, bridges, gateways, etc.
            a. Address
            b. Manufacturer
            c. Description
            d. Warranty
            e. Capacity
            f. Protocols
            g. Routing
            h. Interface cards

    i. Cabling
    j. Transmission speed
    k. Physical location
   2. Workstations
    a. Address
    b. Manufacturer
    c. Software configuration
    d. Hardware configuration
    e. Protocols
    f. Interface card
    g. Cabling
    h. Transmission speed
    i. Physical location
   3. Printers
    a. Local
    b. Remote
    c. Physical location
    d. Address
    e. Description
    f. Print server

 II. Security
  A. Network administration
   1. Alternate administrator
   2. Workgroup managers
   3. User account manager
   4. Other network administrators
  B. Management software
   1. Monitoring
    a. User logs
    b. Audit trails
    c. Intruder detection
   2. Management triggers
   3. Management managers
  C. User
   1. Access rights
    a. Volume
    b. Directory
    c. File
   2. Group rights
    a. Volume
    b. Directory
    c. File

        3. Applications used

    D. Physical security of equipment

III. Performance

    A. Diagnostic testing

        1. Cable tracers

        2. Continuity testers

        3. Diagnostic software

        4. Time domain reflectometers

        5. Diagnostic software

        6. Protocol analyzers

    B. Packets

        1. Send or receive

            a. Too big to count

            b. Too small to count

            c. Miscellaneous errors

            d. Retry count

            e. Checksum errors

            f. Receive mismatch count

            g. Total packets

    C. Buffers

        1. Dirty cache buffers

        2. Packet receive buffers

        3. Directory cache buffers

        4. Original cache buffers

        5. Total cache buffers

    D. Utilization

        1. Processor busy time

    E. File server uptime

        1. Time the server has been running

    F. Memory usage

IV. Operations

    A. Scheduled activities

        1. Daily

        2. Weekly

        3. Monthly

    B. Catastrophe preparedness

    C. Archive of file systems

        1. Test

    D. Restoration of file systems

        1. Test

    E. File system maintenance

      F. Storage of magnetic media
      G. Scheduled maintenance of hardware
      H. Test partition or directory
      I. Testing procedures
      J. Mirrored partitions
      K. Mirrored disks

V. Documentation

      A. Hardware
         1. Warranty
         2. Serial number
         3. Maintenance
         4. Spares

      B. Operating system
      C. Third-party software
      D. Developed software
      E. System outages
      F. Drawings of the network
      G. Offline storage
      H. Availability
      I. Updates

Bibliography

Colin Brown, "CIA Computer Consultant Alleges Massive Conspiracy," *TC Technical Consultant*, August/September 1992. TC Publications, 1916 Rockefeller Lane, Suite #2, Redondo Beach, CA 90278

Colin Brown, "Spies, Lies and Inslawgate," *TC Technical Consultant*, August/September 1992. TC Publications, 1916 Rockefeller Lane, Suite #2, Redondo Beach, CA 90278.

Rob Kelly, "Do You Know Where Your Laptop Is?" *Information Week*, 1992. CMP Publications, Inc., 600 Community Drive, Manhasset, NY 11030.

Lisa Monzolillo and Richard Cardinalli, "Ethics and Computer Crime—A Guide for Managers," *Computer Security Journal*, vol. 7, no. 2, 1991. Computer Security Institute, 600 Harrison Street, San Francisco, CA 94107.

Thomas Peltier, "Policy Statement: The Cornerstone to All Procedures," *Computer Security Journal*, vol. 7, no. 2, 1991. Computer Security Institute, 600 Harrison Street, San Francisco, CA 94107.

Tom Sheldon, *NOVELL NetWare 386: The Complete Reference*, Osborne McGraw-Hill, 1990.

Peter Stephenson, "Implementing the Secure PC LAN—Guidelines for Information Security," *Computer Security Journal*, vol. 7, no. 2, 1991. Computer Security Institute, 600 Harrison Street, San Francisco, CA 94107.

Howard W. Timm, "Who Will Spy," *Security Management*, July 1991. American Society for Industrial Security, 1655 North Fort Myer Drive, Suite 1200, Arlington, VA 22209.

Further Reading

The references presented here can be used to further research specific areas of interest. All of the references presented here are germane to this book.

William Atkins, Charles L. Biggs, and Evan G. Birks, *Managing the Systems Development Process*, Prentice-Hall, 1980.

Robert L. Baber, *Software Reflected: The Socially Responsible Programming of Computers*, Elsevier Science Publishing Co., 1982.

Richard H. Baker, *Computer Security Handbook*, 2d ed., TAB Books, Blue Ridge Summit, PA, 1991.

David Bellin and Gary Chapman, eds., *Computers in Battle: Will They Work?*, Harcourt Brace Jovanovich, 1987.

T. A. Berson, ed., *Local Area Network Security*, Springer-Verlag, 1989.

Terrell Ward Bynum, ed., *Computers & Ethics*, vol. 16, no. 4, Basil Blackwell, 1985.

David D. Clark, *Computers at Risk: Safe Computing in the Information Age*, National Research Council, National Academy Press, 1990.

D. W. Davies and W. L. Price, *Security for Computer Networks: An Introduction to Data Security in Teleprocessing and Electronic Funds Transfer*, 2d ed., John Wiley & Sons, 1989.

Peter J. Denning, ed., *Computers under Attack: Intruders, Worms and Viruses*, Addison-Wesley, 1990.

Philip E. Fites, *The Computer Virus Crisis*, Van Nostrand Reinhold, New York, 1988.

Simson Garfinkel and Gene Spafford, *Practical UNIX Security*, O'Reilly & Associates, Inc., 1991.

Mark W. Greenia, *Manager's Guide to Computer Security: A Sourcebook of Key Reference Material*, Lexikon Services, 1990.

Colin Haynes, *Computer Virus Protection Handbook*, Sybex, 1990.

Deborah G. Johnson, *Computer Ethics*, Prentice-Hall, 1985.

Stephan G. Kochran, *Unix System Security*, rev. ed., Macmillan, 1990.

Richard Levin, *Computer Virus Handbook*, Osborne/McGraw-Hill, 1990.

John McAfee and Colin Haynes, *Computer Viruses, Worms, Data Diddlers, Killer Programs, & Other Threats to Your System: What They Are, How They Work & How to Defend Your PC or Mainframe*, St. Martin's Press, New York, 1989.

Ian Palmer, *Computer Security Risk Management*, Van Nostrand Reinhold, New York, 1990.

Patent, Trademark, & Copyright Law Section Staff, *Software Ownership Confidentiality Forms*, American Bar Association, 1984.

Ralph Roberts, *Computer Viruses,* Compute Publications, 1988.

Marshall T. Rose, *The Open Book,* The Wollongong Group, Inc., Prentice-Hall, 1990.

Gary B. Shelly and Thomas J. Cashman, *Business Systems Analysis and Design,* Anaheim Publishing Co., 1975.

Gary H. Sherman, *Computer Software Protection Law,* BNA Books, 1989.

Mary A. Todd, *Computer Security Training Guidelines,* U.S. Government Printing Office, 1989.

John J. Williams, *Absolute Computer File Security,* Consumertronics, 1990.

Geoffrey H. Wold, *Computer Crime: Technologies for Preventing & Detecting Crime in Financial Institutions,* Bank Administration Institute, 1990.

Will Yanush, *Computer Fraud & Collusion in Customer Service & Billing System,* State Mutual Book & Periodical Service, Ltd., 1989.

Index

About the Author

Dana L. Stern is president of Compunet, where he specializes in the investigation of computer fraud. His past experience with computers includes supporting mainframe operations, implementing manufacturing systems, and testing AT&T's Action 2.0 mobile phone billing system. He also has extensive telecommunications experience, including managing large projects for Northern Telecom and helping to create a worldwide telecommunications network for General Motors. During his career, he has personally documented many acts of fraud for clients, and has testified as an expert witness. He has also developed software for business and government, and has been published in several industry journals, including *Computer World*.